Writing
for
Television

Writing Handbooks

Writing for Television

THIRD EDITION

Gerald Kelsey

A & C Black • London

Third edition 1999
First edition 1990
Second edition 1995

A & C Black (Publishers) Limited
35 Bedford Row, London WC1R 4JH

© 1999, 1990, 1995 Gerald Kelsey

ISBN 0–7136–5092–3

A CIP catalogue record for this book
is available from the British Library.

Typeset in 10 on 12 pt Sabon
Printed and bound in Great Britain by
Creative Print and Design (Wales), Ebbw Vale

Contents

Acknowledgements

The author wishes to thank the following people for their generous advice or assistance.

Mary Bell, Executive Producer, *Father Ted*, Hat Trick Productions Ltd
Zanna Beswick, Script Editor, *The Bill*, Thames Television
Michael Chapman, Executive Producer, *The Bill*, Thames Television
Bill Craig, Writer
Lucy Daniels, Writer
Terence Feely, Writer
Alison Gray, General Secretary, Writers' Guild
Gareth Hale, Writer
Graham Linehan, Writer
Arthur Mathews, Writer
Jean McConnell, Writer
Norman Pace, Writer
Jane Pritchard, Writer
Phil Redmond, Executive Producer, Mersey TV
Anthony Read, Writer
Keith Richardson, Controller of Drama, YTV
Leigh Roberts, *Brookside*, Brookside Productions Ltd
Kenneth Rock, Writer
Ted Willis, Writer
Peter Wragg, BBC Visual Effects
Yorkshire Television Limited for *Heartbeat*

1. Just for Starters

A flip through the pages of any current television programme listings shows that, these days, a considerable amount of air time is occupied by repeats, old films, American imports, quiz shows, game shows, talk shows, football and a variety of other non-scripted programmes. At first sight this appears somewhat discouraging for a 'would-be' television writer – but a study of programme ratings, published each week in *Broadcast*, the weekly newspaper of the TV industry, shows another side of the picture. Scripted television drama is never out of the most-watched top ten programmes, often occupying all positions and only displaced as number one by such events as a World Cup football match. Indeed, *Broadcast's* 'top seventy', published in August 1998, just after the World Cup, showed more than a third of all programmes were scripted.

Very obviously there have been great changes in television in recent years. The single, one-off play, where many talented writers got their first break, is now the exception rather than the regular feature it used to be on both BBC and ITV networks. To some extent it means writers no longer have the freedom to select their own themes, as those writing single teleplays were once able to do. Today they are usually required to write within the guidelines of a programme format; but that has always been a limitation the writer of popular series and serials has had to live with. It can, of course, be frustrating but it can also be challenging and very profitable for those who can embrace the necessary disciplines, for as Sue Stoessl, former head of BBC research services, said in a recent report quoted in *Broadcast*: 'Home-made drama and comedy is what the audience wants to watch.'

Writing for television is a craft in its own right. It has to be learnt, but the effort can be well worthwhile.

It's an awe-inspiring thought, on a single night there could be between ten and fifteen million viewers watching your programme and the following morning, over garden fences, in supermarkets, offices and factories up and down the country hundreds of thousands of people could be talking about your story, discussing your characters or laughing at your jokes.

Fifteen million?

We can recognise the figure on paper. Just imagine that as a crowd!

But that's only the first screening to your UK audience. Successful programmes are usually repeated and distributed all over the world. In the USA alone a networked show can reach an audience of thirty million on a single night. The potential is enormous and many older British TV shows such as *The Saint, The Prisoner, Doctor Who* and *Till Death Us Do Part* to name but a few will, via satellite and cable, continue to be screened for many years.

It is not inconceivable that at some time in the future you could be sitting in an hotel room in Brisbane or Buenos Aires, or in a motel in the middle of nowhere, watching the programme you write next year.

For writers in English have an enormous advantage.

As Professor Randolph Quirk said in his book *The Use of English*, 'A Dane and a Dutchman meeting casually in Rome will almost automatically find themselves conversing in English . . .' 'English is the most international language.'

The entire world is the market for British television productions and for many countries the distributors do not even have to go to the expense of dubbing or sub-titling.

In the next few years there is little doubt that the national and international market will expand. Every week the cable and satellite companies transmit many hours of British programmes throughout the world. Although the majority of drama programmes currently transmitted are repeats the supply is not endless and the appetite for new and original programmes will continue to grow.

And that could be your opportunity.

Probably you would not be looking at this book unless you felt that possibly you could write a television script. Hopefully that feeling has been stimulated by the best work you have seen, not the worst – like a woman I met who told me about a perfectly awful play she had watched and boasted she could write a play as good as that.

And she did . . . and wondered why it was rejected.

The trouble was she was writing for 'The Box' and it showed. Anyone who shares her contempt for 'The Box' should forget about writing for television.

Of course not every script plays as well as the writer and producer hope. At times we all fall short of our own best standards; but television is a mixture of art and craft practised, for the most part,

2

by talented, dedicated professionals and nothing closes an open door faster than hackneyed themes, corny jokes, tired clichés and careless, sloppy writing.

If you want to write for television aim to be as good as the best you have seen not just a little better than the worst.

There are, however, a number of important changes and developments taking place in television production techniques all the time. Very possibly the majority of viewers will scarcely have noticed any differences but for you, as a writer aiming to contribute scripts, they are very significant.

From the earliest days all television plays were produced and shot using three or four television cameras in an electronic studio. Interiors of rooms and somewhat limited exteriors of gardens or buildings were built on the floor of the studio and if wider views or expansive outdoor settings were unavoidable short film clips were specially shot or 'stock' film found and incorporated into the production.

The exception to this was called 'telefilm' (television series made entirely on film) invariably series episodes like *The Saint* and *The Avengers* which were made at studios of the ailing British film industry.

Today some plays and many series episodes are still made by television cameras in electronic studios and incorporate on film the world outside anything that can be built or contained within the limited space of the studio. Most productions, however, are no longer shot with multiple cameras. Many directors now work with a single camera and the majority of plays and major series are made entirely on film. Exteriors will all be shot on suitable locations. The interiors may be done in the studio or they may be shot on locations such as a stately home, village hall or old church that is, with little or no adaptation, the ideal setting for the story. Alternatively the interior scenes may be shot on location in studios improvised in a barn, warehouse or anywhere with sufficient floor space that can be found close to the site of the main outside filming.

The many independent producers who emerged after the establishment of Channel Four, who now take advantage of the Government dictate that 25% of both BBC and ITV programmes should come from the independents, do not, of course, own large studio complexes. Film is well suited to their facilities. It is flexible and of very high quality and both the BBC and the major ITV companies now make many of their productions on film and on location, avoiding the high cost of sets.

The result is that what was always known as a 'teleplay' (a play written specially for television) has to a large extent, become 'A Film For Television' and it is necessary for a new writer to learn, not only how to write a script for production by electronic cameras in the studio, but also the technique of writing a film.

Doubtless many reading this book will have already had some success in writing for other media. For them some of what we have to say will not be new but writing for the screen involves new disciplines that have to be learnt. The writer new to the medium does not need, at the outset, to over-burden himself with a great deal of technical detail. No one will reject your brilliant script because you have neglected to call for 'telecine' where the 'director' will see instantly it is required. Nor will they buy a bad script because the layout and technical jargon are accurate. But anyone hoping to break in to television or the 'Corporate television' market does need an elementary knowledge of the basics of TV and 'Audio visual' production so before we move on we need to define some terms so that we know what we are talking about.

Like any other industry, television has its own vocabulary and in clarifying terms with which you may not be familiar I shall follow the pattern established in the previous editions of this book. The first use of a technical term will be in single quotation marks, followed by a bracketed explanation. There is also a glossary of terms at the end of the book.

To catch up on terms already used:

'Stock' (Film clips obtainable from film libraries inserted in the production, e.g. airport or busy streets)

'Producer' (The administrator in overall charge of production of a collective group of programmes, e.g. a serial, a series, a regular play-spot)

'Director' (The person responsible to the producer for the individual play or episode, directing the actors in rehearsals and the work of the camera crew, sound, lighting and other studio technicians)

'Teleplay' (A play specially written for television)

'Telecine' Frequently abbreviated to 'T/C' and sometimes 'T/K'. (Film or taped scenes for a play shot prior to the studio production. These are frequently exteriors.)

'**Corporate Television**' (Programmes made for marketing, promotional, image-building, educational, social, political and other purposes)

'**Audio Visual**' Film or video productions incorporating both sound and vision.

Television writing in this country falls into two main categories: freelance and staff. Plays, 'Series' (a number of drama presentations using the same theme and leading characters where each episode is a complete story in itself), 'Serials' (a succession of drama presentations which unfold one complete story), Children's drama, Comedies, Light-entertainment sketches, and 'Dramatisations' (rendering a work not written as drama into dramatic form) or 'Adaptations' (converting a dramatic work written for stage or radio into a television script) – these works are invariably written by freelance writers commissioned for each particular piece of work in what may be a single or multi-episode contract.

Neither the BBC nor the ITV companies employ staff writers to script this kind of programme. The reason, when you think about it, is obvious. If they employed a staff writer to provide episodes of a soap opera one month and expected him, as the staff man, to turn in a significant ninety minute play the next and episodes for a situation comedy the month after they would probably be disappointed with the results.

Television writers are mostly specialists concentrating their efforts on serials, series, children's programmes, comedy shows or 'one-off' or 'one-shot plays' (original plays). Like actors, writers often get type-cast. Producers and commissioning editors come to them for the work their track record shows they can do. Thus if an established thriller writer wishes to switch into a totally different stream of production – say situation comedy – he is virtually starting where you start – having to prove himself again. There would, of course, be plenty of evidence that he knew how to construct a television script but none that he could write comedy.

The staff writers working in television, are the people who write the news and current affairs. They are mostly trained journalists with experience on local or national papers. Some documentaries are written by staff, many of whom are writer/directors or writer/producers and might more accurately be described as directors or producers who write; directing or producing being their basic qualification.

Other writers employed as staff by television companies script promotion and presentation material and all major advertising agencies have copy writers who write television commercials. In this book, however, as we talk about 'writing for television' we shall be referring to scripting the many different styles and levels of drama and comedy that are sustained by freelance contributors.

We shall also be looking at the opportunities for freelance writers in the corporate TV market.

Before we move on you may find it helpful if I give you a brief guide to the structure of this book.

Chapter 1, as you have now discovered, is by way of introduction. Chapters 2–4 take you beyond the screen you watch as a viewer to glimpse what happens on the other side of the camera, to see how the script the writer produces is transformed into a television play. Chapter 5 states the obvious that so many would be TV writers forget. Television is about pictures. Think in pictures as well as words.

Chapter 6 is concerned with the substance of your plays – research and finding ideas, while Chapter 7 deals with things you need to know before you start.

Chapters 8 to 13 are the 'Do it yourself' section, so to speak. Chapter 14 deals with what many writers find the most difficult part – selling themselves and their material. Here we have details of production companies and the fees you can expect when your work is accepted. Chapter 15 gives a few other points you should know and Chapter 16 is the tailpiece. Finally the Appendix reproduces excerpts from produced work by established television writers.

Hopefully all that will point you in the right direction but perhaps here we should pause to reflect on the most important asset a dramatist can possess. I'm not referring to his typewriter, word processor or a splendid collection of reference books – rather to those innate qualities and instincts common to every successful dramatic writer. I am talking about imagination, sensitivity and observation.

You can learn, very easily, to lay out a script on the page. You can master all the technical terms but if you can never feel the bitterness of a woman who has lost her child; the anger of a man wrongfully accused; the despair of a young person unable to get a proper job; or the terror of someone facing a madman with a knife, perhaps you should ask yourself whether writing drama really is for you.

Writers have to be like a sponge soaking up incident and atmosphere from all around them. They must be touched by other people's emotions, able to share their joys and sadness – for as the American author, Ring Lardner, once said, 'How can you write if you can't cry?'

2. A visit to a television studio

In television nothing is static for long. Budgets change, schedules change and cameras and other electronic equipment are changing all the time. Broadcasting regulations and government policies change. Uncertainty about the level or indeed the continuation of the licence fee or the renewal of each commercial franchise and the establishment of monopolies which are broken up a decade or two later do nothing for the stability and confidence of the industry.

Not surprisingly fashions and tastes change too and economies have dictated that single plays, like the BBC's Wednesday Play and ITV's famous Armchair Theatre, where many British dramatists first made their names, are now very rare indeed. Replacing them we have dramatisations of novels and multi-part original series involving characters whose lives and adventures audiences are drawn to watch week after week.

Currently, the most hyped change in television is the introduction of digital which promises scores, even hundreds, of new channels and sharper pictures. But this is primarily a change in the way a greater variety of programmes – many of them specialist and minority interests – are delivered to the viewer rather than the way in which the writer scripts a work.

By means of a key-pad viewers will be able to order shopping, do their banking, book holidays or call up favourite film or TV programmes, none of which has any special relevance for the scriptwriter beyond the fact that audiences spread over so many channels are unlikely, on a single night, to peak at the kind of figures previously, and currently, recorded for popular programmes.

But all this is 'tomorrow'. Although the BBC and other television companies are already active in this area the technical miracles may exceed the need and the purse of millions of viewers. It will certainly be many years before the ambitions of the digital pioneers are fully realised.

More important, from the writers' point of view, has been the production of so many television programmes on film releasing directors from the restrictions and limitations of the TV studio and their 'OB' (outside broadcast) vans and maze of cables. Now both the BBC, and ITV companies and the Independent Producers, make the majority of programmes on film and on location.

But this we will look at more closely later. I want first to take you into the kind of electronic television studio you will find at all major television centres. One thing you will notice when you visit a television production centre is that studios come in all sizes from small rooms used for interviews and chat shows to huge aircraft-hanger-size spaces for big drama and spectacular productions. But they all have one absurdly obvious thing in common. There is a positive limit to the number of sets you can get on any particular studio floor.

So let's go in, pausing first to check that the red light outside the door is not warning us that they are recording a programme. 'Keep Out' means 'Keep Out'. Noise, intrusions or distractions can result in the scene having to be shot again – a costly and irritating business. To barge in regardless is no way to win friends and influence producers.

Inside they are engaged in a rehearsal – probably for a serial episode. Let's pause for a moment to get our bearings. From where we stand just inside the door our view is obstructed by the backs of the many sets that seem to clutter the floor. We step forward to get a better view and immediately find ourselves dazzled by hundreds of powerful lights hanging from a network of lighting bars that obscure the entire ceiling. Further into the studio, on the other side of the sets, the world is transformed. The drab wood and hardboard hoarding-like structures that blocked our view become elegant sitting rooms, tropical bungalows, luxury hotel rooms, Victorian slums or whatever the script demands.

But they cost money – a great deal of money these days. If you are working in the dark on your first play, where the major part of the action takes place on interior sets, call only for those that are essential to your story.

We will assume we are watching a multi-camera production recorded on video tape, shot as all TV drama was shot until a few years ago. As we stand watching cameras with trailing cables being pushed from one set to another; actors and actresses taking their places on the sets; sound boom operators manoeuvring the 'fishing rod' (boom from the end of which hangs a microphone) close enough to pick up the dialogue, we realise that a television programme is a team production. You will be astonished to see just how many people are involved.

Staffing levels and titles differ somewhat between BBC and commercial companies but apart from the actors, actresses and 'extras' (small part actors), here on the 'floor' (studio floor), we find the Floor Manager, Assistant Floor Manager, Stage Manager, Camera crews, Sound Boom Operators and a great many others without whose skills and expertise the show would never reach the audience.

In the control room – or control gallery as it is sometimes called – the director sits in front of a bank of 'monitors' (TV screens) each linked to one or another of the cameras on the floor. For an average drama production there will be three or four cameras and the monitors in front of the director will show what each camera has in view and, as the output of each individual camera is selected at a particular point in the story, the picture is duplicated on a master screen so that the director can see that the framing of the picture and the movement of the actors recorded on the master tape is as he intended.

Sitting beside the director we have the 'vision mixer' (who physically presses the buttons that cut from one camera to another to link selected camera output to the video tape recorder). For a drama production the vision mixer works from the shooting script which the director has prepared in advance. This details for each scene which of his cameras is covering the action; which characters it is focusing on; whether it is a 'close up' (CU), 'two shot' (2-shot), a 'group shot' (group-s) or whatever the director wants, and the precise point at which the vision mixer must switch to record the output of another camera.

With them in the control room we find the producer and the 'director's assistant' (PA) and in a connecting room the sound engineer, lighting engineer and telecine operator.

Less obvious but no less vital to the production are the backroom staff: casting director, wardrobe supervisor, dress-makers and dressers, make-up supervisor and make-up artists, set designers, scenic artists, graphic artists, carpenters and set builders to name but a few. Watch the credits at the end of any major drama production and you'll see what I mean.

These are the professionals on whom the writer depends to get his play on the screen. They, in turn, depend on him.

Without the script there is no show.

Let's take a look at a page or two of the script as the writer delivers it. That is a script for a studio production. (NB Layout for a film production is different.)

It looks like this. You will notice it is typed on the right-hand half of the page. This is the usual layout for TV studio productions. You will see why in a moment.

FADE IN:

1   TITLE AND OPENING CREDITS.

2.   INT: LIVING ROOM. DAY.

A COMFORTABLY FURNISHED LOUNGE/ DINER IN A SUBURBAN SEMI. IN THE DINING AREA THE TABLE IS LAID FOR THREE.

FX: RADIO IS PLAYING MUSIC.

JANE, AN ATTRACTIVE WOMAN ABOUT THIRTY, COMES FROM THE KITCHEN WITH A TEAPOT AND PLATE OF TOAST AND PUTS IT DOWN ON THE TABLE. SHE GOES TO THE DOOR AND CALLS INTO THE HALL.

JANE:
It's on the table, Dad.

WALKER: (OFF)
Coming.

JANE GOES BACK TO THE KITCHEN AND AFTER A MOMENT RETURNS WITH TWO PLATES OF EGGS AND BACON. SHE BEGINS POURING TWO CUPS OF TEA AS WALKER ENTERS IN HIS SHIRT SLEEVES.

JANE TURNS OFF THE RADIO.

TOM WALKER, HER FATHER, IS A SMALL, BALDING, CHEEFUL-LOOKING MAN IN HIS MID-FIFTIES. HE COMES TO THE TABLE RUBBING HIS HANDS WITH PLEASURE.

WALKER:
M'm! Bacon. There's no better smell to wake up to.

JANE:
Hallo. Did you sleep all right?

WALKER:
Like a top. (HE SITS) Jim not up yet?

JANE:
No, I think he was awake half the night
worrying about the latest sales figures.

WALKER:
I'm sure it's just a seasonal trend.

(FX: DOOR SHUTTING)

WALKER: (CONTINUED)
Sounds like him now.

JANE:
Yes – but Dad, don't start him talking shop
over breakfast.

WALKER:
Now would I ever . . . ?

JIM ENTERS. HE IS A TALL TOUGH-
LOOKING MAN IN HIS MID-THIRTIES.

JANE:
Yes. – Ah there you are.

JIM:
Sorry if I've kept you waiting love. Morning
Tom.

WALKER:
Morning. Didn't sleep too well, eh?

JIM:
Lot on my mind.

WALKER:
Of course. I think you ought to have a word
with . . .

JANE:
Dad!

WALKER:
What? Oh yes, I remember. Sorry.

JIM:
Remember what?

WALKER:
Oh nothing . . . nothing.

JANE:
I told him not to talk shop over breakfast
and that goes for you too.

JIM:
I see. Where is my . . . ?

JANE:
It's on the stove. I'll get it.

(SHE EXITS)

Let us now look at the same script to see the work the director has
done and how the other members of the production team play their
parts in getting it on the screen.

First a guide to the technical terms used.

'FX' (Sound effects)
'CAMS' (Cameras)
'ACTION' (On the shooting script covers the words and stage
movement)
'SOF' (Sound on film)
'STAND MIC' and 'BOOM' (Microphones)
'FADE IN' or (sometimes) 'FADE UP' (The gradual appearance of a
scene from obscurity)
'FADE OUT' (The scene disappears)
'MIX' (The gradual changing from one scene to another)
'MLS' (Medium Long Shot. This includes the whole figure of the
artist, with a few inches foreground and a few inches above the head)
'TRACK' (To move the camera backwards or forwards or in a
horizontal motion)
'MS' (Medium shot. Cutting a person near the knees)
'PAN' (To move in a horizontal line the direction the camera is
shooting)
'2-SHOT' (Covering two characters)
'3-SHOT' (Covering three characters)

A visit to a television studio

CAMS	ACTION	SOUND
1 FADE UP T/C		SOF

SCENE 1: STANDARD OPENING TITLES.

2 MIX TO		
CAM 1	2. INT: LIVING ROOM. DAY.	
MLS Dining area.		

A COMFORTABLY FURNISHED LOUNGE/
DINER IN A SUBURBAN SEMI. IN THE
DINING AREA THE TABLE IS LAID FOR
THREE.

Track out as JANE
comes forward
to door.

JANE, AN ATTRACTIVE WOMAN ABOUT
THIRTY, COMES FROM THE KITCHEN WITH
A TEAPOT AND PLATE OF TOAST AND PUTS
IT DOWN ON THE TABLE. SHE GOES TO THE
DOOR AND CALLS INTO THE HALL.

STAND MIC

3 CAM 2
MS JANE

JANE:
It's on the table, Dad.

WALKER: (OFF)
Coming.

4 CAM 1
MS JANE

PAN L as she
goes to kitchen.

JANE GOES BACK TO THE KITCHEN AND
AFTER A MOMENT RETURNS WITH TWO
PLATES OF EGGS AND BACON. SHE BEGINS
POURING TWO CUPS OF TEA AS WALKER
ENTERS IN HIS SHIRT SLEEVES.

5 1   BOOM

MS WALKER
HE enters L
for 2-shot

TOM WALKER, HER FATHER, IS A SMALL,
BALDING, CHEEFUL-LOOKING MAN IN HIS
MID-FIFTIES. HE COMES TO THE TABLE
RUBBING HIS HANDS WITH PLEASURE.

Hold 2-shot

WALKER:
M'm! Bacon. There's no better smell to wake up to.

JANE:
Hallo. Did you sleep all right?

WALKER:
Like a top. (HE SITS) Jim not up yet?

13

JANE:
No, I think he was awake half the night worrying about the latest sales figures.

WALKER:
I'm sure it's just a seasonal trend.

(FX: DOOR SHUTTING)

WALKER: (CONTINUED)
Sounds like him now.

MS JANE

JANE:
Yes – but Dad, don't start him talking shop over breakfast.

WALKER:
Now would I ever . . . ?

6 1
_____

MS JIM

Track out as he comes through the door
Pan him L for 2-shot with Jane

JIM ENTERS. HE IS A TALL TOUGH-LOOKING MAN IN HIS MID-THIRTIES.

JANE:
Yes. – Ah there you are.

JIM:
Sorry if I've kept you waiting love. Morning Tom.

7 2
_____

3-shot

Hold WALKER/JIM as Jane exits

WALKER:
Morning. Didn't sleep too well, eh?

JIM:
Lot on my mind.

WALKER:
Of course. I think you ought to have a word with . . .

JANE:
Dad!

WALKER:
What? Oh yes, I remember. Sorry.

JIM:
Remember what?

WALKER:
Oh nothing . . . nothing.

JANE:
I told him not to talk shop over breakfast and that goes for you too.

JIM:
I see. Where is my . . . ?

JANE:
It's on the stove. I'll get it.

(SHE EXITS)

As you now see the writer's script is typed on the right-hand side of the page to allow space on the left for the director's camera instructions.

But let me make it very clear. Writers of studio productions of this kind are not required to concern themselves with the shooting script as shown above. The director and producer would be very resentful of any writer who tried to usurp their position and authority by calling the shots and presenting them with a script like that. It is, as you can see, a very technical business and this short example is included here simply to show you how the script the writer delivers is processed and the extent to which a television play is a team production.

Rehearsal finished, the actors and staff prepare for the performance. The cameramen wearing earphones through which they get the director's instructions wait on their cameras. The floor manager, also with earphones, acts rather like an orchestra conductor bringing in the actors on cue. He checks everyone is in place on the set. The director checks with the floor manager who confirms they are ready to go. Through the speakers in the control room, we hear his voice, 'Settle down studio' and as the actors stand by for the opening scene you can feel the tension rising.

The director orders, 'Start the clock' and the count down begins.

The PA calls 'One minute. We are on the clock.' Half a minute later she calls, 'Thirty seconds'. At ten seconds she starts a verbal count. Ten, nine, eight, seven, six . . .

As the count goes on the director calls 'Cue Telecine'.

The count down ends, '. . . three, two, one, zero', and the pre-filmed title sequence comes up on a monitor. Now on the screen linked to CAM 1 we see the kitchen door through which JANE will appear as the action starts.

As the credit sequence, which is of course precisely timed, moves towards its end the director calls, 'Cue Jane'.

At the precise moment the credit sequence ends, the vision mixer switches to the output of camera 1. The PA calls, 'On 1 – 2 Next.' and on the monitor linked to CAM 2 you see the cameraman is focusing and framing his picture ready for the next shot. Now the director watching the preview of camera 2's shot may call, 'Let's have that shot closer two. Push in tighter.' We watch and see camera 2 move in a little.

When the dialogue and action reaches the place in the shooting script where, as you can see, the director has indicated he wants a different picture the vision mixer presses the button and the picture that is being recorded changes.

As the director works the producer watches detail closely, making notes like, Jane was too slow off her mark as she came from the kitchen in shot 2; the sound boom was visible in shot 5; or you could see the shadow of Jim on the wall just inside the door as he waited to make his entrance. Not infrequently the note will be that the actor muffed his line – a thing the writer usually notices rather quickly.

The process goes on through, perhaps, three or four hundred shots according to the length of the play. Getting it on to the screen requires a large variety of skills and artistic talents. It also takes hard work and great concentration, but the work of the writer is finished well before the script gets to the studio floor.

The pattern of television production changes and will doubtless continue to change over the years. In the fifties all shows were 'live' (transmitted as they happened). If the actors 'dried' (forgot their lines), knocked over furniture or anything else went wrong they had to use their ingenuity to try and cover it. One of the early programmes I wrote was an adventure for boys. I set it on an ex-Royal Navy motor torpedo boat. It was produced entirely in the studio. There were two sets. A small section of deck and wheel-house and the interior of the cabin. We had a sky-blue back-cloth, a wind machine and a stage hand throwing buckets of water over the deck. The camera was on a rocker and we used 'stock film' (film clips from libraries) of seascapes and distant coast lines to give us a whiff of sea air.

It wasn't quite as realistic as *Hornblower* but at least no one got seasick.

Observant viewers did, however, see something of a miracle. An actor stepped off the deck set without noticing a red light showing on a nearby camera indicating it was live. So what the audience saw was a man walking on water which hadn't been done for two thousand years. These days it would all be on film shot aboard a real ship on real water and anyone who stepped off the deck would get very wet indeed!

That is a classic example of the minor things that went wrong. When there was a real disaster the show was stopped and restarted once the problem was sorted out.

In the sixties 'VTR' (video tape recording) was introduced and programmes were recorded and transmitted later, but cutting tape was expensive and time consuming and directors were instructed to keep cuts to an absolute minimum.

By the end of the sixties new developments meant that tape could be cut as easily as film and re-takes of scenes that didn't satisfy the director were as common in the television studio as in a film studio. At that time it was usual to rehearse the play and then start the recording and go straight through so that a sixty minute play was in the 'can' (recorded) in sixty minutes. When it was completed they went back to do any re-takes necessary which were edited in later.

Exterior scenes 'OB sequence' (outside broadcast sequence) could be shot on tape using an 'OB unit' (camera crew, etc) which could be sent to the desired location The OB consisted of three or four TV cameras and a 'mobile scanner' (a small control room on wheels). You may possibly have seen them – a large van bearing the name of the television company on the sides – parked at some sporting event or other open air function that is being televised.

In his mobile control the director previewed every frame of his production on the monitors just as he does in the studio. The problem of shooting exterior scenes in this way was that the TV cameras were heavy and each had to be linked to the control by long cables which were vulnerable. A lot of technical things could, and often did, go wrong. Consequently, while it was worth transporting crews and equipment to shoot a ninety minute football match which couldn't be shot in the studio, taking an OB unit out to shoot a three minute exterior scene in a series episode, which could more easily be done on film, was not looked on with favour.

The next development followed logically upon the new ease of cutting tape. They called it 'Rehearse Record' (scenes were rehearsed individually and then shot in the way films are made). The great advantage of this was that all scenes on one particular set could be recorded together and the set 'struck' (to 'strike the set': dismantle) and other sets assembled in their place on the 'floor' (studio floor).

It meant that larger multi-set productions could, if necessary, be produced in smaller studios and it had the additional advantage that actors, required only on certain sets, were not needed at the studio throughout the entire production. Many series and, in particular continuous serials, are made in this way.

For shooting exterior drama scenes on location film is much the most convenient way although the director is not able to see exactly what he has shot until, usually, the next day, when he gets 'the rushes' (early processed film). This is why film directors always shoot and double shoot from the same 'set up' (camera position) before moving on to shoot the scene again from a new set up.

But outside filming presents its own peculiar set of problems which you need to know about as we shall see in the next chapter.

3. Exteriors and locations

With so much television now made outside the large purpose-built studios and the emergence of a great many independent producers who now have access to the TV screen, it is essential that anyone who aims to write for the media should appreciate some of the problems the director faces when he takes his cameras outside and, in particular, the kind of problems that the writer can avoid if he is aware of them as he constructs his script.

The television studio with its highly sophisticated and expensive electronic equipment demands considerable capital involvement, well beyond the means of smaller independent producers, but they can make high quality films on exterior locations and improvised, 'studios' close by in stately houses, smaller houses, factories, church halls, warehouses and similar premises where they can shoot interior scenes and erect what small sets they need.

An example of this method of production was the serial *Seal Morning*. The book by Rowena Farre was set in the north of Scotland but for various reasons the producers decided to make the television dramatisation in an isolated area of Norfolk where there is, around the coast, a colony of seals.

The producers rented a large house for their production office. The exteriors were shot on nearby beaches and sand-dunes and on the marshes and water-meadows. They found a lonely cottage that looked right for the home of the woman in the story and used exterior establishing shots of the cottage, garden and lane and of the principals and other actors approaching or departing as the story demanded. Cottage interiors that the story called for – living room, bedrooms and kitchen were built inside a huge barn hired from a nearby farmer. It was a very efficient and successful operation.

On the face of it, to shoot scenes outside on a suitable location and avoid the cost of building sets seems an obvious and sensible thing to do but even the most common setting can face the director with formidable obstacles. The first and most obvious, in this country, is of course, the weather. The reason California became the centre of the American film industry was the reliability of the climate. The

19

sunshine makes it possible to get clear, bright pictures and be reasonably sure when you starting shooting exterior scenes that you won't be held up for costly days or weeks waiting for it to stop raining.

In Norfolk, shooting *Seal Morning* in a bitterly cold February one of the production crew actually got so seriously frost bitten that he finished up in hospital. Some days, it rained; others it snowed and then again there were days when the mist coming in off the sea was so thick that outside filming was out of question. But the production was cleverly planned. The days no filming was possible out of doors were spent shooting the interiors in the barn so not too many days were wasted.

But the weather on a deserted part of the Norfolk coast was a minor problem compared with the added difficulties and frustrations producers meet, all too frequently, in many less isolated places. During the outside filming in a London suburban street a young actor playing a policeman was confronted by a woman who wanted to know the way to the post office. The shot was ruined and the camera stopped rolling as he apologised for not knowing and brightly explained his ignorance by telling her he was new on that beat. To have confessed he was an actor and they were making a film for television would have guaranteed a crowd which was the last thing the scene needed.

The woman toddled off and returned five minutes later and walked blithely back into shot. 'Found it,' she informed him, cheerfully. 'It's down the first road on the right. Thought I'd come back and tell you so as you'll know if anyone else asks you.'

Ideally a director likes to work on a controlled location; the interior or gardens of a stately home on days when the public are excluded; small villages or hamlets where the local people can be asked, and relied upon to keep out of shot; road circuits round large factories or through private estates – anywhere appropriate for the setting of the story where the director can be sure there will be no spectators and interruptions.

Ideally! But it isn't always possible. A London street is a London street. If the script calls for shots in that setting without traffic or people about it may be possible to arrange it in the early hours of the morning when the city is deserted. If, as is more likely, the story requires shots of the actors walking, running or pushing their way through crowds of shoppers in Oxford Street or crashing a car in the middle of an identifiable Piccadilly Circus during the rush hour it is going to be a producer's headache and he will undoubtedly change the setting if at all possible – and conceivably the script and the writer if it isn't. Television directors exercise great ingenuity in finding and adapting locations but the writer needs to take care to see that he does not ask the impossible.

An establishing shot of a busy railway station or a crowd coming away from a football match with your actors in the picture may seem simple enough. But not once people see the camera. You can bet your life the moment it is realised they are taking pictures for 'the telly' there will be some idiot determined to get into the picture to wave hallo to his mum or do his imitation ape act which for some reason always seems to be a popular choice.

Of course, cameras can be, and invariably are, concealed for that kind of shot. Bigger problems and considerable expense begins when, for a play set earlier this century or back still further in the past, a splendid Georgian street or suitably isolated Elizabethan cottages are found – sprouting television aerials, telephone wires and electricity cables and every possible camera angle takes in out of period extensions or out-houses and fences; concrete paths, tarmac roads with white lines and traffic signs or advertisement boards.

White lines, modern paving and kerbs in a village street can be easily and inexpensively covered with mud or hay but removing and later replacing street signs, television aerials and the like is a much more complicated business; but when after much searching a location is found that meets the requirements of the story there is frequently no way round it. The negotiations start with the house owners, electricity board, telephone people or whoever and getting permission is sometimes long and always costly.

And when the street signs and telephone wires have been removed there is always a stray dog with ambitions to get into pictures or some- one using a chain saw for the producer to contend with. The prod- uction team need to be on their toes all the time to avoid disasters. They just can't afford to let up. Believe it or not, there was one American western with a distant helicopter in shot beyond an Apache war party.

Selecting the background against which you will tell your story is very important. That alone could determine whether or not it is ever produced. Taking a film crew out to shoot a television programme involves expensive and complicated logistics. If the story calls for an isolated place, well out of town, where they are unlikely to be disturbed by traffic and spectators there may well be difficulty in finding hotel accommodation for the artists and crew, or in organising the arrangements for catering. Transport, hotels and food for a large production unit can be very costly.

One of the reasons the *Seal Morning* programme was located in Norfolk instead of setting it, as in the book, in the north of Scotland, was the availability of accommodation and easier access for artists and production people coming from London and the Midlands.

It is easy to forget, or not to know that, from the producer's point of view there is a great deal more to making television programmes than scripts and camera angles. Shooting that bitter February on the bleak east coast the production office had even to make sure that the cast and crew were issued with thermal underwear.

But by now you are doubtless recalling episodes or plays you have seen set on some beautiful, isolated or exotic location – possibly overseas – and trying to equate that with what you have just read. You are right, of course. Television programmes are filmed in many extravagant settings and, although a lot of cheating goes on, using stock film, if the producing company is keen enough, the script is good enough and the budget big enough they'll make it.

But the dice are loaded against producers accepting and making plays by new and little known writers who arrogantly disregard or are totally ignorant of the economics of the business. Using an experienced writer doesn't absolutely guarantee success but it does guarantee that the bosses or financial backers won't be saying, 'You must be crazy to risk so much money on a play by a writer with no track record!'.

Strangely, it is sometimes cheaper to engage two actors than one. Working on my first television film series I thought I would save the producers money by making the chauffeur who appeared in the first act of the play, also work as the gardener in act three. What, at that time, I hadn't realised, but was very quickly apprised of, was that this meant the actor had to be engaged and retained for fourteen days. He was needed on the set on day one but not again until day fourteen. Quite rightly, the producers would have had to pay him for the time he sat around waiting. Needless to say a second actor played the gardener and the producer paid for two days work rather than the fourteen days my 'economy' would have entailed.

Dialogue on location

One of the problems to be faced shooting exterior scenes on location is the dialogue. Even a light wind gusting into a mic causes distortion. Street noises, distant trains, barking dogs or children at play can render the sound track useless. If, for example, the scene depicts Abraham Lincoln delivering his Gettysburg address and the location is a bit of waste land where the camera can be so angled as to avoid including in the shot the nearby electricity pylon and signs pointing the way to the car park – but on opening his mouth Mr Lincoln's immortal words are drowned by the roar of Concorde passing overhead, the scene will be ruined.

When shooting in towns and cities the problem is so acute that many producers prefer to 'post-sync' (post-synchronise), adding dialogue, music or sound effects, after the mute or partially sound picture (tape or film) has been shot. Which means the scene is played regardless of all ambient sound and later, when the film is assembled, the actors go into a special studio and say their lines again, trying to match their own lip movements. This, however, takes additional costly time for both actors and technicians so the writer should endeavour to keep to a minimum the lines of dialogue the characters must speak on location.

There are, too, particular difficulties when the actors are required to be moving as they deliver lines in the open air. Picking up the conversation of two men as they cycle home from work, for instance, requires a vehicle with a camera mounted on top, driving along just in front of them. The action presents no problem. We've all seen that kind of shot in dozens of movies but the dialogue is something else. Microphones have to be close to the actors to pick up their speech if they are not to pick up, also, all the other noises around – the engine of the car, the drumming of the tyre treads and that jet – the one that always flies over at the most inopportune time.

Of course we have just seen how we get over that. No problem. Post-sync the sound. But what if it is a small budget show and there's no money left for such luxuries?

The writer is expected to use his imagination, skill and experience to overcome the difficulty. The simple way is to have the cyclists stop for their discussion. Open the scene with a few moments of them cycling along together and then let them reach an intersection where they go different ways. Here it is natural for them to pause to say goodbye. Here they can play their scene and say their lines and with the actors stationary the director can get in close with his microphone.

That's another way of doing it.

But they may, for the purpose of the story, be going all the way together and what one has to tell the other – and more importantly what the writer needs him to tell the audience – may be some vital plot point that he has to know before he gets home. You might, of course stop them with a puncture, or a very steep hill at the top of which they need a breather. If you pause and really think about it you could probably find a dozen good reasons. This is where your craft ingenuity comes into play. There is, you see, more to writing television than working out clever plots, creating interesting characters, writing bright dramatic dialogue or funny and witty lines. It is up to the writer to cover the technical-limitation problem in some way that is germane to the story and characters.

One other way of dealing with this problem is 'voice over', sometimes shown in the script as VO. You have your characters in 'LS' (long shot), but their voices in 'CU'.

This convention can be very effective and is accepted by audiences – but not always by directors. It is a style that does not fit well into every production and if you are working with a director or editor it would be worth checking how they feel about it, before you write it.

Where it is acceptable the script would read like this:

| EXT: | COUNTRY ROAD. | DAY. | FILM. |

LS. MARK AND ROY CYCLING SIDE BY SIDE.

> ROY:
> (CLOSE ON MIKE)
> There is something I have been
> meaning to ask you.

> MARK:
> (CLOSE ON MIKE)
> What's that?

> ROY:
> It's something Jane said the other
> night, about you and Dorothy.

For this scene the director would make sure the actors were too far from the camera for anyone to see clearly whether or not their lips were moving. The dialogue would be dubbed on to the film sometime later, but that is no problem if the actors don't have to match lip movement.

When the convention is used you should never introduce new characters in this way. The audience need to meet them first in a normal scene to be able to recognise their voices and the things they talk about.

Frequently an experienced or creative director will solve this kind of problem himself and the writer may never know it existed. Other times and other directors will throw the script back, with, 'It's your script. You created the problem. You solve it.' It helps to be one jump ahead – to avoid creating the problem in the first place or at least to be able to save face with sufficient technical know-how to offer a sensible and practical solution.

This need to know a little about the technique and problems of production affects the nature of the professionalism involved in writing for the screen rather than the printed page. The novelist's work owes nothing to his knowledge or lack of knowledge of type faces, paper quality and printing processes.

But I said, 'at least a little'. Most television writers learn their craft as they write – and from their mistakes as they rewrite.

The script

Before we look at a script designed to be shot on film there is one thing you should note. It is, as you will see from excerpts that follow, an entirely different layout from the tape TV script.

I said in the last chapter, in respect of studio productions, that camera shots are the director's choice so the writer does not have to be too explicit about technical directions. A television film script, however, is essentially a film script where the writer is required to deliver a shooting script which clearly indicates each 'set up' (the scene in the frame of the camera placed in a particular position).

There is a very good reason for this. If the set up is in the script, it is obviously there for some plot or dramatic reason. A director, running his schedule close, may be tempted to shoot scenes quickly which could mean omitting a set up. When he is working within a television studio with monitor screens in front of him any omission is instantly obvious and quickly covered. Not so working with film, which will not come back from the processing laboratory until the next day and will invariably be sequences of disjointed action shot on each particular location regardless of story continuity. In consequence it may not be until they come to edit the film that it can be seen that a vital shot is missing. Then it is too late. That essential shot is gone for ever.

The script for a film must, therefore, be as watertight as possible and story requirements indicated in more detail than for a television studio production.

When writing for film production it is necessary for the writer to indicate where and what the camera is expected to cover. In examples that follow you will see that the writer has stipulated 'LS' (long shot), 'POV' (point of view), 'Another Angle', 'ON HALLET', 'RESUME HALLET' and similar instructions and, importantly, where the action is set - 'STUDIO', 'LOCATION' or 'STUDIO LOT'.

There are, too, other important differences. You will not be long in this business before you come across the term 'Second Unit' (another camera crew complete with director, lighting and sound technicians). While the principal actors are working with the director on the main set or location the second unit film background and establishing shots that are required of other locations.

Where no close shots in which the principals are identifiable are involved DOUBLES are frequently used; but whether it is necessary or desirable to use a double for any particular sequence is the director's decision and the new writer should leave it entirely to him. These excerpts of television film also demonstrate how doubles are used. 'STUDIO LOT' is not actually featured in these particular examples but the term refers to the land and other property that is part of the studio complex – the exteriors of the office buildings; exteriors of storage sheds; roadways, gardens, main entrance gate etc.

88   EXT: STREET.   NIGHT.   LOCATION.   88

POV

THROUGH CAR WINDSCREEN.

A FASHIONABLE AREA OF LONDON.

DOUBLE FOR HALLET COMES FROM A HOUSE AND STOPS ON THE KERB AND LOOKS ROUND.

HE HAILS A CRUISING TAXI AND GETS IN.

THE TAXI STARTS OFF.

                                              CUT TO:

89   INT: TAXI.   NIGHT.   STUDIO   (LIGHT EFFECT).*   89

HALLET (not the double) TURNS AND LOOKS OUT THE REAR WINDOW.

                                              CUT TO:

90   EXT: STREET.   NIGHT.   LOCATION.   90

HALLET'S POV

SHAW'S CAR STARTS UP AND FOLLOWS SOME DISTANCE BEHIND.

---

*This is a night shot – it is done in the studio. The effect of a moving car is simulated very easily with moving lights.

CUT TO:

91   INT: TAXI.   NIGHT.   STUDIO (LIGHT EFFECT).   91

RESUME HALLET   (not the double)

THE TAXI TURNS A CORNER.

HALLET LOOKS WORRIED. HE TURNS ONCE AGAIN AND LOOKS OUT OF THE REAR WINDOW.

CUT TO:

92   EXT: STREET.   NIGHT.   LOCATION.   92

HALLET'S POV

THE ROAD BEHIND IS CLEAR BUT A MOMENT LATER THE CAR ROUNDS THE CORNER AND CONTINUES TO FOLLOW.

CUT TO:

93   INT: TAXI.   NIGHT.   STUDIO (LIGHT EFFECT).   93

RESUME HALLET

HE LEANS FORWARD AND SLIDES OPEN THE WINDOW TO SPEAK TO THE DRIVER.

CUT TO:

94   INT: SHAW'S CAR.   NIGHT.   STUDIO   (LIGHT EFFECT).   94

JOAN IS AT THE WHEEL.

SHAW BESIDE HER.

JOAN:

He's stopping!

SHE SLOWS DOWN.

CUT TO:

95   EXT: STREET.   NIGHT.   LOCATION   95

THE TAXI HAS STOPPED OUTSIDE A TUBE STATION.

SHAW'S CAR IS NEARING AND SLOWING.

DOUBLE FOR HALLET LEAPS OUT AND THRUSTS A NOTE INTO THE DRIVER'S HAND AND RUNS INTO THE STATION.

As you will see above, scenes in the studio use HALLET, one of the principal players. The night location shots – where we see a man hail a taxi and later leap out use the DOUBLE. And there is no dialogue in those scenes. The interior of the taxi and the car are easily done in a 'studio' whether that be a purpose-built studio or a barn taken over for the production. As the movement is actually only passing lights it could be simulated almost anywhere.

The only line of dialogue is in scene 94 (the Int: of Shaw's car. STUDIO) If it had been LOCATION or STUDIO LOT it could have been dubbed without difficulty since, in the darkness, no lip sync would have been required.

Stock film

Hollywood has been called the 'Dream Factory' and much of the business of films and television is concerned with manufacturing illusions; fantasy worlds, peopled with imaginary characters and all kinds of clever technical devices, are used to deceive the viewers and get them to accept, at least for the duration of the story, that the people they are watching are doing the things they seem to be doing in the places where our eyes tell us they are physically present at that moment in time.

We have seen in scenes 89, 91, 93 and 94 above that the taxi and the car are not travelling at night through the streets of London as it appeared to the audience but that is not a difficult illusion to create.

There is, however, a way in which exotic and awe-inspiring outside sequences of far distant places can be incorporated in a low budget film without either the actors or production team leaving the studio or going on location. I am talking about the use of stock film which, as previously mentioned, is the use of clips from film libraries of some sight or location too expensive, or not worth the trouble, or where it is unnecessary to send a unit to make film.

For example, if you want a picture of an aircraft landing at Heathrow there are obviously miles of footage available. If you want shots of crowded beaches or an express train, rush-hour traffic or army war-games there would be plenty of choice from film libraries. It is, of course, all copyright and doesn't come cheap – but it comes a lot cheaper than sending a second unit to bring back pictures of the pyramids or the streets of Hong Kong or hiring a helicopter to shoot pictures of an oil-rig or whatever the story requires.

The problem is matching the picture quality. You can't just include any old piece of film regardless. That would stand out like a sore thumb. But there is a lot of high quality film around and it is sometimes possible to incorporate it into a script very effectively.

For a television film series made at Borehamwood studios for the Independent Television Corporation, the brief to the writers was to devise stories in spectacular settings; mountains, jungles, tropical islands or what have you. The budget was average. There was no money to send film crews around the world to do special shooting. The intention was to find and inter-cut stock film to give a new dimension to what was in other respects a run-of-the-mill series.

I chose to set my story around Scott Base in Antarctica of which there was a great deal of stock available. Unusually, in this case, of 160 shots in my film about half were actually stock film. The scenes below demonstrate how it was integrated into the script.

In the scene that follows special investigators have been briefed and are being sent to check on a suspected breach of an international treaty in Antarctica.

26 INT: GENEVA OFFICE.   DAY.   STUDIO.   26

(Below are the closing speeches of the scene)

TREMAYNE:
Fascinating place, Antarctica. I envy you.

CRAIG:
Oh sure!

RICHARD:
Tell you what – we'll bring you back a penguin.

CUT TO:

27 EXT: ANTARCTIC MATERIAL. DAY. STOCK.   27

PENGUINS

ON ROCKS AND ICE. THEY SCATTER TO THE WATER AS
WE HEAR:

SOUND AN AIRCRAFT FLYING OVERHEAD.

CUT TO:

28 EXT: AIRCRAFT IN FLIGHT.   DAY.   STOCK.   28

AN AIRCRAFT IN THE ANTARCTIC SKY. (A LS. THIS SHOULD
BE A LARGE FOUR ENGINE PROP PLANE TO MATCH AIRCRAFT
SEEN LATER LANDING AT SCOTT BASE). ESTABLISH AND THEN:

CUT TO:

29 INT: AIRCRAFT.   DAY.   STUDIO.   29

A LARGE FOUR ENGINE TRANSPORT PLANE THE REAR OF
WHICH IS STACKED WITH SUPPLIES.

CRAIG AND RICHARD ARE SITTING AT A TABLE LOOKING
OUT OF THE WINDOW. BOTH MEN NOW WEAR ANORAKS
ALTHOUGH THE HOODS ARE DOWN.

CLOSE ON RICHARD
AS HE LOOKS OUT OF WINDOW.
SOUND PROP AIRCRAFT ENGINES.

CUT TO:

30   EXT: ANTARCTIC MATERIAL.   DAY.   STOCK.   30

RICHARD'S POV
AN AERIAL VIEW OF PACK ICE, ICE CLIFFS, ETC. BELOW THEM.

CUT TO:

31   INT: AIRCRAFT.   DAY.   STUDIO.   31

RESUME RICHARD
LOOKING OUT OF THE WINDOW

CRAIG:
A drink?

RICHARD TURNS FROM THE WINDOW.

(And this studio scene plays on until)

32   EXT: ANTARCTIC MATERIAL.   DAY.   STOCK.   32

AIRCRAFT LANDING

A LARGE FOUR ENGINE PROP PLANE COMES IN TO LAND.
WE SEE THE APPROACH AND THE LANDING. THE PLANE
SKIDS TO A HALT.

(At this point we cut away to pick up other characters in the story
who were travelling by sea)

CUT TO:

33   EXT: ANTARCTIC MATERIAL.   DAY.   STOCK.   33

SEASCAPE

A PANNING SHOT OF ANTARCTIC WATERS, ICEBERGS,
PACK ICE, BIRDS FLYING.

A SHIP AT SEA

A SUPPLY SHIP IN ANTARCTIC WATERS. SHOTS OF HEAVY,
ICY SEAS AND SPRAY SWEEPING OVER THE DECKS.

CUT TO:

34   EXT: CABIN PORTHOLE.   DAY.   STUDIO.   34

THE PORTHOLE TO ONE OF THE DECK CABINS. ICICLES
HANG AROUND THE FRAME. THE GLASS IS MISTED. INSIDE
THE CABIN A HAND WITH A CLOTH WIPES THE MIST AND
WE SEE THE FACE OF A MAN PEERING OUT.

WE CLOSE IN AND TIGHTEN ON THE FACE THROUGH THE
GLASS AS THE MAN FROWNS.

CUT TO:

35   <u>EXT: ANTARCTIC MATERIAL.   DAY.   STOCK.</u>   35
<u>THE MAN'S POV</u>
<u>THROUGH THE PORTHOLE</u>
SHOT OF LARGE PASSING ICEBERG.

                                         CUT TO:

36   <u>EXT: CABIN PORTHOLE.   DAY.   STUDIO.</u>   36
<u>RESUME THE MAN</u>
HE TURNS AWAY BACK INTO THE CABIN.
OVER THIS, AND THE PREVIOUS SCENES WE HAVE HEARD
<u>SOUND</u> ROUGH SEA NOISES.

                                         CUT TO:

37   <u>INT: CABIN.   DAY.   STUDIO.</u>   37
ON THE MAN AS HE TURNS AWAY FROM THE PORTHOLE.

(We now play dialogue scene in the cabin before cutting away to other stock material)

In the above instance, by sitting through about five hours of Antarctic travel film, we knew before the script was written what stock was available. It would have been folly to write in shots like an aircraft landing at Scott Base if we hadn't known we could get it.

For this production, too, you may guess they used a lot of polystyrene 'snow' to cover the studio floor for Studio Ext shots that featured the actors.

The amount of 'stock' used here was exceptional. Generally the writer will only need one or two short sequences to establish background and ambience of his story but little tricks like the icy porthole or a matching shadow help to make the transition from 'stock' to 'studio' fairly smooth providing the quality of the stock is not too different from the film being shot.

Night shooting

Before we leave the subject of outside film there is one very important thing that no writer intending to work in television must ever overlook. Night shooting on location is extremely expensive. The unit have to take along huge arc lights plus mobile generators to make the electricity for them and all the technicians will be working on overtime rates. Of course sequences are shot at night but if you are working with an editor or producer it is best to get their agreement before you go ahead and write night scenes.

If you are not in contact with anyone, make the night scenes 'interiors' or set it by 'day' if you can.

But if it can't be an 'interior' and it can't be 'day' and there's no money in the budget for night shooting on location, there is a cheap, but not entirely satisfactory, way round the problem. It is known as 'day for night' shooting. They adjust the camera so that it takes a dull picture. If there is a car involved it has lights on to further the illusion. If the director does it well some of the audience will be fooled into believing the scene has been shot in brilliant moonlight but the more observant will see it for what it is.

One tends to think of film and OB as the only ways of taking a story outside the studio but there are other ways of doing this and although with lighter, hand-held cameras less use is made of these techniques, it is worth having a look at some of the tricks that are used to achieve the effect.

4. The land of mockbelieve

The entertainment industry has, from earliest times, exploited and thrived on clever visual tricks and illusions. In the Victorian theatre they managed to simulate a ship at sea by using a small deck section; spreading a sea-coloured canvas over the stage and engaging small boys to crawl around under the canvas to produce the effect of heaving waves. Old reports tell us it was very effective with audiences ever ready to suspend belief except, perhaps, on one notable occasion when an impoverished company were working with an old and rotten canvas and an over-enthusiastic lad, attempting to create particularly mountainous waves split the canvas and popped up in the 'water' beside the ship. Ever resourceful, an actor is said to have retrieved the situation with the shout, 'Man overboard'.

Nowadays we often hear it said, 'the camera cannot lie'. That may be so, but to use a famous phrase it can certainly be 'very economical with the truth'. Since the invention of the movie camera it is not necessary to ask an audience to stretch their imaginations as far as those Victorian theatre audiences, nor need the showman be a conjurer to fool them into thinking they are seeing something quite different from what is actually there before their eyes.

The early film makers quickly discovered that by increasing or decreasing the number of frames covering the action it was possible to show break-neck speed or slow motion – which those first comedy films exploited with great success. Scarcely able to believe their eyes astonished cinema audiences gasped in horror as great steam trains thundered at speed towards terrified young women chained helplessly to the railway track only yards ahead of them. Motor cars careered crazily through crowded streets missing pedestrians by inches and crashing through brick walls before falling apart bit by bit in slow motion as the driver, with more lives than a cat, stepped from the wreckage unhurt.

Some of the most effective 'cheats' were achieved by camera angles which presented brilliant opportunities to deceive and thrill. In an early film that legendary showman, Mack Sennett, had audiences on the edge of their seats when he perched a mock aircraft on top of a water tower in the hills outside Los Angeles, and by shooting from different angles with three cameras created the illusion of frightening height as a young woman clung desperately to the wing-tip.

And that was comedy!

But this was all day one in the creation of visual effects. The designers and other specialists have come a long, long way since then. For instance, the BBC's Visual Effects Department, which was established in the 1950s, has expanded many times over and had to move out of the Television Centre to separate premises in Acton where they are constantly adding to the facilities and new techniques are devised and developed.

But you don't need to know how to cause an explosion to write one. It is not necessary for the writer, and particularly a new writer, to clutter his mind with details of the many specialist techniques that are currently available to television programme makers. Indeed, with so many new and different creative effects invented and introduced each year, only those working closely with the experts can have any hope of keeping up with all the visual wonders they devise. Theirs is a highly skilled business demanding great imagination, experience and not a little artistic talent and scientific know-how.

If you have written a script that requires some special visual effects you had best leave it to the producer to decide whether he can manage them and whether his budget will stretch to them. When it does, he will probably need to talk to the designers and effects experts to ensure he gets the latest techniques available.

But there are certain fairly elementary things you should be aware of to help your writing. In the last chapter we have seen how the impression of a car travelling along a city street at night can be created in a studio using the very simple effect of passing lights. But what if your car needs to be travelling by day? Well, one way this can be faked in the studio is by the use of 'back projection' (BP). Here a film projector throws a film onto a translucent screen. The actors play their scene on the opposite side while a television camera beyond them records both their action and the moving film. In this way a daytime car journey through busy streets or an express train rushing past a couple standing talking on the platform can be made to look very real without the need to take the actors out of the studio. But BP takes up a lot of space in the studio and the acting area is limited.

We have also seen how, in the Antarctic script, by cutting from a character to his POV on stock film, we have created the illusion that our actors and cameras have been transported at great expense to Scott Base for a dangerous and arduous location shoot. In Chapter 3 we have exposed the 'cheat' of using doubles and, of course, you don't have to have spent half your life working in films and television to know that stand-ins and stunt-men are regularly employed to take the place of star actors in dangerous and long tedious sequences where they are not obviously recognisable.

One of the commonest visual effects that has been used in films for donkey's years is obtained by the very simple device of a 'matte mask' whereby part of the field of view is obscured. Dozens of times, for instance, you will have seen a character put a pair of binoculars to his eyes and in the next shot you see what he is looking at encircled by the rims of the binocular lenses. More ambitiously, using masks, the exteriors of streets and interiors of grand halls can be simulated inside a studio as demonstrated by the illustrations shown overleaf.

In Fig 1 you see the studio set with the studio lights in shot. This is the set on which the actors play their scene and say their lines but the director must make sure they do not poke their heads above the skyline. Fig 2 shows a mask cut to follow the contours of the roof-tops and this mask is then put into the optical printer so that when the film is printed only the unmasked scene will come out. The director then obtains film of a skyscape and the matting expert makes a mask complimentary to the first one as in Fig 3. The film positive showing the buildings is then run through the optical printer with the building masked over while at the same time the negative of the skyscape is run through. The result is the sky is printed on the original positive in the unmasked area. Fig 4 shows the two pictures married together on the same film print.

Television has advanced beyond this basic film industry technique. For many years now masking has been done electronically in the studio by a process called 'inlay' without the need or delays involved in laboratory film processing.

But studios, of course, have no ceilings. Figs 1 and 5 show why. Film and TV cameras need bright light to take clear pictures. To get shots of people dancing in a ballroom, for instance, the director would have to pull the camera so far back that he would shoot over the top of the walls and expose the lights and studio gantries. The ceiling has to be 'cheated' in. So an artist is engaged to make a painting of a ceiling as it would be seen from the POV of camera 1. It doesn't have to be set size but when looked at by camera 2 in a

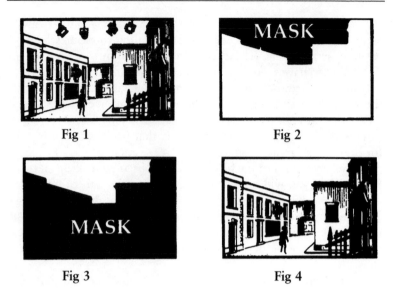

Fig 1   Fig 2

Fig 3   Fig 4

close shot it can be adjusted so that it is in proportion with the set.

With the first inlay developed before the introduction of colour the director worked on a special 'inlay' desk which incorporated a small TV camera that looked at a white screen. On this screen a mask was placed as shown in Fig 7. The output of the inlay camera was controlled by an electronic switch. When the camera saw white it switched in the output of camera 1, (the set). When the inlay camera saw black it switched in the output of camera 2 (the close shot of the small painting of the ceiling). Married together they produced the combined picture illustrated in Fig 8 on page 37.

This kind of inlay has been widely used for years – but not without problems. If an actor got into the unmasked area he disappeared or lost his head, a trick which has, of course, been used many times for comedy effect.

But we live in an age of great electronic advances. With the advent of colour the BBC introduced (CSO) Colour Separation Overlay or Chroma Key as it is known throughout commercial television. Here, instead of the electronic switch being actuated only by black and white as with inlay, it responded to particular colours; at first only blue; nowadays various other colours too can be used to key background changes.

In some electronic studios back projection has been superseded by 'FAP' (front axial projection). This uses a highly reflective screen that

Fig 5

Fig 6

MASK

Fig 7

Fig 8

accepts light thrown directly at it from one position only. Another system known as Paint-box (electronic masking) allows masking to be achieved with a kind of electronic paint brush with which areas of the picture that must be masked are in effect painted out.

Possibly one of the most satisfying and challenging assignments for the visual effects staff are the space epics. Here the latest advanced technology really comes into its own. One wonder is Motion Control Computerised Camera which can be programmed to track in, out, up, down and around while the subject – a model – stays still and the different lenses zoom in and out to give Close Ups or Long Shots as required. Working to a meticulously prepared computer program, space-ships and planets can be flown around the 'universe' through clouds of cosmic dust, narrowly avoiding disastrous collisions with meteorites and alien craft before returning safely to the launch-pad in the studio from which, of course, it has not moved at all. A more recent development is CGI (Computer Generated Imagery).

Of course the uses of such advanced equipment is by no means confined to space epics but if it sounds very technical and complicated it's because it is. The scope of the work of visual effects departments includes explosions and battle scenes, models, monsters and miniatures, electronics and radio controls, robots, sculptures and museum reproductions, fires, lasers and stunt co-ordination to name but a few. It would be a very arrogant writer, new or experienced, who tried to stipulate in his script precisely how some special effect should be achieved. The chances are the professionals would know a different and better way of achieving the result he needed.

As writers we do not need to understand exactly how these things are done but we do need to watch television to see and learn the kind of visual effects being used so that we are aware of the possibilities as we devise and write our stories.

But among all the hi-tech gadgetry many of the old tricks remain. Mirrors and fifty/fifty mirrors which reflect an image on one side only still play their part in the magic of television and destructions and explosions have always been and remain a sensational and favourite visual effect. Not infrequently these scenic destructions appear to be such reckless vandalism that the producers are inundated with complaints as happened some years ago when in a *Doctor Who* episode they blew up an old country church and the BBC received scores of protests.

What was destroyed was, of course, a perfect scale model of a charming old village church that had been featured in the location shooting.

But even blowing up model churches can be dangerous and expensive and there has to be split-second co-ordination between all concerned to ensure safety and efficiency. There is a show-business story about a big film producer who intended to show ancient Rome go up in flames. At enormous expense, he had a wonderful model of Rome built on a hill. To make triple sure that not a flick of flame or wisp of smoke would be missed, he had three film cameras in position, one at the bottom of the hill, one half way up and the other at the top. Then sitting back comfortably in his producer's chair, he called over his megaphone the magic words, 'Roll 'em!' then he had his beautiful model of ancient Rome put to flame. The models of the buildings burnt furiously. Finally when the last embers had blackened to ash, the producer got up and strode over to his first cameraman. 'Joey,' he said, 'you got everything in the can?' Joey mopped his brow. 'Boss, something terrible happened. Just as the flames got under way my camera broke. I couldn't fix it.' Without a word the producer stomped up the hill to his second cameraman: 'Mike, you got the burning of Rome okay?' Mike looked terrified: 'Boss, you're going to hate me, but I didn't get a single frame. My assistant cameraman forget to reload the camera.' Speechless the producer climbed on up the hill until he had the third cameraman in view. Then he raised his megaphone and in a voice touched with controlled hysteria he called: 'Hymie! O Hymie! This is your producer.' And the third cameraman called back down the hill: 'Ready when you are, boss!'

For that fabulous moment of the destruction of the bridge on the River Kwai, legend has it that the producer had six film cameras taken on location to roll simultaneously. Television cannot afford such expense. Instead, everyone in television has to think and co-ordinate a little bit harder.

5. Television – a visual medium

When, in the mid 1950s, television began to take off in this country there were, inevitably, very few writers who had any experience of writing TV drama. It is interesting to reflect, too, that the 'telly' was regarded with unveiled contempt by many authors, playwrights and screenwriters who thought it a very second rate business. It was poorly paid and not something any great number of writers established in other areas felt the need, or wish, to be associated with.

However, because television was broadcasting and broadcasting was the BBC the majority of writers who gravitated to television at the outset were those who had written for radio. They were, in the main, freelance contributors and they welcomed the opportunities of a new and promising market.

In radio dialogue was everything and many of the best writers wrote brilliantly witty speeches, hilarious comedies or articulated thoughts, anguish and depths in their characters that could never be adequately expressed in exclusively visual terms. And it was not only the writers who delighted in the imagery of words. Producers who had grown up in radio appreciated the virtues of good lively dialogue. But in any event, with limited budgets and little of the flexibility enjoyed by television today, very often the only way to get the show on the air was to have the actors tell the audience about things that had happened in another place at another time, thereby avoiding the cost of building extra sets or taking a film camera out to shoot exteriors scenes.

The result was that many of the earliest television plays were rather like radio with pictures.

In the United States in the early 1950s a number of theatre playwrights and radio writers like Paddy Chayefsky and Rod Serling distinguished themselves writing very fine television plays for New York based TV stations. They, too, wrote deep and perceptive characterisations and fine dialogue which received wide critical acclaim but it wasn't long before the large film companies of Hollywood began to dominate production.

40

The film industry had grown out of silent movies where action was all and the writer was the guy employed to write captions for the pictures – surprisingly, in the early 1950s, the 'Talkie' was still only around twenty-five years old. Film men believed actions spoke louder than words; that what a man did had greater impact than what he said and writers and directors who had learned their business in the motion picture industry brought this notion with them to television.

Thus, while the Americans wrote popular drama series that seemed to many British critics to concentrate on action at the expense of characterisation; where conversations were conducted in clichés, slick retorts and an economy of words that seemed positively miserly, British writers wrote lengthy dialogue scenes which American producers and editors regarded as literary diarrhoea.

But as Don Taylor, one of our most creative directors said, in an appendix to *The Generations* by David Mercer, a trilogy of plays published by John Calder, 'Television is not primarily a visual medium. It is not primarily anything. Sound radio is purely aural, and silent film is purely visual. Television like film is an equal partnership of the two.'

Words are the writer's tool and most of us, used to writing for the press, automatically express ourselves in words. Very frequently, however, the words we use are no more than the means of conveying the picture in our mind and television can convey pictorial information without the aid of words.

Obviously a lot of information an audience needs can only be transmitted in words, e.g. thoughts and what has happened outside the time and scenes of the play, but a television writer should always be conscious of the need to avoid telling his audience what they can very well see for themselves.

'Been in a fight?' as a question to a man with a black eye and a bloody nose would get a laugh in a comedy script but is hardly necessary in a serious play. 'Going out?' to a person who has just put on a hat and coat is a waste of words. If the writer cannot find something more interesting to say it is better to say nothing – except maybe 'goodbye!'.

It is said that the British industry follows the USA a few years later. In the current market driven situation Britain has caught up fast with an increasing number of programmes shot entirely on film and much of that on location. The introduction of super-sensitive film stock, high quality, light, hand-held cameras and new production techniques has made it possible for directors to move out of the television studio, avoiding the high cost of studio sets and complex electronic equipment. This gives them the freedom to work on a broader canvas setting stories on locations, too large, too expensive or quite impossible to reproduce in a studio. The emergence, too, of a great many small independent TV-film producers who are no longer kept off the screen by the monopolies of the BBC and ITV companies, has done much to change what was for three decades the established pattern of the British television industry.

Exclusively studio drama plays such as the famous Armchair Theatre, Wednesday Play and others screened under similar generic titles are now largely replaced by one-shot and multi-part dramas made entirely on film, and it becomes increasingly necessary for writers hoping to break into television to learn both studio and film techniques.

When you begin to consciously visualise your story in terms of pictures you will be surprised how often dialogue is superfluous.

If you can show it, show it! Don't talk about it.

Of course it is relatively easy to do that when one is writing an all action detective or mystery adventure that involves a chase or pursuit of one kind or another. The following 'stock chase' sequence from an ITC television film I wrote turned out to be quite exciting and with just two words of dialogue ran for three minutes and five seconds screen time.

This scene, made on film, demonstrates how the studio and location action is shot separately and spliced together later in the cutting room. Note too how a double is used in minor non-speaking scenes to reduce the work-load on the principal actor; to avoid taking him away from the main studio or location filming and cut down the number of days the 'expensive' principal actors are needed for the production.

72. EXT: STREET. SMALL COUNTRY TOWN. DAY. LOCATION.

    RANDALL'S CAR IS PARKED IN THE KERB OUTSIDE BROOK'S OFFICE. THERE IS NOT A LOT OF TRAFFIC ABOUT.

    DOUBLE FOR RANDALL COMES FROM THE DOOR OF BROOK'S OFFICE AND GOES TO HIS CAR.

    ANOTHER ANGLE

    SMALL CAR APPROACHING.

                                    CUT TO:

73. INT: GRANT'S CAR. DAY. STUDIO.

    GRANT DRIVING DOWN THE STREET. SUDDENLY REACTS TO:

CUT TO:

74. EXT: STREET. SMALL COUNTRY TOWN. DAY. LOCATION.
GRANT'S POV (THROUGH WINDSCREEN).
RANDALL'S CAR IN KERB. DOUBLE FOR RANDALL
GETTING IN. THE CAR STARTS.

CUT TO:

75. INT: GRANT'S CAR. DAY. STUDIO.
RESUME GRANT
HE LOOKS AFTER RANDALL'S CAR WITH A PUZZLED
EXPRESSION ON HIS FACE. HE MAKES A DECISION.

CUT TO:

76. EXT: STREET. SMALL COUNTRY TOWN. DAY. LOCATION.
GRANT'S CAR TURNS AND STARTS AFTER RANDALL'S CAR.

CUT TO:

77. EXT: COUNTRY ROAD. DAY. LOCATION.
RANDALL'S CAR TRAVELLING ALONG THE ROAD.
IT DISAPPEARS FROM SIGHT AS A MOMENT LATER:
GRANT'S CAR COMES ALONG THE ROAD AFTER IT.

CUT TO:

78. INT: DYSON'S BARN. DAY. STUDIO.
DYSON IS WORKING IN HIS BARN, MOVING BALES OF
STRAW FROM ONE STACK TO ANOTHER.
SOUND: CAR APPROACHES AND STOPS.
DYSON STOPS WORKING, MOVES TO THE DOOR
AND LOOKS OUT.

CUT TO:

79. EXT: DYSON'S FARM. DAY. LOCATION.
DYSON'S POV
RANDALL'S CAR IS STOPPED IN THE YARD.
DOUBLE FOR RANDALL GETS OUT AND MOVES TOWARDS
THE FARMHOUSE.

CUT TO:

80. INT: DYSON'S BARN. DAY. STUDIO.
RESUME DYSON
HE FROWNS AND MOVES BACK INTO THE BARN AND PICKS
UP A DOUBLE BARREL SHOT GUN.
FROM HIS POCKET HE PRODUCES A COUPLE OF
CARTRIDGES AND PUTS ONE INTO EACH BARREL.
HE THEN EXITS THROUGH A REAR DOOR OF THE BARN
AND WAITS OUTSIDE. WE CAN JUST SEE A GLIMPSE OF HIM.

CUT TO:

81. EXT: DYSON'S FARM. DAY.   LOCATION.

DOUBLE FOR RANDALL IS KNOCKING AT THE FARMHOUSE
DOOR. HE GETS NO ANSWER.
AFTER A MOMENT HE MOVES AWAY TOWARDS THE
BARN. HE ENTERS.

CUT TO:

82. INT: DYSON'S BARN. DAY.   STUDIO.

RANDALL ENTERS AND LOOKS AROUND.

HE CALLS:

> RANDALL:
> Anyone home?

THERE IS NO ANSWER. THE REAR DOOR CLOSES TIGHT,
SILENTLY.
RANDALL TURNS BACK TOWARDS THE DOOR AND IS ABOUT
TO EXIT WHEN HE STOPS QUICKLY AND DRAWS BACK
REACTING TO:

CUT TO:

83. EXT: DYSON'S FARM. DAY.   LOCATION.

RANDALL'S POV

DOUBLE FOR GRANT RUNNING STOOPED TOWARDS THE
FARMHOUSE, REVOLVER IN HAND.
HE REACHES IT AND LOOKS IN THE WINDOW.
THEN HE TURNS AND MOVES TOWARDS THE REAR OF THE BARN.

CUT TO:

84. INT: DYSON'S BARN. DAY.   STUDIO.

RESUME RANDALL

HE LOOKS AROUND AND THEN CROSSES VERY SILENTLY
TOWARDS THE REAR DOOR OF THE BARN.

ANOTHER ANGLE

RANDALL IS VERY CLOSE TO THE REAR DOOR AS IT STARTS TO
OPEN VERY SLOWLY AND CAUTIOUSLY.

HE LEAPS BACK AND DUCKS DOWN BEHIND A STACK OF STRAW
BALES.
HE LOOKS CAUTIOUSLY AROUND THE CORNER.

RANDALL'S POV

THE SHADOWY AND UNRECOGNISABLE FIGURE OF DYSON
APPEARS IN THE DOORWAY.

THE DOOR CLOSES BEHIND HIM.

DYSON COMES CAUTIOUSLY IN AND MOVES TOWARDS THE
PLACE WHERE RANDALL IS HIDING.

RESUME RANDALL

HE EDGES ALONG THE BALES OF STRAW AWAY FROM – AS HE
THINKS – GRANT. AS HE DOES SO HE MAKES A SOUND.

SOUND: FOOTSTEP

ANOTHER ANGLE

DYSON DROPS INTO THE COVER OF ANOTHER STACK OF
STRAW BALES.

CLOSE ON DYSON LISTENING.

ANOTHER ANGLE

ON RANDALL

HE SNAKES ON HIS STOMACH TOWARDS THE END OF THE
BALES OF STRAW AND CAREFULLY PEERS AROUND THE CORNER.

THE WAY IS CLEAR. HE MOVES ROUND. HE WAITS, STOOPING LOW.

ANOTHER ANGLE

DYSON ROUNDS A CORNER AND CREEPS ALONG TOWARDS THE
POSITION THAT RANDALL FORMERLY HELD. HE WAITS LISTENING,
KEEPING LOW.

ON THE DOOR

AS IT OPENS SLOWLY AND SILENTLY AND GRANT DUCKS IN
PURSUING THE MAN HE ASSUMES TO BE RANDALL.

HE STEPS ACROSS TO THE NEAREST STACK OF BALES AND
STOOPS DOWN IN THE COVER OF THEM, LISTENING.

ANOTHER ANGLE

RANDALL PEERING CAUTIOUSLY.

ON DYSON

AS HE STARTS TO MOVE TOWARDS THE CORNER OF THE STACKS
BEYOND WHICH RANDALL IS HIDING.

AS HE DOES SO HIS GUN BUTT DRAGS ON THE STONE FLOOR.

SOUND: GUN BUTT ON FLOOR

ON GRANT

HE HAS HEARD THE SOUND. HIS ATTENTION IS RIVETED ON
THE POSITION FROM WHICH IT CAME.

STOOPING LOW HE MOVES TO A NEW POSITION.

ON RANDALL

WORRIED, ANXIOUSLY LOOKING TOWARDS THE POSITION
THAT DYSON HOLDS. HE RISES BUT STILL BENT LOW RUNS TO
ANOTHER POSITION.

ANOTHER ANGLE

DYSON CREEPS ALONG TOWARDS RANDALL'S LAST POSITION.
SUDDENLY HE BREAKS FROM THE COVER OF THE BALES WHERE
HE HAS BEEN HIDING AND TAKES A NEW POSITION IN ANOTHER
SECTION OF THE STRAW STACKS.

ANOTHER ANGLE

GRANT GLANCES SHARPLY TO ONE SIDE IN TIME TO SEE THE

BACK OF DYSON AS HE DISAPPEARS INTO HIS NEW POSITION. GRANT CHANGES HIS POSITION RETURNING AND GOING AROUND THE OTHER SIDE OF THE STACKS.

ON RANDALL

PUZZLED. HE LOOKS AROUND FOR A WEAPON.

A SHORT DISTANCE FROM HIM, BY A STACK OF SACKS, HE SEES AN IRON BAR. DUCKING LOW HE BREAKS FROM HIS COVER AND GRABS THE BAR.

ANOTHER ANGLE

DYSON CRAWLING TO THE END OF A ROW OF BALES. HE PEERS AROUND THE CORNER.

POV

BACK VIEW OF RANDALL LOOKING IN THE WRONG DIRECTION.

THE GUN BARREL COMES UP INTO SHOT. IT IS CENTRING ON RANDALL'S BACK AS HE DUCKS BACK INTO COVER.

RESUME DYSON

HE KEEPS THE GUN STEADY AND WAITS.

ANOTHER ANGLE

GRANT CRAWLING ALONG TO THE END OF HIS COVER, HE REACHES THE CORNER AND PEERS AROUND. HE RAISES HIS REVOLVER.

ANOTHER ANGLE

ON RANDALL AS HE INCHES FORWARD ONCE AGAIN TO PEER AROUND HIS CORNER.

ANOTHER ANGLE

DYSON'S POV OVER THE GUN BARREL.

RANDALL EDGING INTO SHOT ONCE AGAIN STILL LOOKING IN THE WRONG DIRECTION.
THE GUN INCHES HIGHER TO CENTRE ON HIS BACK.

SOUND: A SHOT

THE BARREL OF DYSON'S GUN DROPS AS RANDALL LEAPS BACK INTO COVER. HE GOES SO FAST THAT FOR A MOMENT WE CAN'T BE SURE WHETHER HE HAS BEEN HIT.

ANOTHER ANGLE

RESUMING DYSON AS HE FALLS FORWARD ON HIS FACE. THE GUN DROPS FROM HIS HAND.

SOUND: GUN CLATTERS TO THE GROUND

ANOTHER ANGLE

ON RANDALL. SUNDDENLY AWARE FOR THE FIRST TIME THERE IS A THIRD PERSON PRESENT.
HE LEANS FORWARD AND PEERS AROUND HIS CORNER.

POV

GRANT, GUN IN HAND, RISES AND MOVES TOWARDS DYSON.

RESUME RANDALL

AS HE REACTS. WATCHING, TAKING NO CHANCES.

ANOTHER ANGLE

GRANT LOOKS AT DYSON. HE IS FACE DOWNWARDS, LYING VERY STILL.

GRANT WAITS A SECOND, GUN AT THE READY. THERE IS NO MOVEMENT. HE DOES NOT BOTHER TO GO CLOSE OR TURN THE BODY OVER. SATISFIED THAT 'RANDALL' IS DEAD HE TURNS AND RUNS FROM THE BARN.

ANOTHER ANGLE

RANDALL GETS UP FROM HIS HIDING PLACE AND MOVES TO DYSON.

HE TURNS HIM OVER TO REALISE THE DEAD MAN IS DYSON.

ON RANDALL'S REACTION

WE UNDERLINE AND CLIMAX THE MUSIC AND THEN:

FADE OUT

The scene we have just looked at is of course a visual cliché. 'Bang, bang, you're dead!'. Doubtless you have seen variations of it dozens of times in British and American television films. It can be exciting in a superficial way but generally we don't know anything about the characters involved as human beings and we don't really care who gets killed. It isn't real life. However, a writer who intends to break into television needs to understand the technique of writing that kind of scene.

Note the LOCATION SHOTS. Numbers 72, 74, 79, 81 and 83 the double is used to avoid taking the actor away from the studio where he is needed for other scenes.

It is, however, possible to write scenes that make a strong visual impact without words that do, nevertheless, still manage to tell us a great deal about the characters involved, as in the following example presented on a 'Tape' (studio) type layout.

This is the start of the play. We know absolutely nothing about the characters as we watch the opening scene.

1. INT: BEDROOM. NIGHT.

SHADOWY DARKNESS.
CU OF MEG ASLEEP IN BED.
SUDDENLY SHE OPENS HER EYES AND RAISES HER HEAD LISTENING.

CUT TO:

2. INT: HALL. NIGHT.

A MAN IS ENTERING THE FRONT DOOR.
FURTIVELY HE REMOVES A KEY FROM THE LOCK
AND QUIETLY CLOSES THE DOOR.

CUT TO:

3. INT: BEDROOM. NIGHT.

MEG RISES AND PUTS ON DRESSING GOWN. SHE
DOES NOT PUT ON THE LIGHT.

CUT TO:

4. INT: SITTING ROOM. NIGHT.

THE MAN ENTERS; STOPS AND LISTENS.

CUT TO:

5. INT: LANDING. NIGHT.

MEG COMES FROM HER ROOM. SHE STOPS AND
LISTENS AND THEN MOVES ALONG THE LANDING
AND OPENS THE CHILDREN'S BEDROOM DOOR. SHE
LOOKS IN.

MEG'S POV TWO CHILDREN ASLEEP IN THE BED.

RESUME MEG AS SHE CLOSES THE DOOR
QUIETLY AND MOVES TO THE TOP OF THE STAIRS.

CU HER FACE WE SEE SHE IS NOW VERY FEARFUL.

CUT TO:

6. INT: SITTING ROOM. NIGHT.

THE ROOM IS DARK BUT WE CAN SEE THE MAN
IN THE CORNER DISMANTLING HI-FI EQUIPMENT,

UNPLUGGING IT AND WINDING UP THE LEADS.
HE PICKS UP ALL THE GEAR AND TURNS TOWARDS
THE DOOR AS THE LIGHT COMES ON.
THE MAN SWINGS ROUND SHARPLY . . .
THERE IS A PAUSE AS HE STANDS CAUGHT
RED-HANDED.

MAN'S POV

IN THE OPEN DOORWAY STANDS MEG, HAND ON
THE LIGHT SWITCH. WE NOW SEE SHE HAS A BLACK
EYE AND A GRAZE ON HER CHIN. HER EXPRESSION
CHANGES FROM TERROR TO ANNOYANCE.

PULL BACK

WE NOW SEE THE MAN, ALAN, PROPERLY. HE IS
THICK-SET AND HE LOOKS AT HER IN A VERY

THREATENING WAY BUT BEFORE HE CAN SPEAK
MEG BRINGS HER FINGER UP TO HER LIPS AND
GLANCES AND POINTS UPSTAIRS, CLEARLY URGING
HIM NOT TO MAKE A NOISE.

HE HESITATES FOR A COUPLE OF SECONDS THEN
TURNS TOWARDS THE SIDEBOARD ON WHICH
THERE ARE TWO PHOTOGRAPHS. HE PICKS UP ONE
OF TWO SMALL CHILDREN. HE LOOKS AT IT AND
THEN SLIPS IT INTO HIS POCKET AND GLARES AT
HER, DARING HER TO OBJECT. MEG JUST WAVES HER
PERMISSION.

CARRYING THE HI-FI EQUIPMENT ALAN MOVES TO
THE DOOR. SHE STANDS ASIDE AND LETS HIM
THROUGH.

SHE HESITATES AND THEN FOLLOWS HIM TO THE
HALL.

CUT TO:

7. INT: HALL. NIGHT.

MEG MOVES TO THE FRONT DOOR AND HOLDS IT
OPEN FOR ALAN. HE PAUSES AND THEIR EYES MEET.
HIS DROP GUILTILY. THEN HE HURRIES AWAY.

MEG CLOSES THE DOOR AND GOES SLOWLY BACK
TO THE SITTING ROOM.

CUT TO:

8. INT: SITTING ROOM. NIGHT.

MEG ENTERS AND CROSSES SLOWLY TO THE
SIDEBOARD. SHE STANDS LOOKING AT THE OTHER
PHOTOGRAPH.

CU PHOTOGRAPH

IT IS OF ALAN AND MEG IN HER WEDDING DRESS,
BOTH LAUGHING AND HAPPY.

CU OF MEG'S FACE

TEARS START TO ROLL DOWN HER CHEEKS.

In those eight short scenes the eyes of the audience have absorbed a lot of story and they will be speculating on a great deal more.

When, in Scene 1 the woman's sleep is disturbed and she lifts her head from the pillow to listen we are awake and listening with her.

In Scene 2 as the intruder removes the key from the lock, quietly closes the door and creeps along the hall we begin to ask questions. Who is he? How is it he has the key? If he has a right to it why does he creep and shut the door so silently?

In Scene 3 as she puts on her dressing gown we get anxious about what she is going to walk into.

Scene 4 confirms our suspicion that the man is an intruder up to no good.

Scene 5 shows us Meg establishing that the noise she heard was not her children and terror now shows on her face as she goes down to confront the intruder.

Scene 6 we have the 'burglar' knocking off very desirable and expensive hi-fi equipment – a common target for house-breakers.

And then the light comes on.

In that moment's pause as he stands fixed to the spot our minds start anticipating what is going to happen. But the moment we take the man's POV – her blackened eye and grazed chin tell us in that one shot what this story is about.

We now know as surely as if we had heard the arguments and seen him beating her up that this is the break-up of a marriage. We know, too, that he is a violent man; that he has left home; that his hi-fi equipment is important to him, that he is too proud or too possessive to ask her for it – or maybe he knows she wouldn't let him take it if he did. But when he accedes to her silent request not to wake the children we realise he is not unconcerned about them. When he picks up their photo to take it with him we know he loves and cares about them.

When the woman agrees he can take it we can guess she is not really vindictive wanting to cut him off totally from his kids.

Scene 7. He pauses at the door for a moment and their eyes meet. Is it really all over between them? Is there a chance of reunion? Then he drops his eyes breaking abruptly the intimacy of eye contact. He can't look her straight in the face and we know he is feeling guilty – perhaps about the violence and the way he has treated her. Perhaps about trying to make off secretly with the hi-fi.

Scene 8. She returns to the sitting room and picks up the photo taken at their wedding. Now it's confirmed, he is her husband – not just a lover and as she cries, even with her bruises and black eye, we can guess she still loves him and would probably take him back given the chance.

All this we can surmise about them and their relationship without a single word and the tension that can be created in that wordless scene is greater than it would be if dialogue was used where attitudes and relationships would be revealed by their intonations and mode of speech.

In 1953 there was a French film, which you may have seen on television, now available as a video, where one very short visual sequence created an almost unbearable climate of tension and excitement throughout the rest of the film. If you saw it you will remember it too but I think it worth recalling because it can't often have been bettered.

It was in the film *The Wages of Fear*.

In order to blow out an oil-well fire two truck-loads of nitro-glycerine had to be transported, as quickly as possible, over about a hundred miles of rough, mountainous roads. The trucks were loaded with drums of the stuff, and two volunteers undertook to make the delivery.

Now nitro-glycerine is, as neither the audience nor the volunteers needed telling, a very powerful and highly volatile explosive. So the boss didn't tell them. Instead he called the drivers into his office and demonstrated. He dropped a rain-drop sized globule about two feet to the ground. As it hit the floor there was a flash and an unbelievably powerful explosion for so small a droplet. From that moment onwards the audience were on the edge of their seats chewing their finger nails at every jolt as the trucks eased their way through rocks and pot-holes towards their destination.

It is hard to imagine what words could have matched the tension created by that one short visual.

But it is not only in action packed sequences that the story, or parts of it, can sometimes be told effectively without words. 'If looks could kill' is an old familiar saying and every actor knows that hatred or love, envy and greed, fury or compassion, and most other deeply felt emotions can be conveyed with a look, gesture or some other body language that can be more subtle and more telling than half a dozen long winded speeches.

Give your actors a chance to act. The best of them will repay you with more imaginative and creative performances. And never forget lines have to be acted. Always ask yourself what your characters are actually doing as they say the words. There are, of course many obvious things. In a domestic scene a woman might be ironing clothes; a man might be using a hammer and saw to make something. Whatever you need them to say don't expect them to stand or sit staring into the camera doing absolutely nothing.

What they are doing can also be used to tell the audience a great deal about the characters. If, for instance, we reverse the activities I have just mentioned, have the man ironing clothes and the woman is using a hammer and saw we have given the audience a great deal of important information about the couple we are portraying. Here we see action revealing both character and the relationship.

51

Very obviously there is no right or wrong balance between the words and pictures. It depends entirely on your story and the way you are telling it. A tale that involves people engaged in physical action unfolding on a broad canvas may provide greater visual opportunities than a claustrophobic story about people living under mental and emotional stress in a small suburban house. And yet the camera recording close ups of nervous gestures, looks of spite or fear, or just a flicker of a smile may tell us more about the character's innermost feelings than he or she is able or willing to articulate.

The things the camera focuses on – particularly when we use close-ups – often speak louder than words. When we see hands clutching a rosary we do not need to be told the person is devout. When, on the wall in someone's house, we see a picture of the Queen we may guess it is the house of a patriot.

The playwright Richard Harris, author of *Stepping Out*, *Outside Edge* and other successful stage plays, started his career as a television writer with a play that showed us a most moving and explicit visual. The picture on screen was of an elderly woman with just one Christmas card, which if I remember rightly, she didn't pick from the mat. She took it from a drawer and placed it on her mantelpiece where it had, doubtless, been placed many times and many years before. Words explaining her loneliness might have sounded a self-pitying whine. The picture told us all we needed to know.

Settings and props also give us the opportunity to offer the viewers interesting and unusual things to look at, and thought and time spent finding fresh and different pictures is never wasted so long as you don't go overboard and ask for the impossible. Remember, too, props can be useful as more than background decoration. They tell us, at a glance, things we should know about the history, hobbies, tastes, profession and status of the people we are watching – but that will be dealt with more fully in the chapter on characterisation.

Comedy sequences lend themselves particularly well to exclusively visual treatment as the silent movies of Charlie Chaplin, Buster Keaton, Harold Lloyd and so many other old-time 'greats' have shown. Chases, accidents and rivalry for the hand of the lady, competition and cheating, always present good visual opportunities as in the following short scene:

1. EXT: VILLAGE HALL. DAY.
CU OF NOTICE: 'PENDLEFORD VILLAGE HALL. ARTS AND CRAFTS SHOW. JUDGE: HONOURABLE MRS WITHSPOON JP. SATURDAY 3rd JULY. 2.00 pm.'

CUT TO:

2. INT.   VILLAGE HALL.   DAY.

BACKGROUND CHATTER.

ON A TRESTLE TABLE COVERED WITH A WHITE
CLOTH JOYCE MERRIFIELD IS SETTING OUT HER
CRAFT EXHIBIT – A POTTERY MILK JUG. AT THE
OTHER END OF THE TABLE MRS HENLEY IS SETTING
OUT HER EXHIBIT – AN ORNAMENTAL POTTERY JUG.
JOYCE SMILES AND NODS AT MRS HENLEY.
MRS H SMILES CONDESCENDINGLY AND SETS OUT A
BIGGER JUG.
JOYCE SETS OUT A MATCHING SUGAR BASIN.
MRS H SETS OUT A BIGGER JUG.
JOYCE SETS OUT A TEAPOT.
MRS H SETS OUT A VERY BIG JUG AND SMIRKS
TRIUMPHANTLY.
JOYCE BEGINS SETTING OUT CUPS AND SAUCERS.
HER TURN TO SMIRK.
BUT WHEN JOYCE SETS OUT THE SIXTH SAUCER SHE
CAN'T FIND THE SIXTH CUP. SHE SEARCHES THE BOX
GETTING INCREASINGLY DESPERATE. IT ISN'T THERE.
MRS H SMIRKS HAPPILY AS JOYCE HURRIES OFF.
MRS H THEN FISHES INTO HER BAG AND PRODUCES
THE CUP. SHE THEN HIDES IT IN THE BOTTOM OF
ONE OF THE BOXES JOYCE HAS UNPACKED.

No words are required. The potential for purely visual story telling in that kind of setting and situation is obvious and can be funnier without words.

Frequently even experienced writers rely on the words when the picture can tell the audience what they need to know.

The writer has at his service both sound and vision and he must learn to use them both to tell the story as vividly as possible.

But there is also another very practical reason why production companies like scripts to tell the story visually. It has to do with overseas sales. A very wordy script requires a great deal of dubbing and when a script is dubbed into a language less concise than English it takes longer to say each line of dialogue. If what is being said is important and won't make sense when cut there is a very real problem of keeping the sound track and vision in sync. In consequence, as British producers seek to increase their overseas sales, it becomes increasingly important to let the picture tell the story wherever possible.

6. Finding material for your stories

Ideas

With literally hundreds of hours of drama produced for stage, cinema, radio and television each week where on earth does one begin looking for new and original ideas? Don't worry.

It's somewhat unlikely that most of us will ever come up with a completely original idea. Most experienced and well respected television writers have had some of their great 'original' ideas returned to them because they happened to be very similar, if not actually identical, to the theme of a play or series episode that someone else wrote before them. One must always be very careful not to steal or plagiarise other writer's work, but the simple fact is that none of us can possibly keep track of all the themes that have been written and are still in copyright, i.e. under EU law, seventy years after the death of the author.

So what do you do?

If you've never read a book or seen a play on the theme you have chosen the chances are that you will treat it sufficiently differently to avoid the accusation that you have 'lifted' it. If it is on a theme you've read or seen then you need to make very sure you really do have a different angle. Probably everyone who thinks seriously about writing for television has a play or plays in mind they would like to write. Once that's written, or is unsuitable for the programme in which you are interested and without sudden flashes of inspiration, where do you find new stories?

In a footnote to an entry in *A Writer's Notebook* Somerset Maugham said, 'This note gave me the idea for a story which I wrote forty years later. It is called "The Colonel's Lady".'

Some ideas take a long time to mature. More often, and especially when writing within the restrictions of a particular television programme requirement, one is so busy with work for which an idea is not suitable that it remains unused for years.

I clipped a newspaper story that intrigued me and kept it in my file for over twenty years. It was about an old woman recidivist who, while she was in prison, read every book the prison library could supply on gracious living and antiques. She became very knowledgeable. She had done a lot of time.

When the opportunity arose I wrote a play inspired by that cutting. I called it *Lady Holloway*.

Newspapers are full of stories – but forget about the headlines. Big, topical and dramatic stories they may be but everyone will have seen them including, no doubt, the editor or producer you are hoping to interest. What you are after is the story the producer hasn't seen and hopefully other writers in direct competition with you haven't seen either. These are stories that don't warrant front page treatment; very small insignificant events in national terms that are frequently major dramas in the lives of individuals – and television is an intimate medium at its best when probing the complex emotions and behaviour of ordinary men and women.

Ideas are the writer's life blood.

If you are serious about writing for television – any creative writing for that matter – start, right away, to keep your own writer's notebook. It doesn't have to be bound in vellum. My 'writer's notebook' is a battered box-file of ideas jotted on the back of an envelope or any scrap of paper that came to hand; word pictures of characters I observed sitting opposite on a bus or tube train; snatches of conversations overheard; newspaper cuttings, along with thoughts about different and original backgrounds and alternative developments of stories sparked by other people's work; as well as roughly typed details of what I like to think are original ideas I dreamed up – or at any rate ideas I have no conscious recollection of having read or seen before.

When you see a good story clip it or note it. It doesn't matter if you have no idea how or when you might use it. In all probability a lot of the stuff you collect you will never use but sometimes an unusual background, a chance remark or short character note that you have harvested will provide you with the basis for a script.

Long before I had ever sold a television script I stood at a bus stop in the East End of London and looked around at the shabby houses opposite. Suddenly I noticed a very old man; thin and frail, seated in an upstairs window watching the activity in the street below and it occurred to me he was now no more than a spectator of life. Years later the note I made at the time was the basis for an episode I wrote for *Dixon of Dock Green*.

It may well be that when you start out to be a TV writer your head will be full of ideas, but when you are successful, particularly if you work on a series, you will discover that television is insatiable. Finding ideas has to be a constant preoccupation. As we search for new and original themes it is very easy to overlook the things closest to us. Use your experience. Journalists, by virtue of their training, have a distinct advantage when it comes to scripting documentaries and dramatised documentaries. But it is surprising how often subjects one knows most about don't seem sufficiently interesting to ever think of writing a play around them and yet, under the spotlight of a truly talented dramatist, the most boring lives can hold us enthralled. Arthur Miller, in his *Death of a Salesman*, made a great play out of the drab and dreary life of an unsuccessful commercial traveller while Arnold Wesker in *The Kitchen* was able to compel our interest in the sordid life behind the scenes of a London restaurant. Neither theme, on the face of it, would seem promising or exciting. But drama is not about backgrounds and things it is about people and their reactions to the circumstances of their lives and the other people they rub up against.

Research

It is important to cultivate the practice of observation and take the trouble to do your research. For programmes like *Heartbeat* which incorporate two of the most popular TV themes – both medical and police work – it is essential. Not only does it help you to get it right, very frequently it provides additional and original ideas you may not have thought of.

For one series I worked on I wanted to write a script about a man who was a compulsive gambler. I had some preconceived ideas about it but I arranged to go to a meeting of Gamblers' Anonymous. It was an open therapy session where men who had managed to give up gambling, and others who were still trying to do so, recounted their personal experiences as encouragement to others.

Nothing I could have invented matched the drama of the stories I heard but after the meeting one man told me, 'If there is one thing that is worse than a man who is a compulsive gambler it is a woman.'

And he was right.

So I wrote two stories. The first about a man that I had set out to research and the second about the woman who was betting the money she should have used for the children's food and getting herself into such a mess that her only way out, she thought, was suicide.

Once you have settled on the theme or background for your story it is not usually difficult to find sources of information to ensure the accuracy of your detail.

The editorial staff of trade magazines are frequently helpful providing information about the particular industry they cover. Writing a script about a disaster in a tin mine I narrowly avoided a very bad mistake by checking with a mining magazine. The story was to be produced in the studio so water – a flood – was definitely out because of the electrical cables covering the studio floor. The best solution seemed to be gas but when I checked I discovered you don't get concentrations of gas in tin mines. We finished up with a roof-fall which suited the story just as well; and I was saved from a very embarrassing mistake.

On another occasion I wanted to know what organ pipes were made of and the scrap metal value, when some enterprising lads stole them from a church while a new organ was being assembled, and tried to flog them to a metal dealer. The editor of a magazine about organs was kind enough to give me all the information I needed, although as I remember it, he was totally appalled at the idea of villains melting down such finely tuned instruments for scrap.

Trade Associations are also useful sources of information. Don't be afraid to ask. They may say 'no' but I am sure you will find, as I have, that people are usually very willing to help.

If you are writing realistic stories about ordinary people and everyday life research is invaluable. As American writer, Syd Field said in his book *Screenplay*, published by Delta Books, 'Research gives you ideas, a sense of people, situation and locale.'

But a word of warning. If you base a character on a living person you must make very, very sure that your fictional character will not be identified as that person. The story I clipped about the woman in prison was a rather sad story. What I wrote was a light comedy developed from the basic thought. And a good many years had rolled by before I wrote the script. Had I wanted to use the idea at the time I read the newspaper report I would, possibly, have made the character a man or very young or added other characteristics to be sure the actual woman was not identifiable.

Not to have done so might have meant the script was libellous.

You should always avoid using the names of well-known people but take care not to fall into the trap of giving your characters highly distinctive names which might just happen to be the name of a living person who could be confused with your fictitious character – a matter which I shall deal with more fully later.

In the *Writers' & Artists' Yearbook*, there is a short section that gives a brief outline of the main principles of the law of libel. It is not, of course, a substitute for specific legal advice if you are unfortunate enough to run into trouble, but writers who know nothing of the law of libel should most certainly get a copy of the book and read it. It points out pitfalls to avoid.

Plagiarism

The other danger area for writers looking for material is the matter of plagiarism.

Don't let other writers tell you their ideas and stories – even your friends – and particularly ideas they are working on or hope to be working on later. The trouble is, long after you have forgotten the conversation you may, in all honesty, hit upon a brilliant idea only to discover later it wasn't your idea at all.

It happened a while ago to a close friend of mine. He wrote a synopsis for a comedy script and a television producer commissioned it. He started work and got half way through the script when something triggered a dream-like memory. He called another writer and asked, 'Did you once tell me a story about . . . ?' and he mentioned the basic theme.

'Yes,' the man at the other end of the line, told him cheerfully. 'Fancy you remembering that. I've just finished writing it for an American film company. They are very excited about it.'

My friend tore up the script and returned the commissioning fee to a fortunately understanding producer. Now anyone who says to him, 'I've got an idea for a play about . . .' is greeted with an immediate, desperate shout, 'I don't want to hear it! Please! Do me a favour! Don't tell me!'

Not only is there the danger that you will unwittingly come up with someone else's idea but, if you talk, there is also the possibility that another writer may come up with your idea.

Like my friend said, Do him a favour. Don't tell him.' And do yourself a favour too. It would be ironic, would it not, if you talked about your idea and knowingly or unknowingly another writer wrote it and sold it while you were writing it for a different company, then you, later, found yourself being threatened with legal action for infringement of copyright?

Could happen!

Copyright

The *Writers' & Artists' Yearbook* also contains a useful guide to copyright law and you certainly ought to be sure you know a little about that to protect and exploit your own work and make sure you don't inadvertently infringe other people's copyright.

But there is one trap it is very easy for all writers – and particularly new writers – to fall into; that is automatically assuming when someone else comes up with 'your' idea that they must have seen your script or synopsis and stolen it. I have known the odd case where that has happened but it doesn't happen anything like as often as most new writers fear.

Sir Basil Bartlett, one time BBC Drama Script Supervisor, writing as far back as 1955 said, 'It is surprising how often a number of writers hit on the same theme at the same time'. My own experience over the years has shown this to be true.

Except when you stop to think about it, it really isn't surprising at all. One of the things I do when I am not actually writing a script is spend time trying to develop new ideas for series and plays. In my files I have a long list of them but more than half have been struck off as one by one they have turned up on the screen. I now have little doubt that if a dozen professional TV writers produced their lists of possible series ideas there wouldn't be many that were not on my list nor many on mine the other writers hadn't also got listed.

The point is well illustrated by a series I once attempted to set up with the BBC. I had been looking for a collective group of people about whom I could tell stories and hit upon the idea of a football team. At that time neither the BBC nor any ITV company had produced a series using that background so I developed and submitted a detailed synopsis for a series I called *Home and Away*. In due course it came bouncing back with a rejection letter. They didn't want it.

You can imagine how I felt when, about a year later they announced they were producing a new series about a football team called *United*.

They have stolen my idea, I thought. What do I do now? Write in protest? Report it to the Writers' Guild? See my solicitor?

While I was still smarting and trying to make up my mind what action to take I met another television writer I'd known for years.

He was fuming! 'Those crooks at the BBC have stolen my idea,' he said.

Yes, you've guessed it. He had submitted the same idea some three months after my submission.

And the truth was that yet another writer that we both knew and respected had, quite independently, come up with the same theme. He'd also found a producer who was enthusiastic about it at a time when the producer happened to be looking for a new series. That's the way it goes. There is always a lot of luck involved in setting up new programmes. Timing is vital. It often depends on having the right idea on the right desk at the right time.

As a member of the Writers' Guild, I have sometimes been asked to take part in an arbitration where a writer has complained a production company or another writer has stolen his idea. Inexperienced writers, in particular I find, are very apt to jump to the conclusion their idea has been stolen when it appears on the screen after they have sent it out somewhere in an attempt to sell it. I remember, early on in my writing career, feeling quite incensed when an original idea I was rather excited about was returned to me by a script editor with a letter that said in effect, it was a very old, corny idea they'd rejected many times before. A few years on I knew what the man had said was true. Of course, ideas do get lifted but like I say, not sufficiently often for any of us to get paranoiac about it. When it seems to have happened it is more likely to be a coincidence than deliberate theft and unless you know for a fact that the other writer has had access to your idea you had best accept the coincidence and save yourself a lot of aggro and possibly a lot of expense.

There is no copyright in basic ideas. It is how you treat them that gives them individuality and makes them unmistakably yours. It is the extent to which you develop an idea that gives it some measure of protection.

You should be cautious, too, about letting people who are not writers, give you ideas. If you know them well as friends or family it can be okay. With casual acquaintances it might be awkward. The late Ted Willis told an amusing story about a dentist he once visited who would have liked to have been a writer. While he was in no position to answer back with his mouth half full of dental equipment the man told him a story he thought would make a super script and suggested that Ted should write it and they could share the fee. When the dentist got his hand and accessories out of Ted's mouth, so that he could answer, he agreed to the proposition on one condition – that he could come in some afternoons and pull a few teeth.

Rewrites

Inevitably there are all kinds of pressures on writers to write this or not to write that. Even people who have never written a word always know exactly how your script should be written and how it could be improved. As H.G. Wells put it, 'No passion in the world is equal to the passion to alter someone else's draft.' Producers, directors, actors, company executives, old uncle Tom Cobley and all, all want a finger in the writer's pie. Can you imagine an artist delivering a painting and the art editor producing a brush to add an extra figure or change the shade of blue of the sky? In television it happens all the time.

There is a splendid book – Splendid? Actually it is a fascinating, tragic/comic story, *Only You Dick Daring* by two American screen writers, Merle Miller and Evan Rhodes, recounting their torments writing a pilot script for an American TV series. After the umpteenth rewrite the producer declared himself happy with the script but a few days later, upon further reflection, he felt it needed additional work. 'Like what?', the writers enquired. And here I quote, 'We need just one additional scene,' the Executive Vice President in charge of programming, said, 'What CBS wants is a kind of friendly lynch mob scene.'

I know a lot of British TV writers who have complained they have had their work mutilated or been instructed to perform the mutilation themselves but nothing quite like a 'friendly lynch mob'.

For a writer rewrites or writing to other people's instructions often goes against the grain but sometimes the producer is right. We all have blind spots. I have written scripts that I freely admit have been improved by a suggestion of the editor or producer.

For all that, the writer can only use his own judgement as he writes his script. He must learn to evaluate ideas – to recognise emotions that are genuine; stories that are original; behaviour that is truly in character; and to reject cheap and corny slants on stories, whether they be his own or ideas thrust upon him by editors and producers; especially when there is pressure on him to delete what he sees as a most vital and sensitive element of his story.

But to resist such pressure you need experience and confidence. It was Ernest Hemingway who said, 'The most essential gift for a good writer is a built-in shock proof shit-detector.'

7. Before you start writing . . .

Okay, lets face it, it probably would help an aspiring writer to break in to television if he or she happened to be married to a son or daughter of the boss of a television company; like it would help you get a start in horticulture if your father owned a large garden centre.

But there is one essential difference. The work of the writer is exposed all the time to colleagues, the public and the critics. If it is no good there is no way anyone can hide it. The writer stands or falls on talent.

I sometimes meet writers who have not yet managed to break in who console themselves believing their problem is that they don't know anyone in the business.

A consolation and a face-saver it may be but it's a fallacy. If it were true most of the writers I know wouldn't be in the business either.

I knew no one in television when I decided to write a TV play. I worked in publishing, at one point as a salesman and later as an editorial assistant. Dick Sharples, who was my writing partner for several years, was in advertising. Other writers I know worked for newspapers. Quite a few were school teachers; several were lawyers; some worked in offices or shops. I know one who was a bank clerk; another who was a taxi-driver; one who was a lorry driver; and another who was a brick-layer and of course many who worked as freelances writing radio, theatre, magazines, novels and children's books.

When they started out few of them had contacts in television. They made their own contacts by writing and submitting scripts and refusing to let rejections defeat them.

Not surprisingly, a lot of actors and actresses write for television. Most of them are not 'stars' and many turned to writing because they had long months of enforced leisure 'resting' between parts. They, it might seem, have the advantage of being known to producers for whom they have worked – but they are known as performers, not writers, and producers don't take kindly to being asked to read speculative scripts which are nothing to do with the programme on which they are working. Invariably they pass it to the script department where it should have gone in the first place.

The real advantage actors and actresses have is that, being around the studio, they learn not to make the kind of mistakes that expose a lack of understanding of the medium and present insurmountable obstacles to production.

In this chapter I want to draw your attention to the sort of blind spots that can result in a rejection regardless of the merit of the script.

Presentation (see also pp 146–8)

For a start, that stage play you wrote but didn't sell . . . You could be right. It might make a good television play. But why bother to type or print it again? It's a good clean copy. Anyone who reads it will see the potential at once.

If they read it. Obviously the layout will be wrong.

Editors are busy people with stacks of scripts to read. Many of them never read a play that starts: 'The Curtain Rises.' an opening that betrays instantly that the play was not written for television; has almost certainly been rejected by theatrical managements for whom it was written; and that the writer lacks either the knowledge, time or interest to present it as a television play.

If it is worth submitting it is worth taking the trouble to do it properly. And if it is laid out correctly as a television script but has got really 'dog-eared', make a new copy. Otherwise you might as well pin a note to it, 'This play has been rejected three times already.'

Target your audience; know who you are aiming at and don't make the mistake of trying to write plays for the critics. Their taste is invariably very much more sophisticated than that of the average viewer. Most television programmes are designed to appeal to a mass audience of ordinary men and women who have never had the advantage of studying drama. If your aim is to write popular television they are your audience and, unlike a captive audience in a cinema or theatre, they can switch to another channel when they get bored – if the play irritates or if it is too highbrow for them.

It needs a fine balance. Great care must be taken not to insult the audience by writing down to them but it smacks of contempt to write above their heads. Any writer who feels impelled to ignore their 'low-brow' taste must not expect to achieve top ratings. Although television attempts to cater for all tastes and minority interests, 'arty', and what many would regard as pretentious plays, need to be very good indeed to get into the schedules.

Watch as much television as you can as a learning process. If you have a video recorder tape and watch plays again to analyse them – something it is difficult to do when you get carried away by the story.

Take note, for instance, how many sets have they used? Are they interiors or exteriors? Is it a film or studio production?

Sets and sound effects

Sets, as I have already said, are very costly. If it's a big prestige production with star performers and well-known writers the sets may be many and lavish. Don't expect that for your first play. It may happen if it is scheduled into a slot where the producer has a big budget and decides you have written a really super script. It is more likely, however, they will look at your script and count the number and cost of sets required, or accessibility of suitable locations where their productions are on film, and if you have been too ambitious return it to you with regrets.

Look closely at the sets as you watch different programmes. There is some very clever 'cheating' going on. The restaurant that looks so expensive may be no more than a couple of 'flats' (backing walls against which a scene can be played) with three or four tables and an ambience of chatter and music to create the illusion of a large, busy place. And if we see first a few seconds of film that establishes of the outside of the Grand Hotel we are very ready to accept that the restaurant is part of the hotel.

In the same way, when we see a film clip of an airport, then cut to a couple of characters seated in a corner, hand luggage at their feet and the sound of aircraft taking off we don't have to build a great departure lounge set to play a short and vital scene. If we have an airport tannoy announce the departure of a flight we don't even need the establishing clip of the airport to locate us. Sound effects can be used very effectively to establish a location and avoid a great deal of expense. Bird-song, mooing cows or baaing sheep will set us in the country. The hoot of an owl will make it night. Traffic noise and the siren of a police car will set us in a city without so much as a glimpse from a window, while the distinctive sound of a ship's siren will locate us near a river or docks and when urgently repeated, in a fog. A lot of costs can be avoided with a little imagination.

Don't demand big and expensive sets for inconsequential scenes and make sure you use all substantial sets you call for to play proper scenes – not just a line or two of dialogue.

You, as a creative writer, must use your ingenuity to tell your story within the limits of the producer's budget and that usually means for a modest hour's play not more than five main sets plus three or four flats or 'cornerpieces' (small section of bar, corridor, shop counter or other limited acting area against which a short scene can be played).

The characters you create may be particularly well drawn – and I will deal with that later – but one way to give your story a distinctive look and feel is to find fresh settings. The office, the pub, living rooms, court-rooms, hotel rooms and restaurants are sets we see on our screens every day. It is hard to avoid them but with many stories the background against which the principal scenes are played is not an intrinsic part of the drama. The same story might be told with advantage against a more imaginative setting. It is well worth while spending a little time and thought to see if you can find different pictures to compliment your story. You may be sure that given the choice between two plays of equal merit, both of which can be produced within the budget, the director will always choose the play that gives him the opportunity to shoot interesting and unusual pictures.

But you must of course be realistic. If you set the play on top of an active vulcano or some equally dangerous and inaccessible spot; if you locate your modest half hour aboard a fully manned Spanish galleon; you must not be surprised when the script comes back faster than a boomerang. And it would be a great mistake for a new writer to imagine that producers would be willing to lavish on a first play the kind of money they might spend on plays by top writers like John Mortimer or Jack Rosenthal. Don't put unnecessary obstacles in the way of a sale by letting your enthusiasm get out of hand.

Characters

Never write in characters you can do without.

There is one very important difference between a feature film and a television production that is most noticable at the receiving end. The cinema has a wide screen that can accommodate crowd scenes with ease and clarity.

On a television screen four is a crowd.

There are usually more than four characters in a play but don't try and get them all on screen at the same time. An exception, of course, are scenes in bars or parties but if you watch closely you will see that this is for background and atmosphere. Dramatic developments and vital plot points are always played close on the characters concerned.

When writing for television it is important to recognise and exploit what the small screen can do better than either a cinema screen or actors on stage. As Rod Serling, one of the first and most successful television playwrights in the USA, was quick to discover, 'The key to TV drama was intimacy, and the facial study on the small screen carried with it a meaning and power far beyond the usage of the motion pictures'.

For any particular play there may be fifteen million other viewers but as the audience sit in twos and threes in their own homes and watch through that electronic window the events of other people's lives they can feel as moved and involved as if they were sitting in on a brawl between guests at their own dinner table. Without the intrusion of an audience around you a TV play can seem a very personal encounter.

Speaking parts

There are two other good reasons for keeping the number of characters in a scene, and indeed in the whole play, down to the minimum your story necessitates. One relates to sharing out the lines and we will deal with that later when we discuss dialogue. The other is the matter of cost.

Actors cost money. Star players can be very expensive. Whatever the budget you will get better leads for your play and a stronger supporting cast if you are economical in the number of speaking parts you write.

'Speaking parts?'

The exact professional status of performers and their minimum fee is laid down by Actor's Equity, the actors' trade union, who have national agreements with all employers. The classifications are, 'actors', 'walk-ons' and 'extras' and it is important for the writer to understand these different categories to avoid unnecessary costs by inadvertently upgrading an 'extra' into a 'walk-on' and a 'walk-on' into an 'actor'.

Actors: Performers with or without lines who are involved in the development of the story.

Walk-ons: A walk-on is identified as a non-speaking performer who at the precise time his movements are recorded has a direct acting relationship with an actor who is simultaneously performing his part as set out in the script.

A walk-on may also perform individually in a special function peculiar only to the trade he is supposed to represent, e.g. a bus conductor collecting fares; a policeman on point duty; a bartender serving drinks. Walk-ons may say a few unscripted words germane to what they, or other people, are doing, at the request and discretion of the director. Thus a bus conductor could say, 'All fares, please', or a policeman, 'Move along there', but such dialogue must not appear in the script.

Extras: A person or member of a group contributing to the overall authenticity and atmosphere of a scene (e.g. drinkers in the bar, diners in the restaurant). They may be dressed in clothing identifiable with a particular trade or calling (e.g. chorus girls, soldiers). Extras can be used for community singing providing it is a well-known song or hymn and the words do not have to be specially learned.

For a first one hour script you should try to keep the number of main speaking parts down to eight or ten plus half a dozen lesser roles. If, however, you are hoping to get your play accepted for a regular play-spot you will be able to see what is acceptable from other productions.

And as you construct and write your play never forget that 'Name' actors and actresses look for 'star' parts and will want to play them. You are likely to get better leads if you keep this in mind.

'Special talents'

But the number of sets and the number of characters are not the only restrictions you need to consider. There are also 'special talents', babies and small children and animals.

'Special talents' can mean an actor's ability to swim, sing, play the piano, speak a foreign language fluently, and so on. If it is essential that a character should have a certain special talent, the director will of course find someone who can do what is required. But don't expect too much, and never casually throw into your 'stage directions' (the scripted description of the set and actors' moves and business) that your leading lady is found doing a Yoga exercise that involves standing on her head, or that your leading man is entertaining waifs at a Christmas party with his sword swallowing act.

Babies, small children and animals

Babies, children and animals all present special problems. Babies can't act. Even getting them to smile or look unhappy at the right moment gives advertisement directors ulcers.

Small children are a little easier in that they may understand what they are being asked to do but that is no guarantee that they will do it. Older children are usually available from stage schools and come complete with chaperons but there are limits to the hours and time they are available. Most directors would rather avoid child actors and you may have noticed when you have watched plays and series that a very high proportion of young married couples seem to be childless – at least until the child reaches its mid teens or thereabouts.

There is an old maxim among actors, 'Never work with children or animals.' If the kids are good they steal the show and animals only have to be there looking dumb and appealing for half the audience to forget who else who was in it.

In the days when television programmes were 'live' animals presented fearful problems. In my ignorance I once wrote a horse into a script and bravely the director actually produced one. In the middle of a comedy scene the animal stepped on the actress's foot.

That was unscripted. The audience thought it was very funny but the poor woman didn't laugh at all.

Everyone who has ever worked with animals has their tale to tell. In a rural scene in a live comedy show they once brought on a set a real genuine cow and without warning in front of the cameras the wretched animal . . . Oh well, we needn't go into that!

Of course, there are many splendid specialist films made these days featuring animals. They require time, patience and under-standing of the creatures involved and are best left to the experts.

Props, furniture and costume

Before we move on there are a few more things you need to be aware of. The first concerns 'props' (properties used for dressing the set), furniture and costume.

There is no problem with modern furniture and furnishings. The studios have store rooms full of contemporary furniture and artefacts, but if you decide to set your play in a different century or even in a different decade you begin to run up the costs because what you require may have to be specially procured or made.

In the same way, in a modern play most of the actors and actresses can wear their own clothes but if the script calls for 'period' costumes the production company has to supply them which means making or hiring which can easily over-stretch a modest budget. (Period means any time in the past.)

And from the past to the future.

Science fiction type props with futuristic control rooms and special effects that must be designed and constructed solely for your play can be well outside a normal play budget and are only likely to be considered for a series like *Star Trek* or *Doctor Who* where the cost can be amortised over many episodes.

If your script is well written and is the type of play they are looking for at that point in time they'll want to produce it. But if it is too costly or presents too many production problems they will more likely return it with regrets. Whatever you suggest must be realistic. An exciting sequence requiring a few hundred Norman soldiers on the cliffs at Hastings is not going to sell your script however brilliantly it is written.

Never forget, as we said earlier, filming outside at night is very expensive. Don't set your scene as: 'Exterior Night' when it can just as well be: 'Interior Night' or 'Exterior Day'. If you do so you simply expose your lack of experience and reduce the chances of producers buying your work.

A new writer, in particular, is well advised to be cost conscious. If the play is worth it and there is money available few directors will not take the opportunity to cast better actors, broaden the canvas by increasing the outside filming or even suggest that it would be better if the writer used additional sets.

But producers are expected to keep within their budget and both the BBC and ITV companies recognising the fierce international competition they face from new technology are cutting budgets and holding down overhead costs. Through satellite TV the door is now wide open for international media companies to share national television advertising revenues. Regrettably these companies are, for the most part, distributors and not producers of TV programmes.

But writers may take comfort in the thought that no one will be rejecting good plays because they are too cheap.

Before we move on it will, perhaps, be helpful if I make a short checklist of points the writer must keep in mind:

DO'S AND DON'TS

a If you are in contact with a producer as you write your script DO find out whether a production would be in the studio or on film and use the appropriate layout shown in examples in Chapter 2 and Chapter 3. If you have no such contacts don't worry about it. Few beginners have. What you must do is present it in the style most appropriate, i.e. a story where most of the action takes place indoors should be presented as a TV studio script. If the greater part of the action happens outside present it as a film.

b DO remember studio sets have to be built and they are very costly. Never call for a set that is not necessary or stipulate a large set to play only a minor scene that could be played against a flat or cornerpiece. (See Chapter 7.)

c When writing a story set on exteriors DO be aware of the producer's problems of ambient sound, unwanted spectators, out of period houses and street furniture, etc., and try and think of settings where he is less likely to be faced with these problems. (See Chapter 3.)

d DON'T make all of your characters speak in exactly the same way. DON'T write faithful reproductions of famous people or people you know. (See Chapter 11.) DO remember that names have connotations of age and class. DON'T write unnecessary words for walk-ons and extras. (See Chapter 7.)

e DO remember modern furniture and modern clothes are easily obtained. Period costumes, period furniture and futuristic costumes and furniture have all to be specially made. (See Chapter 7.)

f DO write in all necessary stage movements clearly and concisely. (See produced scripts in Appendix.) Don't try and be funny. The producer may not share your sense of humour.

g DON'T try to do the director's job for him. He won't thank you. Picture composition and camera angles are his choice. There are two exceptions. It is essential that the writer indicates visual requirements vital to the viewer's comprehension of the story. Thus:

> CU of a tattoo on the back of
> HARRY'S right hand

or:

> HARRY's PV Along the hall.
> His wife is kissing the lodger.

and again:

> ON THE WINDOW
> The curtain blows. A man is
> looking in.

The other exception: when writing a script that will be made on film on location DO see that each set-up is clearly identified. (See Chapter 3.)

The writer's script must also include set description; names and descriptions of characters (see Chapter 14) and DON'T overlook vital sound effects, e.g.

> FX: UPSTAIRS THE BABY IS CRYING

or:

> FX: A JET AIRCRAFT ROARS
> OVERHEAD

h DON'T forget your name and address on the front cover and send a covering letter with your script. DO state the running time of the script on the title page, (30 minutes, 60 minutes or whatever). Check that by reading the dialogue aloud at the speed you intend the actors to play it and time that and all movements with a stop watch. (See Chapter 14.)

i DON'T concern yourself with the music which may be used in the presentation of your play unless the story needs a very specific tune or song and no other will do.

j DON'T write in special effects until you really know what you are doing and unless they are absolutely essential. All this, is, once again, the director's province and he may resent your interference. In any event, it is almost impossible for a freelance writer to keep up with new techniques and innovations when he is not working in daily contact with the production team. Better to omit what isn't absolutely necessary than expose your inexperience and limited knowledge by getting it wrong.

k DON'T send out dog-eared scripts that look as if they've been read and rejected half a dozen times already. (See Chapter 14.) Use A4 paper and see your play is neatly typed with all alterations clearly legible. Never, never send out your only copy.

l And last but not least, if you have a choice between working on a typewriter or word processor you should make the effort to learn to use the latter.

Not only is it possible to produce near perfect pages and keep it working, running off multiple copies while you're entertaining guests or nipping out to the pub, the ease with which one is able to move scenes and speeches around the script; cut lines or add additional lines without the mess of scissors and paste or hours spent on a total retype will more than repay the time spent learning to use it.

For me, alterations to scripts are particularly irritating – mostly, I guess, because I liked it the way I wrote it in the first place. But sometimes they are inevitable and he who pays the piper . . . ! I find the word processor makes the job a great deal quicker and takes out much of the aggro.

8. Writing a synopsis and programme formats

I have occasionally been told by the script editors and producers of series I have worked on, 'Don't bother to write a detailed plot. Just let me have the idea in two or three paragraphs.'

Frankly, I have never found it easy to synopsise my stories in a single page but perhaps that's down to the way I think and the type of stories I tell, for I have sometimes heard television executives say that a good idea can be outlined in a couple of sentences.

I'm not convinced. It seems to me to be one of those pat sayings people trot out without ever properly considering it. The fact is, the essence of some stories can be told in a few sentences and some most certainly cannot.

When you are established and working closely with an editor or producer who has confidence you will not suggest an idea, or commit yourself to write it, unless you are satisfied you can make an acceptable script from it, you may find as I have that they will take you on trust; that you have only to suggest the basic theme they like to be given the go-ahead.

But a writer should not just talk about his ideas with producers and editors he doesn't know. It is best to put them on paper. As we have already seen it is the detail, rather than the basic thought, that provides some measure of protection.

I have talked of plots, storylines, the story synopsis and of formats and before we go any further I had better clarify exactly what is meant by these terms.

A format is the blueprint for a serial or series and will be dealt with in more detail later in this chapter. The plot, the storyline and the story synopsis are terms that are frequently used interchangably. If one script editor asked you for a plot and you delivered to him a synopsis of a story you had developed but had rejected by a similar series, it might still be rejected but not because you had delivered a synopsis instead of a plot. Exactly the same applies to a story synopsis.

Some editors and writers might hold there are shades of difference between the terms. I would myself regard a plot as being very much the bare bones of the story; a synopsis as a brief outline of the story; and the storyline as an extended synopsis but not as detailed as a treatment, a term used more often in film than television and applied to an extended synopsis.

Let me give you an example – a story I wrote entitled:

DEADLY FOCUS

(The plot)

Len and Chris Ashton do a thought transference act in the theatre. Len is about to switch off TV after the channel has gone off the air when he notices what seems to be ghosting behind the 'snow'. They watch as a woman leaves a TV studio and goes out to the car park where a man strangles her.

They assume it is a late night movie but as the picture is so bad call the TV engineer next morning. He says there is nothing wrong; there was no late night movie. It must have been a foreign station ghosting. Chris tells him he is wrong. She recognised the actress, Judy Wilkins.

On the street the TV engineer buys a newspaper. The headline reads, 'Actress Judy Wilkins murdered'. He reports to the police. Detective Grant calls to see the Ashtons. 'How did they know about the murder before it was announced?'

They explain and he leaves unconvinced.

Back at his office his assistant York has something interesting to show Grant – a video of a film Judy Wilkins made three years before. In it she is strangled in a car park.

Later another TV acress Joan Bedford is found dead in her dressing room. She too has been killed in the way she was murdered in a film. Now Grant gets a call from a clairvoyant claiming she saw the murder happen on her TV screen, faintly ghosting, after the programmes had gone off air the previous night.

Grant discovers the same TV crew were making the programme featuring both dead women. He also checks on the actors and technicians in the film murders and traces all except one, an actor named Waltham who has gone out of the business. York is told to try and trace him.

Grant sees the Ashtons. 'How does this thought transference work?' They explain that thoughts and images are in some way transmitted through space.

'Like TV?'

'Who knows. Maybe electrical waves from the brain could be picked up by an electronic TV camera.'

The Joan Bedford play is cancelled. The TV crew are allocated to a late night book show. A former actress Maria Steed has written a best selling novel. At the studio she greets Bob Holt a second assistant cameraman. She tells the make-up girl, she knew Bob when he was an actor – worst actor she ever played with.

Back from the theatre the Ashtons watch the book programme. It goes off air and the ghosting starts. Maria Steed moves across the studio as Bob Holt watches. They recognise Holt as the man they saw in the car park.

Grant at home sits in front of a blank screen. His phone rings. York has traced Waltham. He left acting and resumed his real name. Holt. He is now an assistant at the TV studios. Grant hangs up and gets another call from the Ashtons. They tell him what they have seen.

Maria is still in the dressing room when the door opens and Holt enters dressed in a Regency jacket and hat. He grabs her by the throat. 'Remember "His Majesty's Mistress"? I should have killed you properly then. You and those other bitches ruined my career, upstaging me and stealing my best scenes.'

Grant arrives in time. Holt is arrested. Maria feels sorry for Holt. He was no good as an actor but he had a wonderful talent. He used to entertain the cast at rehearsals reading their thoughts.

As a storyline it would be written in more detail and indicate where and when the scenes would be played, e.g.:

INT: LOUNGE. ASHTONS' FLAT. NIGHT.

In the early hours of the morning, after the TV programmes have gone off the air, Len and Chris Ashton who do a mind reading act on stage notice they have left the set on. Len is about to turn it off when he notices a picture behind the 'snow'. As they watch they see an actress leave the studio and go towards the car park.

EXT: CAR PARK. NIGHT.

In the car park, seen through the 'snow' on the TV set, the woman is attacked by a man as she gets into her car. She is strangled.

INT: ASHTONS' LOUNGE. NIGHT.

The Ashtons think they recognised the woman as Judy Wilkins a well-known actress and assume they have been picking up a late night movie. Set on the blink.

INT: ASHTONS' LOUNGE. DAY.

The following morning they call the TV service engineer. He arrives, examines the set and tells them he can find no fault. They explain the reception on the previous night's movie was terrible. He tells them there was no late movie on the channel the previous night and says it must have been ghosting by a foreign station.
They tell him it was a British film. They recognised the actress. Judy Wilkins. The man leaves.

EXT: STREET. DAY.

The TV engineer buys a mid-day paper. The headline announces 'Actress Judy Wilkins found murdered in car park'.

INT: TV STUDIO. DAY.

Detective Inspector Grant is interviewing the studio staff and actors involved in the production Judy Wilkins was working on. There are no immediate suspects.

INT: POLICE STATION.   DAY.
The TV engineer reports his visit to the Ashtons and that they had told him of the murder and details before it was announced.

INT: ASHTONS' DRESSING ROOM.   THEATRE.   NIGHT.
As they are preparing for their performance Grant arrives to question how they knew about the murder. They explain and Grant leaves, very suspicious.

As you will see this kind of additional detailed storyline allows the producer to form a good idea of the number and kind of sets involved and whether outside filming, if any, will be night or day; the size of the cast; and therefore make a realistic estimate of the cost of a production. It will also fill in details that in presenting a short plot a writer may gloss over. A treatment would include some dialogue.

If you are working entirely speculatively the shorter plot may be sufficient. It will establish whether an editor or producer will be interested in your idea without your spending a great deal of time on a story they may reject as being totally unsuitable or too close to something they have already done.

When you are experienced and editors and producers know and trust you, an outline of the basic idea is often sufficient for them to tell you to go ahead. And if you have a particularly original idea or twist that you do not wish to disclose to people you don't know until you have established a possible interest, this shorter plot may also serve your purpose, but obviously you have to give them enough to whet their appetite to have any hope of selling.

When one is submitting an idea for an existing series the copyright in the series' characters belongs to the person who devised the series or maybe the producers if they bought it outright. A writer contributing an idea to a series has copyright only in characters he creates in depth. Since the principals in a series are all established it is unnecessary for writers, submitting stories, to take up time and space with their characterisations and in consequence the storyline can be that much shorter. When, however, writers are submitting an idea for a play where the characters are entirely their own creation and the plot and background totally original, it needs a very exceptional idea to sell on no more than a single page outline.

It is a fine balance between telling enough of the story to enthuse the reader but not so much as to bore him or make him cast the storyline aside to read another day when he is not so busy. The way you present your material can be crucial, whether it be the synopsis of a play, a plot for a single episode of a series or the format for a brand new show.

Whichever it is, you have got to present a 'selling' document that will capture and hold the interest of people who may be so jaded reading uninspired ideas that their attention span is strictly limited.

If you have not yet written or had your scripts produced on television it is extremely unlikely that you would be commissioned to write anything on the basis of a plot or storyline however original that may be. The only way to prove you really can write is to write and that means you must speculate your time and effort producing a script which they may buy if it turns out as well as you hope but obviously reject if they think it unsuitable or it doesn't fit in with their production plans. But even so, it is not all loss. You learn as you write and if the editor you send it to thinks your script has any sort of promise, he may be helpful and encouraging so that even a rejected script could turn out to be an investment and a key to future success.

That is exactly what happened in respect of the first dramatic writing I attempted. I wrote, speculatively, a film script which the Rank Organisation rejected but the editor who read it was sufficiently encouraging to make me feel I was not wasting my time trying to write scripts. So I was encouraged to try again and not long after I began selling to television.

Most writers get their first break in television with the single shot play where the story and characters are entirely their own creation. The play is written and submitted on spec. Sometimes, and particularly once you have made that first break, a company will read and comment on a story synopsis and you cannot put too much thought and effort into making it both practical and interesting. Don't ever allow yourself to be beguiled by the thought that it doesn't matter much, because it is, after all, only a synopsis and it goes without saying you'd put more effort into the script. Take that attitude and there probably won't be a script. Skimped and careless work shows up like a badly dressed shop window.

Submitting your ideas

Ideas are the life blood of television and established writers have no monopoly of good ideas. If you have an original idea for a series you should certainly try to sell it and if it really is a good original idea you will stand a fair chance of finding a company who will want it.

There are two ways you could go about this. You could write a script and a format and submit them together or you could submit just the format. If you submit script and format they may not be interested in the idea but like your writing and decide to offer you a commission to write scripts for some other series. Or they may like and decide to buy the idea but dislike your script. On the other hand, if you submit just the format and they buy it you would be paid a fee for each episode transmitted, but with no track record, you should not expect the producer to commission you to write all or any of the scripts although you could be sure that any episode you wrote speculatively would be given full and serious consideration by people involved in the production.

But before you start shooting off ideas to companies and producers it is important to make certain what you are offering really is a series idea. Does it have the mileage in it to make a series? Most professional television writers have had the experience of thinking up ideas that seem to promise a long running series only to discover, after they have devised two of three plots, that the potential is exhausted.

Don't risk wasting the idea and good will by going off half-cock. Test it throughly by working out at least half-a-dozen episodes based on the theme. If the six stories come easy you may have a winner. If you get stuck on the third or fourth story, forget it. The primary criterion for any series idea is its potential as a story vehicle. If you approach a producer and he discovers you are scraping the bottom of the barrel after you have written just two or three plots, you may have squandered your chances.

Once you are satisfied that an idea will make at least six and preferably a dozen strong episodes what you now need is the format. In his book *The Way to Write for Television* the late Eric Paice, a writer of considerable experience said of the format, 'This should be reasonably brief, establishing the general ambience of the series, the period in which it is set, the central locations from which it is based, the principal characters who will be used throughout the series and, above all, the conflict implicit in the idea itself.'

Unlike a script there is no standard layout for a format. How you present it and lay it out is a matter for you to decide. Ted Willis, who sold more series ideas than any other writer in this country, used with great success the layout below which he kindly allowed me to reproduce here.*

*Some slight adjustment has been made to Ted Willis' actual type layout, in order to save space.

Although brief, it discloses the full potential of the idea and background and introduces us vividly to the principal characters and general ambience of the series.

There are no original stories included here for obvious reasons but probably you could not do better than follow the style of this presentation.

THE SECRET LIFE OF MR. PRIVETT

by

TED WILLIS

(Notes for a TV film series)

He lives in Surbiton in a semi-detached house . . . The neighbours respect him as a kind and gentle little man . . . he catches the 8.51 to town almost every day to go to his office in Holborn, where he deals in stamps . . . he looks the sort of man you may see on any local railway station anywhere in the suburbs . . .

This is the surface, the public face of Mr. Kenneth Robert Privett. Beneath this . . .

THIS IS ONE FACE OF MR. PRIVETT . . .

On the surface, Mr. K. R. Privett is as suburban as his name implies. Hundreds of men like him may be seen on any local railway station as indistinguishable one from the other as the privet hedges which front their semi-detached houses.

His name is Kenneth Robert Privett, but few are privileged to use his Christian name. To his fellow travellers and neighbours he is always Privett, or Mr. Privett, to associates and business acquaintances he is simply "K".

His conversation seems to confirm his appearance. He has strong, if orthodox views, on cruelty to animals, the devaluation of the pound, the use of artificial chemicals on crops, pop music and the rising generation. He can speak with reasonable authority on flower gardening (carnations are his speciality), cricket and income tax. He is an undoubted expert on philately, though because he prides himself on being a plain and simple man, he will invariably refer to it as stamp collecting.

This, in fact, is his business. He has an office in High Holborn from which he conducts his operations, buying and selling stamps from all over the world. He has a high reputation and collectors find their way up the stairs to the untidy office over the furniture shop in their droves. Nor is Mr. Privett a man to sit and wait for business: he spends half his working life circling the globe in search of rare issues and bargains.

He has a small semi-detached corner house in Surbiton to which he repairs when he can. It is modest, but comfortable and it is maintained in shining order by Mr. Privett's sister, Beryl. She is a hard, unpolished woman with a passion for tidiness and she takes pride in keeping both Mr. Privett and the house up to the mark. The neighbours respect her, but shelter a secret sympathy for her brother. Mr. Privett, however, seems not to need their support. He is obviously fond of Beryl and her sharp tongue does not ruffle him at all. He is patient and kind in his domestic relationship as in everything else.

This is the surface, the public and private face of Mr. K. R. Privett. Beneath this . . .

. . . AND THIS IS THE OTHER.

Mr. Privett is a master-spy in the service of the West. He is the equivalent of M in the James Bond novels: he controls and directs the operations of a small army of secret agents and government couriers.

For this, the stamp business is a perfect cover: many of the people who visit him are agents who have called for intructions and assignments. His own trips abroad are mainly for the purpose of checking on his agents, replacing a weak one, assisting another at a vital moment, setting up a new apparatus or disbanding another. And when the need arises, Mr. Privett will take into his own hands the question of the liquidation of a double-agent or an enemy opponent.

For in his real role, K leaves behind the assumed suburban personality. He is dedicated and ruthless behind the quiet and patient mask. He will not stand cynicism: he believes, and expects his key men to believe, in the importance and patriotic nature of their operations. He is a master-planner, whose ingenious methods and intricate schemes have baffled many rival services. He is a master of disguises also, a man who can sink his identity into that of another character as simply as changing a hat. He can become that person, just as he has become Mr. Privett, the little surburban householder.

Behind the untidy office, there is a larger, air-conditioned room in which the agents are briefed, with an efficient staff and a powerful transmitter which maintains contact with agents operating in Europe. There is another transmitter in the house in Surbiton, operated by Beryl, who is as much part of the set-up as Mr. Privett – and who is not, and never has been, any relation of his. And in Surbiton there is a small experimental workshop where K, Beryl and the odd-job man, Bert, perfect the latest devices for the equipment of their agents.

In the office and at Surbiton, there are the secret scrambler telephones also, which give K direct contact with a Minister, with his boss, or with the Prime Minister, if necessary.

THE STAMP DEALER . . .

So we see him, wearing his bowler hat, neat business suit, carnation in buttonhole, newspaper under his arm, umbrella in hand, leaving the corner house in Laburnum Grove on his way to catch the 8.51 to London. He waves to his sister, raises his hat to a neighbour, steps out smartly and tries to do deep-breathing exercises as he goes on his way. He pauses to post a letter to his Aunt Emily, joins his friend Burlington for the last stretch, discusses the vandalism of the teenagers as they hurry for the train.

He settles into the carriage, exchanges a greeting with his familiar fellow-travellers and sits back to study the paper. He has not assumed the role of Mr. Privett – he is the man. And, in a strange way, he enjoys these hours when he is ordinary and suburban and simply one of the crowd.

Mr. Privett, like hundreds and thousands of others, is on his way to the office.

But in his case, the office is the focal-point for a corps of men and women who walk in danger every moment of their lives. And behind the copy of the Daily Telegraph, K is wondering why his man in Berlin has not reported for ten days: whether he should move in on the Russian spy whom he knows to be operating from the radio shop in Portsmouth, or leave him a little longer in the hope he will lead them to bigger fish: and whether his suspicions that McKenzie, his man in Bucarest, is playing a double game, are well-founded . . .

THE UNIQUE AGENT.

We may be sure that his solution to any one of these problems will tend towards the unorthodox. For Mr. Privett is a far cry from the spy-slugger type of agent whom we meet so often nowadays in our fiction. He will sanction violence only when there is no other possible alternative: and this is not only because he dislikes violence for its own sake, but because he considers it ponderous and wasteful.

He is unorthodox in many other ways. He has, for example, a keen sense of responsibility about his job and the power which it puts into his hands. He deplores the fact that such a job should be necessary at all in a civilised society: and he uses his authority with great care.

His attitude to his agents is also unusual, measured by traditional standards. Not for him the tight-lipped, curt approach, although he can be tough when occasion demands. He has a bubbling sense of humour, a sharp wit and a strong hatred of bureaucracy and injustice. His staff enjoy his constant brushes with the Civil Servants who control the budget on which the Department operates.

And his men know that they will never be abandoned to the tender mercies of a hostile country if K can do anything about it. His staff are never told that they are 'on their own' if caught: they know that the whole weight of the Department is behind them; they know that K will use all his resources and ingenuity to rescue them should they fail in a mission, or be betrayed. They return his complete loyalty in kind.

※ ※ ※ ※

A NOTE ON THE STYLE AND APPROACH OF THE SERIES.

We have an unusual character and background for the series and we should, therefore, make a determined effort to break away from the routine, bang-bang type of secret agent stories and series, and cliché situations which have grown up around them.

We should drift along the Corridors of Power and find problems which only Privett can solve in his own unique way. We should aim to make the audience believe in Privett and in what he is doing, so that they really care about him and are rooting for him all the way.

And just as he is an unusual hero, we should try to avoid the routine cut-out cardboard figures which usually pass for villains: real tension and adventure will come when Privett is pitted against other human beings, as clever and dedicated, and as human as he himself. We should be afraid neither of humour, nor genuine emotions.

The style of production should match this approach. It could be described, I suppose, as a sort of heightened realism. We should aim to introduce the viewers to a new and exciting world, which is real enough to carry conviction, but yet has a mysterious and intriguing quality about it; they must feel that they are really seeing, for the first time, the strange background of power and intrigue and adventure against which the Secret Service operates.

TED WILLIS

9. Plots and story construction

Plots

In recent decades it has become fashionable among some playwrights to regard 'plot' as a dirty word. It is a fashion that causes hundred of thousands of viewers to switch channels.

Old fashioned and unsophisticated? The fact is, the vast majority of the television audience prefer stories that have a strong plot with a beginning, a middle and an end.

There are, of course, a great many splendid plays that don't have a plot in the sense that the word is commonly understood. They are not dependent upon a series of complicated twists and turns like a detective mystery. They may be character studies where the facets of the personalities the playwright is presenting to us are, in themselves, so intriguing that we are captivated as we are captivated by magnetic personalities we meet in real life. Then again they may be narrative stories unveiling a sequence of events that have no direct connection – like a journey full of surprises, chance meetings or unexpected mishaps. And there are many plays with little or no action or development where the wit, humour or sheer brilliance of the dialogue holds us spellbound.

But truly gifted writers are scarce and a television writer who relies on the magic of his dialogue, the insight and integrity of his characterisations, or random unconnected incidents to entertain a mass audience without stimulating them to question what happens next, needs to possess very special talents if his audience are not to be tempted to switch to another programme.

For series and serials – the bread and butter of most television production schedules – the plot is indispensable.

So what exactly do we mean by plot?

Asked, 'What is a plot'?, E.M. Forster said in *Aspects of the Novel*: The King died and then the Queen died. That is a story. The King died and then the Queen died of grief. That is a plot'.

A plot is the relationship of events – cause and effect.

How you go about constructing your plot is a matter for you to decide. Sometimes an idea will come to you in a flash of inspiration and be so full of drama and potential that your problem will be one of selection rather than invention. Brian Clark, writing of *Whose Life Is It Anyway?*, his play about a man paralysed from the neck downwards as a result of an accident, once said that, when he got the idea for this 'talking head' he knew he had a play! If you have seen that play you will know it was a theme so powerful and so dramatic it needed no embellishment.

Failing such inspiration most of us have, all too often, to labour at our plots like a man constructing a wall brick by brick. The theme is the foundation. The plot is the development of the theme – the 'what happens next'.

I suppose everyone knows someone with a great idea for a book or play that stays for ever as a great idea for a book or play. The dilettante will milk it. He will talk it, impressing his friends; dine out on it but if he ever gets round to trying to write it he would discover very quickly that his great idea is no more than a starting point.

Asked, 'How do you write a television play?' N.J. Crisp, one of our most prolific scriptwriters, once said, 'You apply the seat of the pants to the seat of the chair and keep it there until the script is finished.' He was right. Between the basic idea and the finished script there is usually a lot of time and a great deal of hard, concentrated thinking to be done.

When you find the going tough don't get discouraged. Believe me, every experienced writer has faced the situation when, having settled on his theme or found a basic idea he wants to write, he has sat in front of the typewriter staring at blank sheets of paper asking himself the question, 'Where do I go from here?'

In life one must constantly be choosing between alternatives, and which ever alternative one chooses creates a new situation that demands still further choices. As you try to develop your theme into a plot ask yourself questions. 'Given this basic situation how will the character react?' . . . 'What if?'. . . 'Supposing she?' . . . 'What will be the result of the actions?' . . . 'How will it affect other characters' . . . 'What would they do?'.

There is an old joke formula which I expect you know. I can recommend it to you as a way to clarifying your thinking when you are trying to develop your story.

It goes like this: A cashier discovers there is money missing from his accounts. There are two possibilities. Either he finds where the money is, or he doesn't. If he finds it he has nothing to worry about. If he doesn't find it there are two possibilities. His boss will think he has stolen it, or he won't. If he doesn't think he has stolen it he has nothing to worry about . . . but if he does there are two possibilities . . . and so on. I can't remember the pay-off to the joke and it probably wasn't very funny anyway but it's a very effective formula for plotting.

Frequently, of course, there are more than two possibilities but however many the principle is the same. Failing that flash of inspiration when the entire story takes shape without conscious effort; failing that break through when the development of an idea that has nagged for months is suddenly laid out in your mind as clear as an ordinance map, a cool, systematic analysis of alternative courses of action and the different results of each action is an effective way to filter out hackneyed thoughts and construct an original and viable storyline.

And as you fill your wastepaper basket with the ideas you reject there is no reason to feel discouraged. That's how it goes most of the time for most professionals. They too sit at their desks for days and weeks desperately trying to find original ideas or devise unexpected twists and developments for their stories. Experience doesn't actually make it easier but it does teach you not to panic; simply to accept that working out a plot and writing a script requires both time and patience.

Plotting is seldom easy and nearly impossible if you are trying to think of the entire story all at once.

When Dick Sharples and I were writing comedy together and under contract to write two 30 minute programmes each month for a couple of years – which made comedy writing a very serious business – we sat for hours systematically exploring the 'what happens next' possibilities and following alternatives through until we isolated what seemed to us both funny and appropriate developments.

Build your plot in this way – analyse your characters, their motives and their behaviour. Separate each of the elements and deal with them individually. Look for an angle consistent with the spirit of your basic theme and try to make each successive development the springboard for the next development.

The relationship of cause and effect.

And as you ask the questions and find answers try to make them answers that will start the viewer asking questions too.

'Why did he do that?'

'Who was it phoned her?' 'What is she not telling her husband?'

'How are they going to deal with that situation?'

And of course, depending on your theme, there may also be valid questions about your character's emotional behaviour;

'Why is she so depressed?'

'What is he up to now?'

'If he loves her how could he do that?'

Questions, questions, questions!

It is not only in mystery stories you need to create mysteries. One of the surest ways to hold the viewer's attention is to show them behaviour and action that demands an explanation; behaviour that promises, without prematurely revealing, future interesting developments.

A good example of this is demonstrated in the following scene (set out as a tape TV studio production):

LETTER FOR LARRY

by

John Smith

1. INT: BREAKFAST ROOM. DAY.

MODERN, WELL-FURNISHED ROOM. LARRY SMITH IN HIS FORTIES AND HIS WIFE, MARY, ABOUT THE SAME AGE, ARE EATING BREAKFAST. BOTH READ NEWSPAPERS.
FROM OFF WE HEAR THE LETTERBOX FLAP. LARRY THROWS HIS PAPER ASIDE AND LEAPS UP.

LARRY: Be the post. I'll get it.

HE HURRIES TO THE DOOR.

                                    CUT TO:

2. INT: HALL. DAY.

TWO LETTERS LIE ON THE DOORMAT. LARRY ENTERS FAST AND PICKS THEM UP. HE GLANCES AT ONE BUT TURNS HIS ATTENTION TO THE SECOND. HE LOOKS AT IT CLOSELY, THEN SNIFFS IT. HE QUICKLY PUTS IT IN HIS POCKET AND GOES BACK TO THE BREAKFAST ROOM.

                                    CUT TO:

3. INT: BREAKFAST ROOM. DAY.

AS LARRY ENTERS, MARY LOOKS UP.

MARY: Anything interesting?

LARRY: Just the gas bill.

HE SEATS HIMSELF BACK AT THE TABLE AND SLITS
THE ENVELOPE OPEN. HE SNORTS IN DISGUST AND
THROWS IT ASIDE AND RESUMES READING THE
NEWSPAPER.

That short example has suggested a great deal about this man and his relationship with his wife. We know, or suspect, he has a mistress; that he is deceiving his wife. We are going to be inquisitive about them. He could have hidden away a letter for all sorts of reasons. It could have been about a present he had ordered for her birthday, or a second honeymoon he'd secretly booked. It could have been about his over-draft or a demand for payment from his bookmaker; a solicitor's letter threatening proceedings against him or a response to his application for a new job that he didn't yet want his wife to know about.

But not if he sniffs it.

When he sniffs it we know it's from a woman and when he hides it we know he is having an affair.

Or is he?

We are intrigued.

The action demands an explanation and starts us asking questions.

As a scene in a television play the action tells a lot of story with very few words.

It also avoids heavy plot laying. The point that the man has a mis-tress – if indeed he has – could have been made in dozens of different ways but few would have been more succinct than his sniff at that letter.

Yet we could find an innocent explanation for that. We are left guessing what the odour was. While traces of an exotic perfume might reinforce suspicions of a mistress the smell of moth balls or the scent of lavender might be explained by the fact that the letter was from an aged aunt who kept her note paper in a drawer with lavender bags or moth balls.

The man's action in concealing the letter from his wife might be equally innocent. Perhaps he knew Auntie's letter would be bad news he wanted to break tactfully at a more convenient moment.

The audience will always be trying to out guess you and you should aim to be one jump ahead of them, never forgetting the need to avoid the obvious if the individual viewer's interest is to be retained.

To quote Sir Basil Bartlett again, 'What writing for Television really means is that the author is trying to tell a story to a single individual, who is not obliged to listen to it, who has not paid for his seat, whose attention must be well and firmly held if he is not going to switch off his set.'

When the viewer can anticipate the developments and ending of your play he will probably start looking for something more original.

But a word of caution. Audiences who now watch so much television drama are becoming very perceptive. An unexpected or unusual development in your story that does not ring true will infuriate many viewers. They resent being cheated. If you expect the viewer to accept your characters as normal intelligent human beings they must behave consistently. You will destroy the characters and lose your audience if, having established a complicated relationship, or an intriguing situation that is not easily resolved, you slide out of it by making your people behave as no normal intelligent person would behave.

Teasers and hooks

This ability to switch programmes so easily has imposed its own particular form on popular television series. It is responsible for the 'teaser' or 'hook' as it is sometimes called. (A short pre-credit sequence designed to grab audience attention and ensure they continue to watch after the first commercial interruption – which in the USA comes within the first two or three minutes of the start.)

American productions, segmented by dozens of advertisements, invariably start with a teaser. In contrast British productions usually opened at a more leisurely pace spending more time setting up the background and characters. This pattern continued here even after the introduction of commercial TV because the Independent Broadcasting Authority regulations stipulated the number of commercial breaks permitted in a single hour and do not allow the intrusion of advertisements within minutes of the start of the programme. The result has been that plays and series produced for the home audience have been able to develop theme and character in a more balanced way.

When programme makers are aiming for overseas sales the 'teaser' is important and many British series particularly those made by commercial companies and independents conform to the established Hollywood pattern with a dramatic, attention grabbing opening.

So vital was the 'teaser' in making an American sale that the writer's brief on one series was to think of a opening that presented a seemingly 'impossible' situation and then develop a story that solved it. A challenging assignment.

A beginning, a middle and an end.

Sam Goldwyn is said to have instructed his writers to 'Start with an earthquake and build up to a climax.' That would surely tax the inventiveness of a genius. Can you wonder that American screen-writers are so highly paid? The problem about starting with the earthquake is that everything thereafter is likely to be an anti-climax unless the writer is capable of great imagination and inventiveness.

Story openings

But whether you are writing solely for the domestic market, a pro-gramme designed for overseas distribution or a joint production, financed in part with foreign money, a really strong opening is vital. British audiences are well used to fast moving American style openings and many series producers here insist, if not on an earthquake, at least on a few threatening rumbles as a harbinger of stirring things to come.

But the 'teaser' is no more than a taster. The true beginning is the 'first act', which in a half hour play or episode means the first fifteen minutes and for a sixty minute play is usually the first twenty minutes.

The opening of your story, whether physical action or just two people sitting talking quietly; whether it is a 'one off' play or a series episode is very, very important. You cannot take too much care and trouble about it. When your play is screened you need to capture audience attention as quickly as possible but long before that you have to capture and hold the interest of the company script editor who has the job of reading unsolicited manuscripts and, with a great stack of scripts to read, needs to be persuaded early on that yours is a script worth spending more of his time reading.

Story construction

What you are offering is a drama and drama is about conflict, physical or mental, and men and women are the material of drama.

At one time there was one important difference between a play written for the BBC and a play written for a commercial company. A one hour commercial television play – which usually means fifty-six or fifty-seven minutes actual screen time – is played in three acts of approximately twenty minutes. This imposed a discipline on the writers not very different from the discipline involved in writing for the stage.

The one hour play for the BBC was sixty minutes. However, since they began showing their archive material on the UK Gold satellite they have been insisting on the right to cut completed programmes to make room for advertisements. Plays written for commercial companies are constructed so that the commercial break falls like a curtain drop at the end of the act heightening the drama and holding the audience in eager expectation, ensuring they will still be watching when the advertisements are over. The BBC may now require writers to do the same for some programmes. But one thing is sure; well written series episodes do not lend themselves to this kind of 'convenient' cutting – especially by people other than the original writer. It is not unlikely that many highly regarded programmes will be spoiled. Not to say ruined.

In the first section of your play you need to set the scene; establish your principal characters; and introduce the audience to their problem.

However, you should never forget as you write the early scenes of your play that none of us care much about plight of characters we don't know or characters with whom we have no immediate sympathy. Our aim must be to stimulate the viewer's interest from the outset. 'Another Indian bites the dust?'. That body falling from the horse might just as well be a sack of corn for all we care. But once we have met the man; seen him playing with his children; talking tenderly to his wife; or when we recognise the justice of the cause for which he is fighting, we are concerned.

Identification is the key to emotional involvement.

We read a report of a motorway pile-up or an aircrash in which dozens of people are killed with a shudder but never a tear, but when some person we know – be it ever so slightly – is involved we too are involved.

And yet, very obviously there are circumstances, situations and characters where the audience need to know very little about those concerned to arouse both sympathy and anxiety.

Take for example the following opening scene (set out as a TV film script):

1. EXT: COUNTRY ROAD.	DAY. 1.

A CAR IS BEING DRIVEN ERRATICALLY ALONG THE ROAD.

CUT TO:

2. INT: CAR.	DAY. 2.

TWO YOUNG MEN, THE DRIVER AND PASSENGER. THE PASSENGER IS

DRINKING FROM A BOTTLE. HE HANDS THE BOTTLE TO THE DRIVER
WHO ALSO TAKES A SWIG. THEY START TO SING.

CUT TO:

3. EXT: ROADSIDE.   DAY. 3.

TWO BOYS ARE PLAYING WITH A BALL ON THE VERGE BESIDE
THE ROAD.

CUT TO:

4. INT: CAR.   DAY. 4.

PASSENGER:
Come on, don't hang about. We're late!

THE DRIVER PUTS HIS FOOT DOWN ON THE ACCELERATOR AND THE
CAR SPEEDS UP.

We don't need to go any further. Already audience emotions are
involved. We don't know who the boys are but we are concerned
about them. We don't know the men drinking as they drive but
already we hate them. We have to know whether the boys are hurt
or killed; whether the car crashes and the occupants are injured or
even whether the car stops after the accident – if there is an accident.
We want to know if there is!

Of course plays do not necessarily require catastrophe or the
expectation of physical violence to grip the viewer's attention. The
'earthquake' can be personal and emotional, shattering the lives and
happiness of our characters – and any event that produces an
upheaval with which the viewer can identify, about which ordinary
people may be apprehensive, is far more significant for most viewers
than a mountain falling into the sea in some far distant land or a
space war adventure involving futuristic weapons and multi-headed
monsters. The strength and appeal of programmes like *Coronation
Street* and *EastEnders* is that the audience know, recognise and
identify with the characters. The problems they face are everyday
problems that viewers may themselves sometimes experience.

The closer to the reality of our everyday lives the greater the impact
and, incidentally, the greater the responsibility upon the writer to be
aware of the effect the play may have on the audience.

Having established the characters and their problem, the middle
of the play must be concerned with the effect it has on their lives and
how they face up to it. Here you will see we are back to the questions
and the alternatives . . . If this, what? . . . If that, how? . . . If not,
why or when or who? . . . 'To be or not to be,' as Hamlet agonised.

Problems, conflicts and decisions, creating new problems requiring yet further decisions.

'The drama may be called the art of crisis', said William Archer in his book *Play-making – A Manual, of Craftsmanship* which, published around seventy-five years ago, is concerned with writing for the theatre. The statement applies equally to writing for television. You should always endeavour to construct your play so that it leads up to a crisis – either physical or emotional – a crisis that becomes a turning point in the lives of your people. Thus we meet a man full of joy and confidence and see him tested and maybe destroyed or we find him desperate and humiliated and watch him triumph over his adversity. This reversal of the circumstances is an old and well-tried formula but none the worse for that. The Greeks had a special word for it. They called it the 'peripety', the change of fortune, but you don't need to turn to the plays of Euripides or Sophocles for examples. You can see them any week on your TV screen as when a man, well established in a secure position is suddenly made redundant with no prospect of other employment, or the man we know to be innocent is found 'guilty' but subsequently proved innocent and the guilty person arrested. Yet another common example, which we have all seen on our TV screens many times, is the man who visits the doctor to seek advice on some trifling ailment and leaves half an hour later knowing he is doomed to die.

How tragic, how momentous the crisis will depend on the type of programme you are writing. An episode for a soap opera that left the set littered with corpses – even if you spared the principals – would be unlikely to endear you to the producer or be appreciated by the regular viewers. Tragedies and crises come in all sizes. A lost purse with little money in it can be a greater heart-break than a lost fortune; The fatted calf is killed for the prodigal son while the lad who stayed dutifully at home goes unrewarded.

Any unexpected reversal whereby the viewers discover the situation is not as they thought or that a character is not driven by the motives they thought, or that he holds, or does not hold, powers they believed he held can be a very effective turning point in your story. More by luck than judgement I got into television with a short thriller that depended on such a switch.

It went like this:

A man is sitting at a desk writing. A gun slides into shot levelled at his head. The gunman is a bully. He demands money and the car keys and as the man stalls he slaps him around getting sadistic pleasure at the power the gun gives him. The victim says he has no money in the house. The robber cocks the gun and presses it against the man's temple. The victim looks terrified. Then his demeanour changes. There is money in the house. You can have it on one condition. 'I want you to kill me!'

He explains. The paper on his desk is a suicide note but he is worried about the effect of a suicide on his impressionable daughter. But as the victim of a murderer . . . !

The power of the gun has gone. The robber will not risk swinging for a few quid. (At that time the penalty for murder was death.) He refuses the deal. The man is a nut! He starts for the door as the man produces a gun of his own. He tells the intruder, 'Shoot me or I shoot you'. The robber drops his gun. It wasn't loaded anyway. Now the man at the desk taunts him, reducing the bully to a trembling wreck, glad to be handed over to the police when they arrive.

That, briefly, was the story. In the thirty minutes we saw a complete reversal of the fortunes of the two characters involved.

The third act or final part of your play should be concerned with the resolution. You have got your characters into some awful trouble or particularly tricky situation. You have placed them in peril of life and limb or presented them with emotional and psychological problems that cannot be easily resolved – because if the solution is easy and obvious the audience will be there before you and feel cheated.

Many years ago there was a famous radio series called *Dick Barton – Special Agent*. He was a private detective and the series had a large following. Week by week he was involved in hair-raising adventures and each episode ended with a 'cliff hanger' – like he was alone, bound hand and foot in a dungeon that was slowly filling with water or left in some other equally perilous situation. The following week, at the start of the next episode, his escapes were usually highly imaginative and sometimes so incredible, that 'With one bound Dick Barton was free' became something of a catch phrase.

A modern television audience expect more.

The ending of your play is just as important as the beginning. Some would argue, more so. A play needs a positive direction but it is unlikely to have positive direction if you have no idea where you are aiming from the start. The ending is the destination and your story must move steadily towards it all the time.

I confess I have, on occasions, started writing a script hoping the action and development would suggest the ending as I went along. Sometimes my luck has held and it has worked out very well.

Sometimes I have not been so lucky and it has worked out badly. And sometimes I have been out of luck and have found myself with a great deal of rewriting to do.

Unless you know precisely where you are going from the beginning it is all too easy to let a bright idea or some interesting, but minor, character you have created take over your story or start you off down a blind alley. And when that happens you frequently find yourself stuck and trying desperately to write your way back to the storyline and make it work.

Unless you know exactly where you are going from the start you can finish up with nine tenths of a brilliant script and no idea how to end it in way that does not ruin it.

I mentioned earlier 'heavy plot laying'. It's a common fault; worst of all when it comes as a kind of 'Butler and Maid' exposition where the two characters tell each other for the benefit of the audience why someone behaved in a particular way or plot details the author has not taken the trouble, or had the ingenuity, to disclose in a more subtle manner. In badly written detective stories it sometimes happens after the event when, having totally confused the viewers, the author winds up his story by having the brilliant detective explain to his idiot assistant how the crime was committed and why some small piece of evidence nobody has mentioned is after all the vital clue that solved the mystery. Surprise endings are great but they must grow inexorably out of character or situation or both and not as a result of startlingly relevant information the audience has been unfairly denied throughout the story. An explanation that seemingly inexplicable behaviour makes sense, after all, because 'she was really his illegitimate daughter,' 'his dead brother's wife' or some equally momentous announcement deserves to be more than a 'P.S.' at the end of the play.

It is sometimes said there are only seven plots. I have never been quite sure exactly which they are supposed to be but most stories revolve around one or another of the following very basic human emotions: love, hatred, revenge, fear, greed, jealousy, and ambition. They are all very primitive and powerful motivations. They are the raw material of drama.

When you are plotting be clear in your own mind about the motivations. Don't overload the story. It tends to confuse both the theme and the audience and sometimes the writer too, if the action stems from uncertain and mixed motives. One must always try to avoid the fortuitous, be particularly careful not to seek cheap effect by piling excessive problems and adversities on the characters. It would not be very difficult to write a story about a man who has lost his job, who is about to be evicted from his home, whose wife is dying and whose children are delinquent. He have would have plenty to complain about and innumerable opportunities for conflict and action but would any of it seem credible? With so much adversity it would be almost a comedy. But try writing a play about a man who is happily married with two or three bright, loving children; a man who has no money worries or health problems; a man without tragedy or grief in his life. What do you say about him? The superficial and the melodramatic will provide an easy story. The writer has to dig deeper to write plays about ordinary people in ordinary circumstances which is what true drama is about.

As G.K. Chesterton said, 'Death is always more tragic than death by starvation.'

With so much television it gets harder by the month to find new and original plots and themes as every professional television writer discovers all too quickly when, after spending many hours writing a storyline, he is told by the producer or editor that one of his fellow writers has pre-empted him.

Before we move on there are a few more points I want to make. The first is about sub-plots.

A play may have a straight line development or it may digress from the main theme and principal characters to introduce a sub-plot with additional characters and activity that is in some way germane to the overall story. In the early years of television when programmes were 'live' or when cutting tape was time consuming and expensive the sub-plot was used to allow actors to move from one set to another or time to change costume. It was and still is used to indicate a time lapse, and it can also be very effective when heavy dramatic content needs to be broken up with light relief. Shakespeare regularly used the sub-plot in this way.

But a sub-plot is not essential. You use it if it works for your script – where for instance you need to introduce and follow the activities of minor characters which early in the story may seem to have nothing to do with it but at a later stage play some crucial role. It can be used like a 'meanwhile back at the ranch' exposition or to accentuate facets of character contrasting, for example, in alternate scenes the behaviour of a brave man and a coward or two men towards their wives.

Hobbies, chance meetings, articles lost or found, old loves, new loves, ambitions, superstitions, knowledge or ignorance have all been used as the basis of sub-plots in plays I have seen in recent years.

There is no limitation to what you can use but it mustn't be allowed to over shadow the basic story and to be truly relevant it must ultimately flow into the main theme and become a vital part of it, like a stream joining and losing its own identity in a river.

A final point about plotting. Learn to be selective. If you allow yourself to be hooked by a bright idea – a development or a scene that is out of place in your story and find yourself trying to bend the plot to accommodate it – you are usually storing up trouble. It frequently happens that the scene you like best is one that has to be cut. Not so long ago I had a situation where I had written myself into a paper bag. I was stuck and couldn't find the way ahead. I read the script to my wife who said when I finished, 'Scene 26 is the problem', putting her finger right on it. When she said it I knew she was right. What is more I had known all along that it was scene 26 that had messed me up but I liked it so much I couldn't bring myself to admit it and do what I had to do – throw it out.

A writer has to be ruthless. Situations that are unbelievable; actions that are out of character; indulgent scenes that do not advance the story; splendid scenes that run too long must all come out! It'll break your heart to junk a good idea but professional writers do it all the time. You learn with experience that what you leave out is often as important as what you leave in.

10. Dialogue

'Natural' dialogue

What your play does not need is genuine authentic natural dialogue.

If that surprises you, as it does some people, I suggest you try a little experiment. Set up a recorder and tape your friends or family talking without letting them know what you are doing. What you will hear will be genuine, authentic, natural dialogue and unless your friends are exceptionally brilliant conversationalists you will find it quite impossible to listen to them.

The experiment will demonstrate to you that what we take to be natural dialogue when we hear it coming from the mouths of television actors is nothing of the sort. It is very carefully edited and contrived.

Most of us, when we speak, hesitate. We 'um' and we 'ah'. We start to say something and change our mind in the middle of the sentence. We lose the thread of what we are saying. We stop when other people interrupt us and we interrupt other people when they are speaking. We mumble. We speak too quickly. We take a dozen words to say what could very easily be said in half a dozen. We often never actually get to the point at all.

As you attune your ear to listen critically – not just to your tape but to precisely what people around you say and, importantly, what they avoid saying, you will find a great many sentences are never concluded. They trail off because what the speaker intends to say is so obvious it is unnecessary to continue; or they stop abruptly because the speaker realises what he or she was about to say is indiscreet or tactless or is so painful they can't bring themselves to mouth it.

Dramatic dialogue for a script is simulated 'natural' dialogue. It is honed and filtered and meticulously selected and, unless the character you are writing is intended to be dull and boring don't, whatever you do, give him totally realistic natural dialogue lines to say. Play dialogue needs to be a great deal wittier and sharper than most of us produce in natural conversation.

It is sometimes said the best ad libs are the scripted ones and it is true that many people, particularly in the entertainment business, work very hard on their image by creating, collecting and storing witty sayings and wise-cracks that make their conversation sparkle and enhance their reputation. But that isn't just a twentieth century show biz trick. There is an interesting story about Oscar Wilde. Leaving Oxford one day he is said to have stood at the window of his train carriage and regaled his friends with a stream of brilliant witticisms. But the train was delayed and at the scheduled departure time he waved goodbye, pulled up the window, sat down and opened a book leaving his disconcerted friends to straggle away with an embarrassed wave. Seemingly he had used up that day's quota of brilliant original Oscar Wilde quips and epigrams and did not propose to risk tarnishing his image indulging in dull every day small talk.

Sharp, interesting dialogue is usually the result of hours of concentrated thought and if your play is to catch the attention of script editors and producers you cannot pay too much attention to it.

Some years ago I met a young actor who was interested in script writing. One of the companies was running a competition for a half hour play and he had an idea he thought might be suitable. I agreed to help him work out the plot. We spent a few hours together and he went away to write it. He came back early the next day. He'd done it! Now you may not be surprised to know it didn't win the competition. It certainly didn't surprise me. I wouldn't have attempted to write a half hour play in the time. His dialogue was made up of the first lines that came into his head and that, as most professional script writers know only too well, is seldom good enough.

There is an Oscar Wilde story that bears on this point too. It demonstrates the care even great writers must take with the detail of their work. He is said to have told someone he had spent all the morning deciding to put in a comma and all the afternoon deciding to take it out.

Such care over a comma? It is not hard to guess how much time and thought went into those sparkling speeches in his plays.

Working to television deadlines I do not recommend you spend even half an hour on that comma but do spend half an hour – a couple of hours – or as long as it takes to write lines for your people to say that the audience will find more interesting than the boring everyday inconsequential chatter you recorded on that tape.

Slang, dialect and idiom

Writing dialogue for a play it is necessary to write the words and sentences exactly as they are spoken. To the unpractised eye it may look strange on the page but play scripts are not written for the eye. They are written for the ear. The actors will produce the accent but the writer should script the slang, dialect and idiom; abbreviations and combinations of words like, y'see, I've, we've, 'is, 'ers, m'self, t'morrow, that reflect the way his characters speak.

Look, for example, at these speeches from *Where The Difference Begins* a play by the late David Mercer.

> WILF: And I've nobut one question to put to thee, Edgar.
>
> EDGAR: What's that?
>
> WILF: What's ta going to do with thy two lads?

Or again at these speeches from Alan Owen's play, *Lena, Oh My Lena.*

> GLYN: Hi, Lena. (Lena ignores him. Glyn steps in front of her) I said, Hello.
>
> LENA (to PEG) Y' don't half get some muck round this midden!
>
> GLYN: Don't mess me about, lovely girl.
>
> LENA: (turning on him) Don't come any of that lovely girl stuff wi' me!
>
> (GLYN grins)
>
> And you can wipe that soft grin off your daft face an' all.
>
> (GLYN still grins at her)
>
> PEG: Eeh – he is cheeky!
>
> GLYN: (still smiling) Shut up!
>
> PEG: (furious) I won't be insulted by your sort!
>
> GLYN: Then push off and mind your own!

Characterisation by dialogue

When you start writing your play be very careful about the lines you give your principal characters early in the script. These may determine irreversibly the person's nature and attitudes. One clever flip remark, sharp retort or wisecrack that pleases you so much that you can't bear to strike it from the script, may create a character totally different from the one you'd intended and even more importantly have a knock-on effect on the attitudes of everyone else in your story.

A reply by a teenager to her father could set the pattern and determine the relationship for the rest of the play as the following example demonstrates:

> FATHER: Don't argue with me. I'm your father!
>
> DAUGHTER: So what?
>
> FATHER: So do as you're told!

Here we have a father who expects to be obeyed. The girl is slightly resentful and gives a pat cliché answer but the man's final remark is a clear indication of his authority and their relationship.

Now consider this second example:

> FATHER: Don't argue with me. I'm your father!
>
> DAUGHTER: And that makes you right?

The same line from the father but a more intelligent answer from the daughter. It suggests she is capable of the logical deduction that paternity has absolutely nothing to do with the merits of the argument. And she is right. If he replies, as he does in the first case:

> FATHER: . . . do as you're told!

it suggests he is impatient; not capable of, nor prepared to enter into an argument based on reason and unless he can come back with some very sharp retort he comes out of the exchange as the weaker character.

Now let us look at a third case:

> FATHER: Don't argue with me. I'm your father!
>
> DAUGHTER: You sure?

Now we have a totally different relationship suggested by her saucy answer. If she is smart she doesn't stay around long waiting for her father's reply which might well be a smack across the face. She might be well advised to use it as a dramatic exit line for unless the line is delivered in a way that makes it quite clear it was meant as a joke there is implied contempt in her words.

But the way her father reacts is crucial to the characterisations for the rest of the play. If he hits her it establishes him as a bully whose answer – when he doesn't have an answer – is violence. If he ignores it we conclude he is a weak ineffectual sort of man who has no real control over the girl. On the other hand if he comes back with a sharp witty retort – even a joke about it, it would show us that they have a easy, relaxed and uninhibited relationship. But then again if he picks it up as a serious question and becomes defensive it might suggest he actually has some doubt as to whether he really is her father.

And what of the mother? It brings into question her fidelity and morality and whether the girl has a genuine reason to suggest some man, other than the husband, might be her father.

Very obviously one flip remark or smart retort, that might seem as you write it to brighten up the dialogue, can leave you stuck with attitudes you had not intended and that do not fit in properly with the rest of the story.

And if you have to start changing other characteristions, written or planned, to accommodate that odd bright line you need to look very closely at your overall story to be sure the alteration does not undermine the integrity of the theme. When, with the greatest reluctance, you decide that it does you must be ruthless and cut it.

The way people speak and the vocabulary they use are usually positive indications of their class, background, occupation, temperament and attitudes. It frequently happens that a short telephone conversation with someone we have never actually met leaves us with an indelible impression of what the person is like. Of course the impression isn't always accurate – as people making blind dates often discover. Vocabulary and accents can and are commonly used to deceive even when the substance of what is said is true.

But as Lewis Herman says in his book *A Practical Manual of Screen Playwriting*, 'A person's innate character is mirrored in the tempo of his speech. The stubborn bite off each word with clipped determination: the meek meander along with faltering 'uh's' and 'ah's' and interjected 'ands'; the pedantic use long-winded sentences; the strong willed speak with determination; the aged speak slowly, contemplatively; the young gush out their thoughts like a spring freshet; poetic folks use high-flown tropes; the dull and unimaginative resort continually to clichés.'

A drama writer needs to be sensitive to the nuances of language and train himself to be constantly alert for colourful expressions and snippets of conversation to broaden his understanding of human nature; flesh out his characters; and bring originality and individuality to his work.

If you listen attentively to what the people you meet have to say you will without doubt pick up some gems. I met a sad woman one day, as I was walking my dog – sad because her dog had died. I knew she had been fond of that dog and offered my condolences. In return she presented me with one such gem which I later used in a script. Near tears she said, 'In a way he's still with me. I've got him in the garden under a ten-shilling lily.'

A ten-shilling lily! At that time before inflation and decimalisation ten shillings was a lot of money for her to pay for the flower. But it was a mark of her love for her dog but more importantly, from a writer's point of view, it was a colourful and interesting facet of the woman.

The speech patterns and vocabulary of your various characters must vary. Beware of making them all talk as you do. The actor may impart the proper accent for a Scottish football fan or a church of England Bishop but you, the writer, will determine what words he uses and that has to be appropriate to his standard of education, social background and profession.

Speech patterns can easily be distinctive if you are playing a middle class character against someone with a working class background. But if all your characters have similar backgrounds, speech mannerisms will help to distinguish them. You might have a character who injects into his speech the term 'By the by', which has colour because most people say 'By the way'; or there are such mannerisms as ending sentences with 'Do you get my drift?' and 'Are you with me?' These are mechanical approaches, but they can be useful.

Jargon is particularly interesting. *The Concise Oxford Dictionary* defines it as 'A mode of speech familiar only to a group or profession' and it is important when you are featuring members of a particular speech-community that you get it right. You shouldn't attempt to write dialogue for members of the Asian or West Indian immigrant community unless you are familiar with, or take the time and trouble to research, their speech patterns and vocabulary. Failure to do so may result in an offensive caricature for television very quickly exposes careless and phoney dialects. In the same way it is necessary to get professional jargon right. Pop musicians, for example, use a lot of words that are not common in every day English. If you wish to portray a pop musician as one of your characters you need to acquaint yourself with his speech patterns and at least some of the words of his vocabulary to make the character sound authentic.

But a word of warning. Don't overdo it. Some jargon – particularly professional jargon is quite unintelligible to the average viewer. I once wrote a script that called for the professional, technical conversation between the pilot of an aircraft approaching London Airport and the control tower. I got from British Airways a script detailing precisely the exchange that takes place from the moment the aircraft starts the communication with the Heathrow air traffic controller. Most of it was clear but there was also some very technical stuff that I did not understand at all and I knew the majority of the viewers would not understand it either. As such detail wasn't important to the story I cut it, leaving what I required for the purpose of my story and sufficient to sound fully authentic to all but pilots and control tower staff. But the television company called in an expert adviser and he instantly put back all the lines I had filtered out – boring technical jargon that slowed up the action and told ninety nine per cent of the viewers absolutely nothing at all. They had no idea what he was on about and were only interested in what was going to happen when that aircraft landed.

So much for accuracy! You mustn't expect the ordinary viewer to understand or be gripped by the incomprehensible utterings of scientific men and technical experts.

From jargon to clichés.

Language is a living thing. It is changing all the time. Policemen become Bobbies, become Coppers, become Rozzers, become the Jacks, become the Fuzz, become the Filth, become the Bill and so on. Today's bright witty 'with it' expression is tomorrow's cliché and yesterday's cliché can sometimes seem bright and colourful to a generation of viewers who have never heard it before.

There are, of course, innumerable hackneyed clichés in common use in rather carelessly written movies and television programmes – and not so carelessly written programmes too. Some are so corny and so melodramatic that the audience might find them funny if they actually listened to the words rather than hearing them without registering precisely what is said.

You will have noticed, I am sure, 'Bolts always come from the blue', 'Blessings in disguise', 'We take our lives in our hands' and leave people 'To stew in their own juice'. We 'Turn an honest penny' and 'Live in the lap of luxury.' 'Louts', of course, are always 'Clumsy' and 'Coast's clear' which enables us to see 'The ships that pass in the night'.

There is no end to them; all part of the rich fabric of the language but many so stale they must be used with care, if at all.

Thrillers, because the dramatic situations are in themselves so often clichés, are particularly vulnerable. An example of cliché situations and phrases by Malcolm Hulke demonstrates this rather well.

Situation 1. The hero is searching a room. Another man enters quietly and asks:
Cliché 1. 'Looking for something?'

Situation 2. Up to now the speaker has been the hero's seeming ally. But now he is holding a gun at our hero and reveals he is really on the other side. The hero says:
Cliché 2. 'I should have known.'

Situation 3. But the hero didn't. The traitor escapes. Now the hero learns that the heroine is held prisoner in the villain's fortified country mansion. He tells the heroine's young brother, who happens to be a promising concert violinist, that he (the hero) intends to rescue her. To heighten the audience's expectancy for blood, the young brother enumerates the terrors to be faced – alligators in the moat, mad dogs, machine guns at every window. All our hero can say is:
Cliché 3. 'That's a risk I'll have to take.'

Situation 4. Which he does – and gets caught! Now he is chained to a wall, a laser beam pointing his way. The villain with his hand on the switch, says:
Cliché 4. 'Before I kill you, tell me what you have told your associates.'

Situation 5. Naturally our hero tells him nothing but says with a touch of gay defiance:
Cliché 5. 'You'll never get away with this.'

Situation 6. Which of course the villain doesn't, because the young brother tricks his way into the mansion, finds the hero and releases him. The hero asks the young brother how he slipped by the alligators, mad dogs and machine guns. The young brother answers:
Cliché 6. 'There's no time to explain.'

Situation 7. Just as well since we, the audience, saw how he did it. And anyway the villain is now returning to kill his prisoner. In the fight the young brother is wounded. But by an act of tremendous courage the hero defeats the villain. The heroine is released and the young brother is tended by a helpfully handy doctor who just happened to be in one of the other dungeons. The hero has a brief word with the doctor, then goes on to report to the heroine.

Cliché 7. 'He's going to be all right. Your brother will play the violin again.'

The challenge in thriller writing is you cannot avoid the situations, but you must try and think of original replacements for 'That's a risk I'll have to take,' and all the others.

It is, however, a fact that in everyday conversation many people do use clichés and if you are writing dialogue for the kind of man who uses clichés in his normal speech, true characterisation demands that you show this. For example, the ex-army man in *Coronation Street*, Percy Sugden, very properly spoke in military clichés. If you watch the annual TUC conference on television you will see that Trade Union leaders have their own particular brand. And these days it is hard to imagine a professional football player who is not 'As sick as a parrot' about the goal he missed, 'Over the moon' about winning a cup or thinks 'The lads' had a great game.

When you are writing these characters, this is the way they talk and this is the way you have to make them talk if they are to ring true, but here again one must try to think of original replacements, analogies and expressions that seem somehow to have a familiar feel about them even though they are original to you. It is worth spending time to give your dialogue an uplift in this way. You may be sure, when you come up with something fresh and colourful, producers and script editors won't miss it.

Between the words

Talking of dialogue one thinks automatically of words but it is important never to forget the spaces between words. Pregnant pauses and choked emotions can sometimes say more than half a page of talk. A suspect under questioning may, by over long hesitation, tell his interrogators more than he does by his words. A scene between sadly parting lovers will need far fewer words to fill three minutes screen time than a bitter quarrel between them. And, incidentally, as a quarrel gets more heated sentences generally get shorter and the speech faster until a squabbling couple are almost snapping at each other like a pair of bad tempered terriers.

The characters in your play are different people and they need to have a different speech rhythm. A busy young business executive speaks as he is, sharp, impatient. You will have to provide him with a lot more words for thirty minute play than if the principal characters were old aged pensioners. A politician or college lecturer will be used to articulating slowly and distinctly and carry something of this over to his every day conversation. A market trader may be used to gabbling and his speech patterns will reflect it.

Stress

All of us judge people not only by what they say but the way they say it. The stress they place on individual words can change their meaning and our understanding of what is said and indicate the mood, attitude and disposition of the speaker.

In the following scene taken from an educational programme I wrote the word the actor was required to stress is underlined. You will see to what extent it changes the intention of the statement.

> SIX PEOPLE ARE SITTING AROUND A TABLE.
> ONE OF THEM IS LOOKING INDIGNANT AS
> THE FIRST MAN TURNS TO HIM:
>
> 1ST MAN:
> I never said you were stupid.

No particular stress – A straight denial.

> 2ND MAN:
> I never said you were stupid.

The 'I' is stressed implying someone else said it.

> 3RD MAN:
> I never said you were stupid.

But he thought it!

> 4TH MAN:
> I never said you were stupid.

So which of them was he talking about?

> 5TH MAN:
> I never said you were stupid!

So you didn't actually say stupid. What did you say?

Speech directions

When you write dialogue and words that are open to different inter-
pretation it is extremely important to make sure that your meaning
is unambiguous and where a particular word needs to be stressed to
carry the intent of the sentence it is permissible to underline it to
avoid confusion. But don't underline the obvious. Directors and
actors loathe a proliferation of unnecessary speech directions and it
is a sign of inexperience to produce a scene like this:

EDGAR: (HOPEFULLY)
I think you once really loved me Priscilla.

PRISCILLA: (TENDERLY)
I am still very fond of you Edgar.

EDGAR: (WITH YEARNING)
And could fondness turn into love again?

PRISCILLA: (ANGUISH)
Don't ask me that, Edgar.

EDGAR: (STOICALLY)
It's all right, Priscilla, you don't have to be kind.

PRISCILLA: (EXPLAINING)
I'm not being kind. It's just that . . .

EDGAR: (HELPFULLY)
Just that what, Priscilla?

PRISCILLA: (PAINFULLY)
Just that I don't actually love you, Edgar.

EDGAR: (FULLY AWARE NOW THAT WHAT
WAS ONCE IS NO MORE, YET STILL HOPING
AND AT THE SAME TIME KNOWING IN HIS
HEART THAT THERE IS NO MORE HOPE)
Oh.

Not surprisingly, many directors and actors feel insulted when a
writer gives them a script that seems to assume they are idiots and
cannot interpret the sense and feeling of very obvious and straight
forward lines without such fatuous assistance.

However, there are certain technical speech directions which can
be helpful. In a multi-handed scene, it may be useful to make clear
to whom a remark is being addressed:

MICHAEL: (TO FRANK)
Why don't you ever speak the truth?
(TO BETTY) He's always lying to me. Always . . .

BETTY: I think you're imagining this.
If only you'd be more reasonable –

Two other useful technical directions are (CUTTING IN) and (CONTINUING). So to conclude our example:

MICHAEL: (CUTTING IN)
I am always reasonable!

BETTY: (CONTINUING) – and listen to
what he is trying to tell you.

When an important move comes in the middle of a speech it is advisable to revert to stage directions and then pick up the speech again with (CONTINUING). When one character is speaking and another character interjects a remark which is ignored by the 1st speaker it is necessary for the writer to indicate his intention with the instruction (CONTINUING OVER) or (OVER ABOVE).

In the following scene two lads, REG and BRIAN, have returned to REG's room to count out money they got by mugging a shopkeeper on his way to the bank. They have agreed to share the loot with their informant, WARREN.

(THE MONEY IN FIVE POUND BAGS IS
SPREAD OUT OVER THE FLOOR)

REG: (COUNTING) . . . Hundred and
ten . . . fifteen . . . twenty . . .

BRIAN: Christ, it's a lot more than Warren said.

REG: (OVER ABOVE) Twentyfive, thirty,
thirtyfive, forty, fortyfive.

(THAT IS THE LAST BAG. HE WEIGHS IT
IN HIS HAND)

REG: (CONTINUING) This one's not full.

BRIAN: Who cares! That's three into a hundred
and fortyfive . . . That's . . . er . . . that's . . . er . . . (THE
ARITHMETIC BEATS HIM) How much is that each?

Regional and foreign accents

It is never long before a writer working for popular television programmes is faced with the problem of handling regional and foreign accents. Don't write phonetics to indicate a regional or foreign accent. It insults the actor's intelligence. If it is not clear from the characters themselves that a particular accent should be used, indicate it at once in their first speech in the play. Thus:

> ROBINSON: (FRENCH ACCENT) I am very
> pleased to meet you Mr Smith.

It is important to invest your regional and foreign characters' dialogue with fitting phraseology and words. In the north of England they say, 'Can you not'. In the south they say, 'Can't you'. If you are offered a late night drink in the Midlands it means a beverage, in London it means alcohol.

A civilian might say on HMS So-and-So; Navy personnel will say *in* HMS So-and-So.

The many different dialects and accents of the British Isles are strong and colourful and since British audiences, through television, are now so familiar with them, writers from other speech communities need to handle them with care if they are not to be exposed as spurious.

Terminology often betrays political attitudes. Left wingers say 'the Soviet Union', 'a Chinese', 'Mrs Joan Smith', and 'Britain'; those on the right say, 'Russia', a 'Chinaman', 'Mrs John Smith', and 'Great Britain'. (These are extreme generalisations. They are here to prompt you to listen to how people talk rather than for you to copy.)

If your play is set entirely in a foreign country and all the characters are nationals of that country, write the dialogue in normal English. When foreign characters are playing against English speaking people it is necessary to make this clear by a careful choice of words and sentence construction. In that connection it helps if you have some knowledge of the grammar of the language you are approximating but how ever well you speak a foreign language it is unacceptably pretentious to write long speeches which the majority of your audience will not comprehend. It can be guaranteed to infuriate them. As with technical jargon it is sufficient to use a few familiar 'tourist-type' words 'Merci M'sieur' or 'Oui Madame', 'Guten Morgen' and 'Bitte' or 'Señor' and 'Gracias' to add atmosphere to the scene.

Doubtless you have noticed, foreigners, who speak English well –
but not as a native – frequently follow their own sentence construction and seldom use colloquial abbreviations. In consequence
the dialogue often seems pedantic and distinctively un-English. One
is able to use this device to invest the dialogue with a foreign flavour
as in this scene from a radio play, *The Picture Beyond The Canvas*,
which I set in Paris.

The setting is a street café. A man waits for service.

WAITER: Bonjour M'sieur. What can I get you?

WALTON: Café, s'il vous plait.

WAITER: Au lait?

WALTON: Merci.

WAITER: Tout de suite, M'sieur.

CAMILLE: (APPROACHING) Excusez moi M'sieur.

WALTON: Oh, bonjour, sister. You are collecting for
your convent? I am not sure I have any change.

CAMILLE: No, no M'sieur. I do not want your money.
I would like to talk to you.

WALTON: For the good of my soul? No, if you'll
forgive me, sister, I really don't . . .

CAMILLE: Not for your soul, M'sieur. Can I sit, please?

WALTON: If you wish. My friends are never going to
believe it when I tell them I was picked up by a nun in
Paris.

CAMILLE: Have no fear M'sieur Walton. You are safe.

WALTON: You know my name?

CAMILLE: Ah oui, M'sieur. We have met before.

WALTON: Oh? I'm sorry. I'm afraid I don't recall . . .

CAMILLE: That is not strange. It was many years ago.
I am – I was Camille.

WALTON: Camille? Camille! No, I don't believe it!
You, a nun?

CAMILLE: As you see M'sieur.

WALTON: No wonder they couldn't find you. We all
thought you must be dead.

CAMILLE: I am now dead to the world, M'sieur. I live
only for God.

> WALTON: But you recognised me?
>
> CAMILLE: Oh no. I knew you would be here from the newspaper. I had to see you.
>
> WALTON: Why?
>
> CAMILLE: I have trouble, M'sieur. Only you can help.

The accent which the actress used made that scene acceptably Parisian.

As you mix with, and listen to, other nationals talking you will hear a number of common phrases and words that are not precise translations. Germans, for instance, frequently say, 'We have the possibility to go ski-ing next year' when the word we would use would be 'opportunity'. Again, asked where he lives a German may tell you, 'In the near of Bonn' whereas a native English speaker would simply say 'near Bonn'. This kind of non-standard language tells us instantly a person we are meeting is not English and it can be used effectively in a script for the same purpose.

Never be without a notebook to jot down colourful phrases and expressions you hear. This, after all, is one area where the writer is rather lucky. The air-waves are full of raw material that will give life and texture to your dialogue. You have only to harvest it.

Always read your work aloud to make sure the speeches you have written can be said. It is easy to write lines that look and read perfectly well but, when the actor comes to say them, turn out to be impossible tongue twisters.

Another problem for the actors that writers sometimes create is caused by ending two speeches in the same scene with the same or similar words:

> TED: We called on every house on the estate but couldn't sell none of the stuff.
>
> MANAGER: You really went to every house?
>
> TED: Honest. But there's no money around. If you want to know what I think, we're not going to get rid of any of the stuff.

Part of the actor's memorising technique is to be motivated by cues. The manager's cue to say 'You really went to every house?' was motivated by Ted's '. . . none of the stuff'. When Ted ends a speech with '. . . any of the stuff' it would be all too easy for the manager to be 'thrown' (put off balance, or temporarily mentally confused) and forget which of his lines is to follow. I once saw a stage play where a speech-ending in the third act was identical with a speech-ending in the first act. Fifteen minutes into act one the actress came in with the line from act three and the play was heading up fast for the final curtain until they stopped it and started over again. It's not too great a problem in television where the tape or film can be cut but it can destroy the actor's confidence and adversely affect his performance.

Most actors and directors prefer the cut and thrust of an exchange of short, sharp sentences between characters. It helps to inject life and spark to the scene. But long question and answer sessions, except in law courts or police enquiries, are best avoided. They are unnatural. Conversations between ordinary individuals are not usually interrogatory. Direct questions are sometimes evaded or countered with another question. Often a person ignores a question and switches to an entirely different line of thought.

Long speeches are best avoided but sometimes it is in the nature of the character to be verbose and when you create such a character you need to make sure that what he has to say is of some significance. Your audience may listen attentively to Napoleon explaining to his Generals how he intends to conquer Russia but would quickly get bored by a woman telling a neighbour full details of a less than eventful trip to a supermarket.

If you are writing series drama, make sure the series leads get most of the good lines. If you are writing a situation comedy give all the funny lines to the star, even to the extent of losing potentially funny lines because – for plot reasons – they could only be delivered by a minor character. A great many star and lead actors are, to say the least, somewhat egocentric. Maybe they wouldn't be in the business if they weren't. It is not uncommon to find them counting the lines or counting the laughs to make sure supporting actors don't outshine them and if they do, as writers often find to their cost, demanding that the script be rewritten to accommodate them.

In chapter seven I mentioned 'sharing out the lines' and said we would deal with it when we talked about dialogue. Great care should be taken about the number of people included in any particular scene. A two-handed scene is not difficult but three or more characters may present problems – not the least being making sure the principal actors get the lion's share without leaving the supporting cast 'stooging' (standing with nothing to say and no business) for too long. As you write your play check back through the scene to see that everyone present has some line or business in the scene. Multi-handed scenes are always more difficult to write than two-handers but you mustn't dodge them. A play consisting of one two-hander after another can be rather dull.

Naming your characters

One final point. Names are important. First names, in particular, can in themselves be clichés. At this point in time Agnes and Agatha suggest an elderly woman, Susan and Samantha someone much younger. Fred and Bert are almost certainly manual workers while Frederick and Bertram are not. Names go in and out of fashion and they carry with them an association of class and time and geography. Unimportant as it may seem names must be chosen with care.

11. Characterisation

The tendency of writers to produce interchangeable dialogue is a common fault, about which script editors and directors sometimes complain. Characters are not created by writing names on a script. If speeches can be switched from one player to another without any trimming or adjustment they may serve to tell the story and advance the plot but they are unlikely to be establishing or sustaining a character.

Too often the story then becomes flat, played by cardboard cut-outs to be saved, if at all, by creative performances from the actors who try to give the part more than the writer has done and probably more than it deserves.

It would be misleading to imply that every bit player must be given distinctive characteristics that are instantly apparent for the two or three minutes he is on screen. If you people your script with walk-ons who stutter or extras who limp or other minor players with nervous coughs or convulsive twitches you are likely to get it back by return post. Leave the walk-ons and extras to the director. Your concern is with the principals and supporting cast and you must give the actors something to work on.

The character of a person is not exhibited by such superficialities as a limp or a stutter, although either may have a bearing on it, making them feel inferior and bitter or strong and determined not to let the handicap beat them.

Character is the sum total of the qualities that make one man or one woman different from the next. Even identical twins are different people with their own unique personalities. Character is revealed in a person's temperament and behaviour; in attitudes and prejudices; through fads and fancies. It is born of the many different factors we inherit and the pressures and influences of our own particular upbringing and surroundings. It may be expressed through the way a person dresses, the kind of home they choose to live in, the sort of friends they make; through their hobbies, through the way they speak, the words they use and by no means least the tone of voice. It is through speech and actions the character is portrayed.

We have talked about plots but plots can be mechanical things piling incident upon incident holding our interest but needing more to involve us. It is the way in which the lives and actions of the characters in the story are affected that keeps us watching. What we are all most interested in is people. Secretly, we are all would be eaves-droppers and 'Peeping Toms' incurably inquisitive about other people's lives, habits and behaviour – and particularly about their private behaviour which, in real life, is usually carefully concealed behind shut doors and closed lips. The continuous serial – the ever popular soap opera with audiences in Britain close on twenty million for every episode – is sometimes described as 'keyhole drama'. Those who use the phrase patronisingly might reflect that all drama is a window through which we goggle avidly to see how other men and woman live, love and die.

When characters are well drawn we quickly find ourselves envying them, pitying them, loving them or hating them and often learning from them, which does not happen when all the writer is offering us are functional plot-laying speeches attributed to one or another of the names on the page.

In his book *Play-Making* which I quoted earlier, William Archer said, 'A drama ought to bring out character as a photographer's chemicals bring out the forms latent in the negative' but to achieve this the writer needs to be clear, from the outset, who his characters are and what makes them tick.

It is sometimes said that characters write themselves. They don't! But it can happen that a particular character seems so familiar that instead of needing to wrestle mentally to give life to this being the writer can anticipate his every word and action as he might anticipate the words and actions of his wife or closest friend. Invariably the character who seems so familiar is familiar. Often, subconsciously, there are elements of autobiography – personal experiences and attributes of the writer himself. Or it may be biography, the ghost of some long forgotten acquaintance or composite of a number of people known or observed.

Because drama is about people, it is not so much what you are writing about as who you are writing about that is of prime importance; and knowing who the character is involves more than giving him a name and describing his physical appearance.

But there is no time or room in a television play to delve back into the life history of the characters as one might in a novel although some television writers find it useful to develop life histories of their people as a working blueprint that ensures a consistency of attitude and factual details. This is particularly important if one is writing a series or serial spread over a number of episodes and weeks. But in a series or serial the character can be allowed to develop over a period of weeks or months. In the time span of the average play the characterisation must be sharper and more immediate, demanding of the writer care and observation.

Television throws a spotlight on the people it portrays and false, shallow lack of characterisation turns the spotlight back on the writer exposing him as one who has not taken the trouble to properly observe nor properly motivate the men and women he is writing about.

Many, possibly most, truly dramatic stories do not start with a plot. They start with a character. Writing a crime story you may think of your crime and then decide what sort of person shall commit it or you may decide on your character, evil or deprived, weak or arrogant, settle in your mind who he is and what he wants to achieve and then decide what crime he commits and how he goes about it which will inevitably be determined by the type and nature of the person you have chosen.

Which comes first plot or character is a 'chicken and egg' question but it has been said that the one thing that all great plays have in common is memorable characterisation. The writers have created individuals. They have taken the trouble to get to know and understand their hearts and minds.

Having decided upon your character and settled what their objective or problem is, it is what they do rather than what they tell us that illuminates the character. Actions speak louder than words.

To illustrate the point I cannot better a splendid example from the film *Three Into One Won't Go*. It showed a middle aged man driving his car. A pretty girl with a rucksack thumbed for a lift. He slowed, and stopped some yards beyond her, leant over to unlock the nearside door, and looked back as though expecting her to run up to the car. Instead, she remained where she was, hand on hip, waiting for him to back up to her. Not once had he smiled at the prospect of young female companionship, yet he did back up just as she wanted. Without a word, we knew about his pent up middle-aged emotions, and about her self assurance and knowledge of the power she had over a man of his age.

Brilliant!

A girl who crosses herself, a man who kicks a dog, a child who darts impulsively across a dangerous road, a lad who picks a pin from the floor and sticks it in his lapel or a woman who takes an empty gin bottle from her shopping bag and slips it into a street litter-bin are all exposing facets of character that may be trusted to tell us rather more about them than their words.

Character may also be expressed through the use of sets and props. A personalised number plate on a car (letters matching the owner's initials followed by the single digit '1') a drawer full of pill-bottles, a room lined with books a meticulously kept garden or an untidy bedroom with dressing table cluttered with cosmetic jars all signal very clearly the kind of person we might expect.

You will have seen other examples of the use of props that define character in Chapter 5.

The important thing is for you to know the character you are writing.

Know?

Very obviously if you are writing about a murderer it is unlikely that you will have been lucky or unlucky enough to have actually made the acquaintance of such a character and if writers limited their work in this way that most popular entertainment, the murder mystery thriller, would probably be somewhat rare. Few of us know political dictators or archbishops or, happily, confidence tricksters but it would be somewhat inhibiting if that were allowed to prevent us writing about them.

This is where your research and creative talent meet. Learn all you can about persons of the type you wish to write – and note I say persons, plural, rather than person, singular. You are intending to create a character not make a faithful reproduction of a distinctive individual – which could lead you into trouble unless that person is dead. Your character may be a composite comprising general rather than specific and exclusive features of actual people. Thus you may create a personable young entrepreneur in the record business but if he also runs an airline or goes ballooning you are on very dangerous ground indeed.

Having settled on the character you must now by creative imagination make him truly yours. Think about him. Concentrate on him. Get inside his skin. Know what motivates him, whether it be fear or love or greed or whatever. Know his weaknesses – the obvious ones of course – drink, women, gambling – but pay particular attention to the less obvious ones like pride, a bad conscience, an inferiority complex, inveterate lying or a reckless competitive aggression that comes to the surface only when he is driving his car. These are the kind of personal traits that put flesh on the bare bones of your people and help us to recognise them as familiar, albeit unique, human beings.

A writer of drama should never forget that motives are the starting gate for action and action strips away the verbiage and exposes the heart and soul of the character.

If you take the time and trouble to develop your principal people before you start writing, when you get down to the actual scripting you will know exactly how they should behave and whether the lines you are giving them are lines the person you have created would really say.

But it is not enough that the lines are apposite. Is the character interesting or sympathetic? Are the audience going to care? Will they be stirred to love or loathing or laughter? It matters not which as long as they are stirred in some way because the worse thing that can happen is that the viewers will be totally indifferent to the fate of your people.

A drama without drama!

The importance of the supporting cast is sometimes overlooked. A writer who will take great trouble to define his lead characters may flag as though he has used all his time and creative energy on them or has decided the secondary characters are not worth bothering about anyway. Supporting characters are, all too often, presented as clichés; hearty vicars, stuffy civil servants, sex-starved spinsters, obsequious domestics, or other stock characters who are given only tired cliché lines to mouth.

And strangely at times almost the reverse happens. It is not uncommon – particularly in series – to find your minor characters trying desperately to steal the limelight.

Note, I am not talking about actors. I am talking about characters the writer has created.

More often than you would ever think likely, a 'child' to whom you have given birth can quickly become your favourite, poking his nose into scenes where he is not needed, hogging the best lines and demanding that the part be built up well beyond anything conceived of in your original storyline. This is the character who 'seems' to write himself. Without the writer planning or intending it he grabs attention to which he is not entitled. He is wittier than everyone else or funnier than everyone else and may even be capable of turning your tragedy into a comedy and your gentle comedy into a broad farce. In a play that is entirely your own you may feel you want to accommodate him, deciding his vitality warrants altering your storyline to give full reign to this gate-crasher, but in series and serials it can be a disaster, infuriating the lead actors as they find the interloper overshadowing them; landing you with massive rewrites and a reputation for being incapable of writing to the brief.

Sadly every writer has to learn to murder his darlings.

Never, never, never allow yourself to be seduced by these lesser characters. If they are that interesting write them a play of their own. And that, all too often, is when you discover they really have feet of clay or as writers and producers often put it, 'no mileage in them'.

Of course it sometimes happens that a secondary character in a series is so well cast, so well written and so well liked by the viewers that the producer decides to elevate him or her to a main supporting role but that is the producer's decision not the writer's.

Writing television series is 'service writing'. Writers who do it successfully know it is their job to provide scripts for the regular series cast that are not only the right kind of story but essentially scripts designed to exploit the talents and established characteristics of the principal actors involved.

As between two police series or two family comedies the basic storylines might be interchangeable. It is the characters and characterisation that make them better or worse but essentially different.

12. Writing comedy

When people say 'I am a comedy writer' they tell us as much about their work as anyone who says 'I am a painter' for there is as great a difference between the work of television comedy writers as there is between the work of the Impressionists and Surrealists in visual arts.

Comedy on television comes in many different forms, from solo performers like Victoria Wood and a host of other well-known names, through double acts, such as Mel Smith and Griff Rhys Jones and the unforgettable Morecambe and Wise, on to situation comedy – which is an art form that television has made very much its own.

Writing comedy is, word for word and minute for minute, the highest paid television writing. It is also the most exhausting and requires a rare talent which is why it is so highly paid.

It is sometimes said, usually by people who don't write, that everyone has one novel in them. I doubt it is true. But one thing I have no doubt about is that everyone does not have one comedy script in them. I have known quite a few established dramatic writers who have decided to turn their hand to comedy without success. I have also known quite a few established comedy writers who have decided to turn their hand to drama with considerable success. As somebody once said, 'It's harder to make people laugh than it is to make them cry.'

I am sure that's true but if you are one of those lucky people with a well developed sense of humour; whose wit, turn of phrase and off-beat ideas keep your friends amused; if you believe it possible you might have the talent and aptitude to write TV comedy material you should invest a little time and effort to find out. It could be well worth while. There is not so much first class, original material around.

It would, however, be misleading if I did not tell you that the discipline that writing comedy imposes – and especially in scripting situation comedy – is more severe than that imposed by writing straight drama. When you are bashing your brains trying to find a funny line or a comedy situation only a funny line or comic situation will do. You will doubtless think of a hundred lines that would make the point of the story; a dozen situations that would serve to develop the plot but none be worth so much as a titter. More than in any other form of script writing comedy writing demands that the writer go on and on sifting though and throwing out ideas until he finally comes up with something that is exactly right.

But success brings it's own problems. The killer is that, when you have used up all your bright hilarious ideas – the ones that got you the show to write in the first place – you sit without a funny thought in your head and begin to suspect you will never think of a truly funny line or situation again.

Then the panic sets in. And the clock ticks on remorselessly towards your deadline.

Deadline! There's always a deadline. Everyone delays making decisions and then they want the script the day before yesterday. One of the principal differences between drama writers and comedy writers is that the writer of television drama is usually given weeks even months to write his play. The successful comedy writer has to produce on time, week after week for as many weeks as the show runs.

As Denis Norden once said, 'In comedy they say, don't make it art, make it Tuesday'. Indeed, it sometimes happens that the producers are so thrilled with the ratings of a new comedy that the writers are hardly given breathing or thinking time between scripts; a haste that has killed off many a promising series as the writers become exhausted long before the audience.

In England situation comedy was invariably written by pairs of writers. Many of these coupled names roll easily off the tongue: Ray Galton and Alan Simpson who gave us the unsurpassed *Hancock* and *Steptoe* series, Dick Clement and Ian La Frenais to whom we owe, among many other shows, *Auf Wiedersehen Pet* and *The Likely Lads*. We have to thank Jeremy Lloyd and David Croft for *'Allo, 'Allo* and David Croft again, with Jimmy Perry, for *Hi-de-Hi!* and *Dad's Army*, while among the more recent pairings we find Richard Feegen and Andrew Norris with *Brittas Empire* and Andy Hamilton and Guy Jenkin who won awards for *Drop the Dead Donkey*.

Writing with a partner if one is lucky enough to find one with whom one can agree, or perhaps more importantly disagree without actually falling out, provides something of an insurance against stylistic variations.

121

But there are other advantages. Humour can be very personal. For all of us things are sometimes funny only by association. If your partner also thinks a line or situation funny the chances are a good many other people will think so too. If he stares at you blankly as you split your sides, demanding 'so what's funny about that?' it is not unlikely that a high proportion of the audience won't laugh either. But by no means the least advantage of a partner is, in moments of despair when the going gets tough, the comfort of feeling, like a co-defendent in the dock, someone else is sharing your troubles. The downside is, you share the fee, too.

But a very real bonus is the laughs you get as you build together, developing the situation or topping the joke. Here again, is where the discipline comes in. You think of a funny line; both roar your heads off and as your partner wipes away tears of laughter he says, 'Very funny! Can't use it'. If you actually avoid murdering him at that point and let him explain, he will probably tell you the joke doesn't fit. 'It's out of character!' Or too broad or too subtle or too corny and if you are honest you will sometimes reluctantly agree. Then you screw it up; throw it in the waste-paper basket and start all over again.

Obviously there are many different kinds of humorous writing. A brilliant piece of slapstick; a clever satirical line; a sophisticated wisecrack; and a hilarious comedy of manners would probably mix together very badly in the same script – probably because anything is possible.

You need to make up your mind about the kind of script you are writing. If you are writing a 'comedy' – and by that I mean a script about perfectly normal intelligent people in amusing situations – make sure you don't stray into farce, defined by the *Oxford English Dictionary* as 'a coarsely comic dramatic work based on ludicrously improbable events'. That sounds derogatory but no one should forget that farce has a long and honourable tradition. It fills theatres and has audiences falling out of their seats with laughter.

In television light entertainment 'farce' comes under the general heading of comedy and audiences enjoy both without concerning themselves about definitions. The writer, however, needs to be careful to recognise the limits. It may be an easy way to get a laugh but you will destroy the integrity of your script if you introduce absurd and totally unbelievable characters – even caricatures – into a script where the audience are expected to accept that the other members of the cast are ordinary sensible individuals.

Some time ago I saw a play that, on the strength of the idea, I would have voted the play most likely to become a smash West End hit. The first act was hilarious; recognisable types in amusing circumstances and relationships. But the second act fell apart. The author introduced new characters who were so broad and unbelievable that they completely destroyed the credibility of everyone else in the play. We, the audience, laughed at them at first and then we got annoyed. Nobody, but nobody – and certainly not the characters we met in the first act – would tolerate these ridiculous people in their house and lives.

The play would, I am sure, have got a different reaction if everyone in the play had been comedy rather than farcical characters. It was the mixing of comedy and farce – reality and absurdity – that killed it.

In America, which can claim to be the birthplace of television situation comedy with programmes like *I Love Lucy*, scripts are usually produced by a team of writers. Indeed many stars boast their importance by the number of writers working for them, unlike the situation in Britain where lead players, particularly comedians, often demanded a script credit for their input.

A fairly recent development in Britain follows the American pattern where, as with *Birds of a Feather*, a team of writers script different episodes of a series. It remains to be seen whether this practice grows here. The standard of individual programmes does tend to fluctuate putting at risk the integrity of the characters and it is unlikely that the most successful and talented British comedy writers would willingly risk a mutation of unique characters they have created by agreeing to imput by other writers.

Currently the majority of British comedy shows seem to be scripted by single writers. Notable among them are Roy Clarke with *Keeping Up Appearances* and *Last of the Summer Wine*, Carla Lane whose work includes *Butterflies* and *Bread*, Roger Hall *Conjugal Rites*, Simon Nye *Men Behaving Badly*, Jennifer Saunders *Absolutely Fabulous*, Bob Larby *As Time Goes By*, David Renwick with *One Foot in the Grave* and Victoria Wood with *dinnerladies*.

What is generally called 'Situation Comedy' is, in fact, very frequently 'Character Comedy'. In some cases the star of the show has been established as a comedy personality in earlier work and the show has now to be specially designed and written to exploit a particular talent. Dick Sharples' *In Loving Memory* starring Thora Hird is a good example. This kind of show depends principally on the 'character' previously established. The 'situation' may be slight but the script is designed to allow the artists to give the audience the performance they expect of them.

A different vein of character comedy is seen in the late Johnny Speight's *In Sickness and in Health*, where the actor Warren Mitchell made Alf Garnet his alter ego.

New writers hoping to strike the vein of gold that is successful comedy writing might learn a great deal by taping and analysing shows written by top writers.

Different as these programmes are the one thing they have in common is outstanding characterisation. Comic situations, of course. Funny lines, certainly, but what distinguishes them from other less successful shows are memorable characters. Roy Clarke's Hyacinth, the suburban snob with delusions of grandeur; Carla Lane's Mrs Boswell, the strong, competent mother piloting her wayward family through the problems of life; Johnny Speight's Alf Garnet, the outrageous bigot with his blinkered aggression; Galton and Simpson's 'Steptoes' with the love hate relationship of father and son. And not least David Renwick's Victor Meldrew, never happy unless he has something to complain about. All are characters the audience will not easily forget. None of them is ridiculous. None is farcical. There are shades and facets of each of them that we can recognise in ourselves and people we know.*

Submitting situation comedy scripts

In an article published recently in the Writers' Guild magazine, Jeremy Hardy of the BBC TV Comedy Script Unit had this advice for situation comedy writers. 'An ideal submission is one completed half hour script along with five synopses of subsequent episodes to demonstrate that the idea will sustain a series. Character biographies and background notes should be avoided as all the necessary information should be conveyed within the script. Most importantly the script must be funny! "Gently amusing" is simply not enough. One very funny scene or a funny character is worth a million pages of competently plotted gentle amusement. All characters should have an original slant, comic potential and a weakness or two that keeps getting them into trouble. They need to interact with each other to

*See Appendix for an excerpt from the script of *Father Ted*.

create comedy but at the same time be believable. The humour needs to be driven by the characters and the stories not just by people saying "things in a funny way".'

The running gag

The running gag is a particularly effective comedy device. The following sketch demonstrates its use.

Sid, the principal character, has just bought a smart-looking secondhand car. He drives it proudly away from the showroom. As he arrives home a neighbour, Joe, comes out to look at it.

> EXT: STREET. DAY.
>
> SID AND HIS NEIGHBOUR JOE STAND LOOKING AT THE CAR.
>
> SID: Look at the condition of that bodywork. You'd never think she was five years old, would you?
>
> JOE: It's fantastic. What's the engine like?
>
> SID: Beautiful! Listen.
>
> (HE STARTS THE ENGINE AND LETS IT TICK OVER)
> SID: Music, isn't it?
>
> JOE: Yeah. Sounds great! . . . Just a minute. Rev her up a bit.
>
> SID PRESSES THE ACCELERATOR.
>
> JOE: Yeah . . . thought so.
>
> SID: What?
>
> JOE: You've got a bit of a knock.
>
> SID: Knock? I can't hear it.
>
> JOE: Well, you haven't had my experience. Take my advice. Get it looked at.
>
> SID LOOKS WORRIED.

A little later we find Sid getting the car filled with petrol.

> AS THE GARAGE MAN RETURNS TO SID WITH HIS CHANGE, SID STARTS HIS ENGINE.
>
> SID: Just a minute mate. Can you hear a knock in my engine?

THE GARAGEMAN COCKS HIS EAR TOWARDS
THE ENGINE AND LISTENS AS SID REVS UP.

GARAGEMAN: No, I can't hear a knock. It's
more of a rattle, I'd say.

Later still Sid parks on the car park outside a pub where he meets a
friend who is admiring his new car. The engine is still running.

SID: Listen, Tom, you're good on cars. Can you
hear a knock or a rattle from that engine?

TOM: (LISTENS) No . . . no . . . there's no knock
or rattle there. You've got a bit of a whine! Got a dry
bearing, I should think.

By now, very worried, Sid visits another friend, Bill, and calls him
out from under a car in his garage.

SID: Do me a favour. Listen to my engine. Can you
hear a funny noise?

BILL: What sort of funny noise?

SID: Well, like a knock, a rattle or a whine.

BILL: (LISTENS) Oh yeah. I hear it.

SID: What is it?

BILL: Well, it's definitely not a knock or a rattle.

SID: You reckon it's a whine?

BILL: No, it's not a whine. It's more a rumble
going on towards a clatter, I'd say. Sounds expensive!

By the time Sid is driven almost desperate to get rid of the car the
noise turns out to be only a loose spanner vibrating in the tool box.

Visual comedy

Television comedy should, like other television programmes, exploit
the visual wherever possible and it's a pretty thin idea that doesn't
present opportunities for visual gags. One has only to look at some
of the old silent slapstick films to see how cleverly the props and the
situation can be milked. A modern example was Eric Sykes' short
film *The Plank* where that particular prop is, of course, fully relevant
to the story.

126

Props can sometimes be effectively used for more gentle humour and when you start to think visually about your story and characters you will frequently find very ordinary everyday articles and events will provide you with comedy possibilities

But your speciality is words. Verbal jokes play their part in most TV comedies and completely straight lines can be very funny given the right situation and pictures.

In one script I wrote, under the impression he was digging for hidden treasure, a rather foolish man was persuaded to excavate a basement where the householder feared there was an unexploded bomb. As he dug enthusiastically for the 'treasure', of which he'd been promised a share, the man said, 'If I hit the jackpot you won't see me for dust' – a straight line that the audience thought very funny.

The metre and balance of the line is vital too. Writers who have written radio comedy have learned to construct a line so that the actor can place full stress on the key word in a gag. In television comedy it is also important for the writer to learn 'to place the key word in a calculated gag in just the right rhythmic position to make the line explode', as Walter Kerr puts it in his book, *How not to write a play*.

You, as the writer, have four means of making your audience laugh. Situation, characterisation, visual and verbal funnies. You can't afford to ignore any of them.

Comedy sketches

So far I have talked largely of situation comedy which many writers would regard as the pinnacle of success, and indeed audience ratings show they are consistently among the most popular programmes screened. But situation comedy is not the only market for television comedy; in fact at present, with so many imports and repeats, it is one of the smallest and without doubt the hardest markets to crack. But you will have observed from screen credits there are many writers contributing comedy sketches and additional material to Light Entertainment programmes for such performers as Dave Allen, Russ Abbot, Rowan Atkinson, Rory Bremner, Jasper Carrott, Ronnie Corbett, Ben Elton, Harry Enfield, Victoria Wood, Hale and Pace, Griff Rhys Jones and Mel Smith – to name but a few.

These programmes usually welcome material from freelance contributors and payment is by the minute of screen time.

If you are a beginner aiming to sell sketches there are points you should keep in mind. Unlike the situation comedy which usually occupies a thirty minute slot, there is no uniform length for a sketch. Some are short plays lasting several minutes. Others are quickies – virtually animated cartoons which make their point and win their laughs in a fraction of that time. A three-handed, ten-minute sketch submitted to a solo artist or a fast talking double act is unlikely to be accepted. Neither the producer nor the comedian will change the established pattern of the show to accommodate it however funny it may be. Save the stamp. Use it to submit the sketch to the right artist.

Watch the number of characters you involve. Keep speaking parts for supporting cast to the minimum. And make sure the star gets most, if not all, of the funny lines. Many comedians build a reputation working a particular theme – be it golf or motoring or medicine. Dave Allen, for instance, frequently works religious sketches, while the late Les Dawson was strong on mother-in-law gags. This thematic style offers clear guidelines and an open door for a writer who makes sure the script on offer is apposite.

Star vehicle sketches need to be tailor-made. It is not enough that it is funny. Material that is right for one artist may be totally unsuited to another. For this reason a writer must study a comedian's work to be sure the sketches and gags offered exploit strengths and avoid weaknesses.

Television, of course, provides the perfect opportunity for such a study, but artists working on top TV shows will almost certainly be using their own scripts or scripts from proven comedy writers. Unless what you have to offer is funnier and more original than material he is getting from other writers the comedian is unlikely to want to change.

Now if that sounds like a wet blanket on your hopes let me tell you the experience of a well-established writer I know. He was contracted to write TV comedy sketches for a certain famous comedy artist. He delivered one to the producer who loved it. 'Funniest thing you've ever written', he said. The star congratulated him. The director roared and the production staff giggled for hours. When they started camera rehearsals the crews nearly fell off the cameras laughing. But you can only laugh at any joke for so long. Soon the star was walking round looking very unhappy. He was concerned about that sketch. Now he'd had time to reflect he didn't think it was as funny as he'd first thought. There was a crisis meeting at which the writer, director and producer tried to convince him his worries were unfounded. All to no avail. The sketch was cut and replaced by a sketch the star had played for years at Blackpool. He felt safe with that. He knew it always got a laugh.

That is the kind of problem a comedy writer has to live with. Alan Simpson, talking of their work with Hancock, once said they had to put up about three ideas before they could get Tony to accept one. And oddly enough, when writers produce a particularly good script that the star raves about, it is always very, very much more difficult to get the next idea accepted without endless argument and rewrites.

The fact is insecurity is the occupational disease of actors – and comedy stars more than most. When the audience don't find the material funny; when their most desperate efforts are met with stony silence; the comedian 'dies the death' as the expression is. His future seems all in the past.

It is important for the writer to understand this. It makes it easier for him to deal with star temperament.

Happily not all comedy shows rely on the popularity of stand-up comics or established comedy actors. Some of the best have been written and so well cast with character actors that they have become, for ever more, inseparably identified with the part they play. *Steptoe*, for instance, was cast after it was written.

Of course you would think, when the writer creates an entirely new character and the producer and casting director find an actor or actress to play the part, all the writer's problems would be over. You would be wrong. Something of the writer's frustrations were voiced by the late Marty Feldman. Talking of writing for other artists, which he did before he became a performer, he said, 'You invent some characters and a few weeks later they're telling you, "I wouldn't say this, it's not me!" . . . and they didn't even exist a few weeks before.'

With all the reorganisation and changes that have taken place in British television over the last two decades I should tell you that while some well-written, unsolicited comedy sketches may earn very welcome 'pocket money' the chances of a writer without a track record being commissioned to write sketches for star comedians, much less a new situation comedy, are slim. With a brilliant idea, outstanding talent and a lot of luck a beginner might make it. But failing that . . .

Where and how, then, does a comedy writer get started?

You start in the same way and the same places as the performers with whom you aim to work. There is always room at the top but the way to the top starts from the bottom. More than a few highly regarded television comedy writers began their careers by attaching themselves to the coat-tails of up and coming comedians with whom they were able to establish a professional relationship. A newcomer who is seriously interested in a career as a comedy writer might find a way in by developing such a relationship with a comedian on his or her way up – one who has not yet hit the headlines.

Half a century ago, most successful comedy writers learnt their trade by producing material for comedians working variety theatres up and down the country, in particular the Moss Empire circuit, while in London, the famous Windmill Theatre boasted not only it's glamorous nudes but also a stream of promising comedians who topped the bill and were destined to become household names in the age of television. But the variety theatre has been a casualty of television and those that survive have little room on their bill for any but top audience grabbing acts.

But it is not all gloom.

The stars of tomorrow can be seen at work in clubs and pubs around London and the provinces. This is where the action now is. This is where you will find young ambitious entertainers – often struggling with material that does less than justice to their talent – who will welcome a writer with new and original ideas.

And that could be your chance.

Do the rounds. Find yourself a performer who has real promise; one whose style and work interests you; make the contact; discover what he is looking for; let him see some of your sketches; tailor-make one or two for him. In doing so you will be following the path that has lead to fame and fortune for the dozens of writers who have sustained the TV comedy scene over the last fifty-odd years.*

---

*See Appendix for examples of produced comedy sketches by Hale and Pace and Gerald Kelsey, and comedy quickies by Ken Rock.

13. Specialised programmes

Not so many years ago, in addition to one-off television plays where a newcomer might get his first break, there were a number of television series that were open to contributions from freelance writers.

To obtain a commission on such series the writer needed to have a track record and the right idea or, if he had never had anything on television before, he could write a script speculatively and if it proved good enough it would be used and the writer commissioned for further episodes.

Producers of series are on something of a treadmill and they need the reliability of experienced writers if they are to sleep at night. It is for this reason they are reluctant to take risks with new writers. Any beginner who hopes to get a chance to write episodes of a series has no alternative but to study the programme carefully and then write an entire script as a sample of his work. Series like *The Bill* and *Casualty* which use a great deal of material may be willing to look at scripts written speculatively if they contain original ideas or new slants on old ones.

There are two kinds of serial currently used on television. One is the serial written by a single writer, like the late Dennis Potter's *The Singing Detective*. The other is the continuous serials like *Brookside*, *Coronation Street* and *EastEnders*. A new writer would have little chance of selling his own serial unless he had all or most of the episodes to show; the producers liked them; and they fitted in with the company's production schedules.

The continuous serial is different. The would be writer has the opportunity to study the programme and get to know the characters and settings. He is not going to be commissioned to write episodes without specimens of his work that will have to be as good or better than scripts by the existing writers, but although a specimen script could not be used – obviously it would not slot in with storylines of a continuous serial – it is likely that the producer and editor would be ready to give a chance to a newcomer who was able to show he could write to the standard required.

Adaptations and dramatisation

One kind of programming that presently occupies a high proportion of available screen time is the production of material originally written for other media.

Where the existing work is already in dramatic form what is required is an 'adaptation' (the rendering of drama written for stage or radio into a television script).

Where the existing work is in non-dramatic form what is required is a 'dramatisation' (converting a prose work such as a novel or biography into a television script).

The writer is paid more for a dramatisation than for an adaptation but the payment for either is less than that paid for an entirely new play since, if the original source material is still in copyright, an additional fee must be paid to the copyright owner.

From the scriptwriter's point of view there is obviously less work involved in an adaptation, where the material is set out in scenes and acts and the dialogue has already been written. In a dramatisation one has from the book the story, characters and settings but, very frequently, too many characters and too many settings and often a good deal of introspective thought-stream material that cannot be used in that form in a visual media. At times, too, the author has taken the 'God Almighty' position from which he sees all, hears all and knows all and reveals it to the reader as and when appropriate.

Unless 'God' is one of the characters on the screen the scriptwriter must find some other way of progressing the story.

On the face of it, a dramatisation looks as if it might not be too difficult. In point of fact it is often considerably more difficult than writing an original script. Authors writing prose can take all kinds of liberties that a scriptwriter cannot get away with. Things that can be passed over quickly in a paragraph or two or thrown away in a casual aside in the book can present fearful problems when one attempts to transfer them faithfully to the screen.

Over the years there have been a great many series based on short stories by famous writers, and it is not unusual, where the pro-gramme has been popular, for the producers to continue the series after the source material has been exhausted. To do this they have commissioned writers who have worked on the dramatisations to devise original stories using the same characters. Most of the writers I know, and I myself, have often found it easier to devise and write these original stories than make a script one is really happy with from some of the original stories without taking a great many liberties with the author's work.

This is particularly so when dramatising popular fiction, written fifty or more years ago, for readers who had not, at that time, been quickened by exposure to regular television dramas. The television camera acts like a spotlight illuminating and exposing any 'cheating' or inconsistencies in the story and unless the scriptwriter covers them you can be sure the producers will get letters from observant viewers pointing them out.

But in case that sounds as though I am knocking the writers of the original books, which I am not, let me hasten to say that the scriptwriter's work copies the pattern, characters and general ambience created by the author and is, at best a counterfeit, albeit one that sometimes displays better than the original in the show-case of television.

The problem for most writers working on a dramatisation is respect. If the writer really likes the work he may be overawed by the talent and reputation of the author and bend over backwards to avoid the sacrilege of mutilation. He will be struggling hard to find ways to keep in the script things that would be better out. That may mean dispensing with characters who are extraneous to the main theme of the story and who, although lovable and attractive, simply slow up the action. Equally the only way to progress the story may be to create new characters who will tell the audience things which, in the book, the author himself has interjected from his God-like 'all seeing' perspective. Occasionally the book will have introduced a character, full of promise, who for some reason the author has failed to exploit. It may be necessary to build and develop this character to make him work for the script. Sometimes it is possible to composite existing characters, incorporating into a single one the habits, attitudes and relationships of two or several thus avoiding losing some of the texture and colour of the book.

Yet again, making it work as a television script may necessitate deleting entirely a sub-plot because the story has to be condensed into the finite time slot that has been allocated to the programme. Technical reasons or economics may demand that a flood be changed into a fire; that a wind storm substitutes for a blizzard; that a voyage on a ship becomes a journey on a train; that the period is changed or the story is set in a totally different location as happened with the programme *Seal Morning* which I mentioned in chapter three.

Dramatising a book you have to approach it as if you are writing an original script based on source material. What you use is the basic story and principal characters and some, but not necessarily all, of the development. To do it successfully a writer needs both technical knowledge and talent and for this work producers generally engage experienced screenwriters.

In the last few years the mini series – two or three one-hour episodes usually a dramatisation of a best selling novel – has taken over slots formerly allocated to the popular domestic series and 'one off', drama plays. We have seen our own home produced versions as well as productions from Australia and of course the USA. It is not a type of programme that is likely to go away and since it is occupying screen time that might otherwise have been available to new television writers it is worth examining what chance a new writer has of breaking through here.

Well, to be brutally frank the chances of a writer new to television being commissioned to write a dramatisation are pretty slender. But don't let that discourage you entirely.

Many people reading this book will have written novels or biographies. Some may by the owners of copyright inherited from relatives or friends. If you control the copyright of a book that you think would make good television it may be worth doing a dramatisation and submitting it to the BBC or one of the production companies safe in the knowledge that so long as you own the copyright no one can rip you off.

Every salesman needs a sample of his wares to effect a sale. No one likes buying a pig in a poke and television producers are no exception. Indeed, because of the high cost of production they have to be more careful than most. Your dramatisation may not be a story that appeals or fits in with their production plans but if it is really well done there is a chance you may be able to persuade them to give you an opportunity with some subject they have decided to do.

Again, if it is a copyright you control, but they don't go for your script, it may prompt them to make you an offer for the television rights, which wouldn't be exactly what you wanted but at least some consolation.

There are also, as everyone knows, hundreds of thousands of 'out of copyright' books. Many of the more famous ones have been made into films and television plays but you may know of some super book that has so far been overlooked (which you can check with film reference books in public libraries). Of course if you don't own the copyright you have no protection against a sharp producer deciding it is a good story but a lousy script and without so much as a thank you, getting someone else to write it and then proceeding to make the programme without you.

I can't guarantee that won't happen but I think it unlikely. In any event, if you want to break in you have got to take that risk. But here again there is a chance that even if they are not interested in the story, they might be impressed by the way you have done the dramatisation and offer you work on some other project.

If it happens that they reject your script, but go ahead and use the source material you suggested, it is not all loss. You may take consolation from the fact that your instinct about the material was right. You have actually written a script and will have learned a lot in the writing. You will have enjoyed writing it and although it was rejected you will have, when it is screened, the rare opportunity to compare what you wrote with the way the more experienced professional handled the dramatisation and that could stand you in very good stead for your next script.

Writing for children

Could children's television make your fortune?

This was the title of a panel discussion chaired recently by Jocelyn Hay, Founder and Chairman of the 'Voice of the Listener and Viewer'.

The answer from Richard Morss, Controller of Children's Programmes, United Film and TV was a positive 'no'.

Yet youth culture is one of the most interesting and fastest growing areas of programming. It is probable there are more children's programmes in production than anything else at present. Carlton TV alone screens nearly 40 children's programmes a week.

But as to the fortune?

Richard Morss explained that when he suggested there is a worldwide need for children's scripts there is also a worldwide resistance to paying for them. So you probably won't make a fortune. Most writers don't but if you have good ideas, talent and determination; if you study the market and refuse to be discouraged; you may get your foot inside the door.

And then? . . . Who knows!

Programmes transmitted in the afternoons and early evening are frequently shorter than material used elsewhere and consequently might provide a 'way in' for the writer trying to get started. But it would be a mistake to assume anything goes because the money is tighter and it is, after all, only kids' stuff. Highly imaginative, unusual and original work often finds a market here and programmes are getting better, broader and more exciting all the time. There is no place for the makeshift.

Writing children's programmes is no less exacting than writing for adults. In many ways it is more so. The scope of children's television ranges from toddlers to teenagers and it is vital that writers select and target their audience very precisely. Great attention must be given to storyline, relationships, characters and language to be sure all are suitable to the age and experience of viewers for whom the programme is designed.

It is a mistake to imagine children are less critical and demanding than adults. They are not prepared to wait and see if a story gets better. They will switch channels or be off to their mountain bike or latest computer game if they are bored or bewildered. You, the writer, face fierce competition. You have to be more fun or more exciting if you are going to retain their attention.

But it is not all limitation. There are a lot of pluses. As Kate Fawkes, Creative Director of Hit Communications, told the panel 'In animation you can take the lid off your imagination and do anything'.

And not only in animation. Spooks, space epics and supermen all provide rich and imaginative material.

You will, of course, have noticed, in the past children's television used a lot of 'period' pieces. These tended to be dramatisations of classic books but because period productions are disproportionately expensive to produce, due to costumes and settings, it is invariably experienced writers who are commissioned for this work.

From a new writer's point of view a modern play or serial with a contemporary theme is a better bet. You may have an advantage here if, as a parent, you have a close knowledge of activities and specific areas wherein children are involved. For example, one writer I know utilised the time spent waiting while her small daughter had riding lessons to research and write a popular pony serial. There was also an entertaining programme set in a dancing school which might well have been conceived by a mother during the hours spent waiting to pick up her budding ballerina.

If you are a teacher your knowledge of children in that environment provides you with rich material. It has done so for others with great success. It is an interesting fact that children, who profess such relief and delight when released from the classroom, devour so avidly stories and dramas set in just that background.

Youth club leaders too may well be able to utilise their experience to good effect.

Writing realistic drama for children in such familiar settings as the home or school the writer faces a very real responsibility. It is not possible to pretend that bullies and other unpleasant people do not exist; children discover for themselves, all too soon, that they do. Indeed such characters are the stuff of conflict. The struggle of the just against the unjust has always made compelling drama but a very careful balance must be struck. This is not to suggest that any obvious moral stance is called for, but the writer must appreciate that his work can have a remarkable impact and influence on the juvenile mind. It has been fashionable to scorn this but researchers at Nottingham University announced that the pundits who claimed violence on TV does not influence youngsters appear to have been wrong. In an age of increased vandalism and violence it has to be a matter of grave concern – and not only here. In the USA it was suggested that the impressions TV can make on a child's mind are so deep and lasting that all programmes intended for children should be viewed by a panel of child psychologists before permission to broadcast is granted. It hasn't yet come to that and hopefully it never will but writers must be ever mindful of the dangers.

Adventure stories have always been popular and will undoubtedly remain so. Here again, if you have any special knowledge that could determine the basic setting you should take advantage of it. If you have personal experience of life on the farm, down a mine, 'messing about in boats' or some other exciting activity your story will draw us along with conviction and children will sense your authority.

As with all drama it will be the characters you create who will sell your work. If you choose to tell your tale through a group of youngsters, it is good policy to mix them as regards to sex and type but your chances of selling are better if you make it a small group to keep down the cost.

Children love weird creatures that never lived on land or sea. They feel safe with them. They can get involved in quite frightening situations, but the child knows all is well because those 'things' don't really exist – any fool knows that. The adventures can be quite alarming, but they are never threatening because they can never really happen, can they? Flights of fancy such as the famous *Doctor Who* fall into this category. Terrible inventions like the Daleks may even end up being lovable. The hideous ET proved simply to be a little chum after all.

There is always a place for a new fantasy creation. You have only (only?) to get the style right, then small children may peep at it with a thrill of delight from behind the sofa, but they won't get nightmares. It is fun to watch something scarey, just so long as it doesn't relate to real life. And if, as the writer, you do get it right, your creation is liable to end up on tee-shirts and, providing you have been careful to retain at least a share in the merchandising rights, you could end up very rich indeed.

There is endless controversy about the amount and type of violence on children's programmes. Tom can beat the living daylights out of Jerry and it is okay. It seems it is always okay so long as no one bleeds and so long as the victim gets up afterwards. Or maybe so long as it is the villain who gets the chop. The question of violence is constantly in dispute and usually subjective. That very violent show *The A Team* screened here a few years ago was notable for the fact that, despite the mayhem and everything getting blown skyhigh in ever more elaborate, inventive and noisy ways, you seldom see anyone actually killed. The villain ends up sorry for himself and that is more satisfying than if he ends up dead.

Heroes with faculties the rest of us do not possess are always attractive. We get vicarious pleasure from the abnormal abilities of Superman since we, ourselves, are obliged to get by without them. To children it must sometimes seem that to have a magic sword is the only answer to life's problems.

Smaller children are swiftly won over by warm attractive characters, no matter what shape or form. Note *Postman Pat* or *Thomas the Tank Engine*. A cynic might say any audience will become a fan of anything if it is thrust at them mercilessly enough and we can all name programmes whose ratings grow unaccountably. But children are discriminating and, once won, intensely loyal.

Another stream of programmes widely used by children's television consists of stories told by a narrator with accompanying illustrations. Many are based on legends and myths and this provides an opening that might appeal to some newcomers. Searching around for subjects and stories that lend themselves to presentation in this way could prove rewarding.

Animals, of course, have always been a big favourite with children. They relate strongly to their innocence. Puppets, stories with drawings and cartoons work well but using real animals presents serious problems as we have seen in an earlier chapter. Drama with real animals only works properly on film where trick camera effects can be used.

Anyone contemplating writing television for children needs to study carefully the many different kinds of programme on offer but it is, perhaps, worth pondering that a good many children, these days, are addicted to the Australian 'soaps', and when you come down to it, these are stories of uncomplicated people, living a pleasant sunbathed lifestyle, with problems that are usually resolvable.

And if there is not actually a duck-billed platypus by the fireside you get the feeling that animals are never far away.

So how to go about breaking into the children's market? No differently from the way you have to set about breaking into the series and serial market for adult television. If it is a serial you are trying to sell you need to write at least the first script. Better two or three and a detailed synopsis of other episodes. Best of all, the entire serial if it is no more than half a dozen episodes. Yes, it is a lot of work but with a good children's story you have some chance of selling as a book if television reject it.

For a series you need, at least, the first story. Better two of three to show it is not just a flash in the pan. You then need a synopsis of other stories you aim to tell and character notes on the principal cast required. The third thing you must show is the settings – where the action of the story takes place – obviously very important to allow the producers to estimate what sort of cost would be involved in making the programme.

Documentaries

As a new freelance writer you can forget, right away, all dreams of a few idyllic weeks on sun-kissed islands as they shoot your idea about Greek legends, or a month in Spain, all expenses paid, while you research for a programme on the traditions and customs of Catalonia. Other people got there first.

Television documentaries are more often the concept and work of directors or writer/directors, and of television journalists rather than scriptwriters who are not involved beyond writing the words. The film may be shot off the cuff and the scenes cut together later, or they may be shot, strictly in accordance with a camera script the director has carefully prepared in advance. Generally they do not include dialogue. Such words as may be necessary to explain the scene or action usually takes the form of a voice over commentary which can be written and recorded after the film is shot.

For a new writer to sell a script for a documentary programme to a major television company it would have to be an original idea based on a subject he had properly researched, or about which he had expert knowledge. It is the kind of programme where, perhaps more than any other, it is necessary to work in close co-operation with the producer. However since legislation that provides increased opportunities for independent film companies to get their work on to both BBC and ITV screens many independents welcome bright ideas from freelance writers.

A high proportion of documentaries are, of course, concerned with social problems and where these involve interviews they are frquently the work of journalists but programmes on music and art, motoring, sport and other popular activities are in constant demand.

There is, however, one form of documentary programme that falls well within the compass of the freelance scriptwriter. This is the dramatised documentary that has recently become known as faction. Here actors are engaged to play famous contemporary, or near contemporary, characters exposing their strengths and weaknesses and highlighting moments of crisis and decision in their lives. Facts about, and speeches of, the principal and secondary characters are adhered to as closely as possible but inevitably a good deal of incident and dialogue is created by the writer to bridge gaps of secrecy and privacy in order that the story can be told.

What you have is, in effect, a modern historical play about a principal character recently deceased – and in one notable case still living at the time of transmission. It also features secondary characters – both living and dead – whose lives and fates were closely involved with the life of the principal.

Two famous examples of these productions that you have probably seen are the American offering, *All the President's Men*, and a home produced epic, written by Ian Curteis, *Churchill and the Generals*.

To have any hope of interesting a television company in this kind of programme the subject has to be a person of major importance and the writer needs to be very careful not to find himself landed with a libel action by characters, still living, who played their part in the events featured in the play.

Not an area of programming recommended for the novice but could be of considerable interest to experienced journalists.

Instructional programmes

A flip through the pages of the programme journals reveals, if anyone had any doubts, that a great many hours are devoted to informative and instructional programmes from art to zoology. If you have some special or expert knowledge of a popular leisure activity or a profession, be it cooking or computers, languages or law, dogs, diet or 'Do it Yourself', it is worth considering whether you can channel your training and experience into a television programme.

You may, of course, find you can use this experience as the background for a play, but drama is a small part of the overall television output and many popular programmes which appear unscripted have to be written in the same way as the totally visual sequences shown earlier – with the writer specifying the props, equipment and other visuals required; what the demonstrator must do and precisely what the camera and audience are intended to be looking at.

This sort of programme may be presented by someone who is totally familiar with the subject and therefore talks freely off the cuff as the director follows a camera script that specifies the visuals required. Often however, the relaxed 'off the cuff' commentary is scripted, perhaps by the presenter himself, but not infrequently by a writer who has spent time and thought constructing the words to match the pictures and make points that must be made while avoiding digressing or spreading the commentary beyond the allocated time.

When one of the commercial companies decided to make their first adult educational programme, *Headway* Dick Sharples and I were invited to write the scripts. The substance of the lessons was provided by two university professors. Our job was to present the teaching material in a visual, interesting and amusing way that would make our target audience – young people who had missed out on educational opportunities – watch the show for interest and entertainment.

We were engaged to put the sugar round the pill, so to speak.

Some time later I scripted for the BBC episodes of their series, *English by Radio and Television*, which was distributed all over the world for the benefit of English language students. This material was presented in the form of short dramatic situations that 'worked' the particular words and phrases each lesson was designed to teach.

A programme of this kind may start in the production office with an executive who thinks of the idea, or it may start with a freelance who suggests it to the producer. But it is not enough for the freelance to say, 'I've got this idea for a programme about knitting or pottery' or 'How about a series on diet?'. The obvious and popular subjects have been done time and again and will doubtless be repeated, revised and remade for ever more.

If you are a leading expert on a subject they may, perhaps, come looking for you. If you are not you have got to approach them and show how the material can be presented in a fresh and interesting way that will attract and hold an audience who will, in all probability, have seen programmes on the subject many times before.

Writing for television starts with thinking for television; scouring the mind for themes and subjects that have been missed. Who would have thought, for instance, that fishing would make fascinating television until someone put it on the screen? Finding new ways of telling old stories or rekindling interest in well worn material by revealing to the viewer unfamiliar and unexploited facets can open the door to a newcomer.

Videos

By far the greatest number of video films available are 'name actor' feature films produced originally for cinematograph exhibition by major film companies and made available for video distribution when the circuit run is over.

You will also have seen many favourite shows – particularly comedies, thrillers and children's stories – produced by the BBC and other national television companies. This is simply further exploitation of work and the writer's payment for this use is covered by agreements between the producers and the Writers' Guild.

Larger video shops and libraries also stock informative and instructional films covering hobbies and popular activities such as home decorating and car repairs and writers with technical knowledge or those prepared to do the necessary research may find an opening in the ever growing market for these instructional videos.

Industry, business and public service organisations now make extensive use of educational and training videos and although many of the companies making these films use their own 'in house' writers others use freelances who know how to script television programmes.

Companies taking advantage of the opportunity to make these programmes tend to be companies who have been involved making documentaries and industrial films. Such companies now provide a far wider market potential than the restrictive monopolies of the national and regional television companies and writers – particularly those with experience in advertising and public relations – may find that time spent learning the tehnique of television writing will pay off even if they are uanble to get a break into national television programmes.

Freelance scriptwriting in the corporate or business television and video market is dealt with more fully in the next chapter.

14. Marketing your material

At a Writers' Guild meeting a few years ago one member, asked what he was working on, said, 'I've just started on my third volume of rejection slips.'

Now there is a man who will probably be successful sooner or later because with such a volume of work and such persistence he is going to land the right script on the right desk before very long. And that's what it is all about most of the time.

If you are sure you have written a good script based on a good idea don't let a rejection by a single company or producer – or even half a dozen of them – put you off. Good scripts are regularly rejected because they don't fit in with the company plans; because the schedules are already full; because they are too similar to something already in the pipeline or a play you didn't see, that went out a week or two before, while your TV was switched off and you had your head down writing your script. That happens to us all believe me! Then again, it may be rejected because it would be too expensive to produce; or because one man – just one man – doesn't like it or even because the editor is a fool or, all too frequently, so inexperienced that he wouldn't know a good script or an original idea unless his boss said it was. But even more likely, the rejection would be because it just doesn't happen to be the kind of idea the producer is looking for at that particular moment.

Don't get depressed or embarrassed by rejections. You stand in good company. Towards the end of his life Bernard Shaw said, 'I finished my first book seventy six years ago. I offered it to every publisher on the English speaking earth I had heard of. Their refusals were unanimous; it did not get into print until, fifty years later, publishers would publish anything that had my name on it.'

And if you think Shaw's experience is exceptional listen to Rod Serling, the American television writer I quoted earlier.

'I remember a bad moment when my diet consisted chiefly of black coffee and fingernails. I'd written six half hour television plays and each had been rejected at least five times.'

To be successful a television writer needs more than talent. He also needs a little luck and a lot of determination to go on writing; to go on writing; to go on writing. Selling yourself and your ideas in the competitive market that exists in television is never easy, even for established writers. It sometimes seems that a thick skin is more important than a good idea.

The comedian Victor Borge used to tell an amusing story about his grandfather who, he said, invented a soft drink which he called 'One-up'. He tried to market it but it failed, so he tried again with a drink he called 'Two-up'. That failed too but the old man, refusing to admit defeat, kept trying. 'Three-up' 'Four-up' 'Five-up' and 'Six-up'. They all failed. At this point grandfather lost heart and gave up. Then along came this guy who invented a drink called 'Seven-up' and made a fortune.

It may be your scripts from 'One-up' to 'Six-up' will be rejected. 'Seven-up' may be the one for you – the script that will open the doors to fame and fortune but you'll never know if you give up at 'Two-up' or 'Six-up'.

Script writers all start as amateurs. We write because we want to write and enjoy doing it. That is a reward in itself. If you sell it too you are doubly paid.

Some writers are, by instinct or training, good businessmen and that is a big advantage because selling scripts, like selling anything else, is a business enterprise. For those who are not sales orientated it is useful to have a 'hungry' agent – one who is not so prosperous that he can live comfortably on the percentages he takes from a string of established clients. The bigger agencies pick and choose who they represent and there is no compulsion on them to try and do anything for a new, unestablished writer. For the first year or two it may possibly involve work and expense for little or no return. The problem is, however, a 'hungry' agent cannot afford to spend time working for a new writer unless the writer shows outstanding promise. Indeed, no agent can afford to spend his time reading piles of scripts by unknown writers in the hope that he may come across one he has a chance of selling. Experienced agents will tell you, it's like panning for gold. You've got to sift through great stacks of rubbish before you hit a single golden nugget and there is no guarantee there is one to be found in any stack you tackle.

So it boils down to this: you have got to make that first break on your own. Then when you approach agents with your second play – your first having been produced, screened and hopefully well reviewed – you will not have much trouble in finding one who will want to represent you.

'Great!' you say. Sounds as though you do the really hard bit – getting the first break – why bother with an agent after that? It's a good question. We'll look at that later.

In the meantime let me offer you this encouragement. Many script editors are especially interested in the work of new writers. It almost seems as if some seek to crown their own unremarkable careers by being able to boast of some truly talented dramatist, 'I discovered him. I bought his first play.' You will also find a lot of Independent Production Companies who make a point of saying in their entries in trade guides and yearbooks that they are, 'Interested to read new writing', 'Delighted to see new work', 'Very interested in scripts by new young writers' and similar invitations to beginners.

A writer living in the regions will probably find it easier to get started there than in London, where the competition is at its fiercest. If you live somewhere 'out in the sticks' you may be surprised to learn that writers from the regions would appear to have an advantage over writers born and bred in London. There are a great many writers from all parts of the UK working for London based producers while maintaining their contacts with their home based companies. Relatively few native London writers work for regional television companies.

Presentation

Now you have written your script. You want it to look as professional as possible so let's check on some of those obvious things it is all too easy to forget.

Never submit a script without your name and address on the front cover and your agent's name, too, if you have one. The letter you send to the editor or producer may get detached from the script and lost.

Always state on the cover page the running time of the script.

How do you check that? With experience you develop an instinct – you can look at the number of pages, the number and length of the speeches on the page and guess within a minute or two how long the script will run. This, incidentally, is why producers like scripts presented on their standard layout. However, until you are experienced there is only one safe way. Read the dialogue aloud at the rate you want the speeches played, remembering characters do not all speak at the same speed. As you read the words act out the movements checking the time against a stop watch. If, in the script, the telephone rings you must allow time for the actor to cross or enter the room to answer it. If the person on the other end of the line is saying things the viewer cannot hear, you need a few seconds silence as the person in vision listens. Again when there is a knock at the front door and someone answers it seconds must elapse before they re-enter with the visitor.

You need to be aware that we are working with two different conceptions of time; actual time and 'stage time'. One may take liberties with 'stage time'. Four or five hours later that day may in reality be just thirty seconds later as shown by the watch on the viewer's wrist. We all happily accept a character who goes off screen for a five mile run can be back, panting, five minutes later. And he might well pant. He would have done the run at sixty miles an hour! But we can take no liberties with time when actors are required to actually do something in vision. The time it takes is the time it takes and you must allow that in full when estimating the running length of your script.

Your second page will be the cast list indicating principal actors and extras. This should be set out on a single sheet with brief details of the physical appearance and characteristics if this is particularly relevant. As for example: SUSAN a pretty blonde aged 17 or 18. Or ROBERTS 40ish, very fat. A Scot.

The third page should show the settings. Here it is useful to indicate whether these are Interiors or Exteriors and whether Night or Day.

Lets take a look at the layout of these pages.

ANYONE HERE SEEN KELLY?

A play for television

by

John Smith

Running time sixty minutes

John Smith
34 Barcelona Crescent
London NW11 5ZX

Agent: Wm Baxter
1 Dawkins Street
London WC1

<u>CAST LIST</u>

BOB PRICE (A pensioner around 70)

DETECTIVE INSPECTOR BROWN (near 50)

DETECTIVE CONSTABLE RAWLINGS (25ish)

MIKE BYRD (A tearaway, late teens)

SPENCER (Irish. A car salesman, aged about 40)

JUDY (A pretty suburban mother, aged about 30)

JOYCE KELLY (Thin, drained, 40ish)

BARMAN

BARMAID

<u>NON-SPEAKING</u>

KELLY

POLICE CONSTABLE

PETROL PUMP ATTENDANT

WOMAN IN STREET

<u>VOICES</u>

TELEPHONIST

NEWSPAPER SELLER

<u>SETTINGS</u>

INT:	BOB'S BEDROOM	Night and Day
INT:	BOB'S LIVING ROOM	Day
EXT:	SUBURBAN STREET	Day
INT:	MIKE'S FLAT	Day
INT:	D/I BROWN'S OFFICE	Day
INT:	PUBLIC BAR	Day
EXT:	SCHOOL	Day
EXT:	PETROL STATION	Night
EXT:	MAIN ROADS (Various)	Night and Day
INT:	CARS (Two)	Night and Day
EXT:	WASTE LAND	Day

The writer working for a production to be made in one of the film studios will sometimes indicate his scene is set STUDIO, STUDIO LOT or LOCATION as you have seen from examples elsewhere in this book. However, when submitting a script speculatively, without any idea whether it will be produced as a studio production, studio plus filmed exteriors or shot entirely on film it is better not to attempt to be too precise.

If the BBC were making a programme that called for the settings indicated above it is probable they would shoot it as a studio production with Telecine inserts. A Film Producer with his own studio would mix Studio, Studio/Lot and Location. A smaller Independent Producer, without his own studio, making the play entirely on film would shoot it all on location renting premises that would be suitable, or could be adapted, to accommodate the interior scenes called for in the script. (See Chapter 3.)

At this stage in your script writing career it is enough to indicate the settings essential for the purpose of your story and leave it to the producer to decide where and how he will shoot it.

There is also no need for you to stipulate the position of the commercial breaks. If it is a BBC production there are none and it can be agreed later with the editor if the play is bought by a commercial company.

You should submit two copies of your script neatly typed. If you are aiming for a studio/tape production you should use the layout shown in Chapter 2, page 10 leaving the left-hand side of the page clear. Use single line spacing between the lines of dialogue; double line between the speeches; and double line spacing between speeches and stage instructions which are in capitals.

If you are aiming for a TV film that will be shot mostly on location you should adopt the film type layout shown in Chapter 3, page 26 and elsewhere in the book. Here you will see all scenes start on the far left of the page with just a 2.5 cm margin with the scene number both sides of the page.

The name of the character is centred and the dialogue starts 4 cm from the margin. This is single line spacing. Stage instructions are again in capitals and given single line spacing but a double line space is given between two or more quite separate instructions such as camera action, actor action, and sound FX (effects), as shown in the Antarctic script illustrated in Chapter 3.

But don't lose sleep worrying as to which layout you should use when you don't know, if your script is bought, whether it will be produced on film or tape. The really important thing is to make sure it is laid out clearly so that the reader knows exactly who is talking to whom; where they are; and what they are doing. No one will reject a first class script because it is not laid out in the style they normally use. Different companies use slightly different layouts. It is the quality of the writing that counts.

One thing you must always be careful about. Never under any circumstances send out your last and only copy.

If you make errors correct them neatly and clearly in ink.

Use A4 paper and if you are making carbon copies keep the bottom one for your file to be sure that any you send out are fully legible.

Number all the pages and bind or staple them together in some kind of folder.

The script will speak for itself. In the letter you send with the script it is enough for you to say, 'I am enclosing two copies of my play entitled, 'So-and-So'. I look forward to your reaction when you have had a chance to read it.'

Enclose a large stamped addressed envelope for the return if they are not interested in the play.

Send it by ordinary first class mail. Recorded delivery smacks of the amateur.

Wait a month or so before you phone or write to know what they think of it. If they reject it you won't change their minds by arguing. It would actually make some editors less interested to look at your next play.

And as soon as you've sent off your first play start work on the next. The only way to get to be a professional writer is to write.

Marketing

So now your script is ready. To whom do you send it?

Editors and heads of drama are frequently changing so there is little point in telling you here and now to send it to a particular individual at a particular company. To keep right up to date on that you need a copy of a book called 'CONTACTS' that is published annually by *The Spotlight*, 7 Leicester Place, London WC2H 7BP, from whom it can only be obtained direct. Otherwise a telephone call or letter to the company you hope to interest will point you in the right direction.

Unless you have established contact with a particular producer or editor you should address your script to:

The Drama Script Editor, (name of the company)

If you are attempting to contribute to an on-going series it should be addressed to:

The Editor, (name of the series and name of the company)

Comedy material should, however, be addressed to:

Head of Light Entertainment, (the name of the company)

BBC Television addresses

BBC
Television Centre
Wood Lane
London W12 7RJ
tel. 020 8743 8000

BBC Documentary Features
White City
201 Wood Lane
London W12 7TS
tel. 020 8752 5252

BBC Birmingham
Broadcasting Centre
Pebble Mill Road
Birmingham B5 7QQ
tel. 0121-414 8888

BBC East
St Catherines Close
All Saints Green
Norwich
Norfolk NR1 3ND
tel. 01603-619331

BBC East Midlands
York House
Mansfield Road
Nottingham NG1 3JA
tel. 0115-955 0500

BBC North
Broadcasting Centre
Woodhouse Lane
Leeds LS2 9PN
tel. 0113-244 1188

BBC North East
Broadcasting Centre
Barrack Road
Newcastle-upon-Tyne
NE99 2NE
tel. 0191-232 1313

BBC North West
New Broadcasting House
PO Box 27
Oxford Road
Manchester M60 1SJ
tel. 0161-200 2020

BBC South
Broadcasting House
Havelock Road
Southampton
SO14 7PU
tel. 023 8022 6201

BBC South East
Elstree Centre
Clarendon Road
Borehamwood
Herts WD6 1JF
tel. 020 8953 6100

151

BBC South West
Broadcasting House
Seymour Road
Mannamead
Plymouth PL3 5BD
tel. 01752-229201

BBC West
Broadcasting House
Whiteladies Road
Bristol BS8 2LR
tel. 0117-973 2211

BBC Wales
Broadcasting House
Llandaff
Cardiff CF5 2YQ
tel. 029 2032 2000

BBC Scotland
Broadcasting House
Queen Margaret Drive
Glasgow G12 8DG
tel. 0141-339 8844

Broadcasting House
5 Queen Street
Edinburgh EH2 1JF
tel. 0131-225 3131

BBC Northern Ireland
Broadcasting House
Ormeau Avenue
Belfast BT2 8HQ
tel. 028 9033 8000

Independent television companies

Anglia Television Ltd
Anglia House
Norwich NR1 3JG
tel. 01603-615151

Border Television plc
The Television Centre
Durran Hill
Carlisle CA1 3NT
tel. 01228-525101

Carlton Television Ltd
101 St Martin's Lane
London WC2N 4AZ
tel. 020 7240 4000

Central Television plc
Central Court
Gas Street
Birmingham B1 2JP
tel. 0121-643 9898

Channel Five Broadcasting Ltd
22 Long Acre
London WC2E 9LY
tel. 020 7550 5555

***Channel Four Television
  Corporation**
124 Horseferry Road
London SW1P 2TX
tel. 020 7396 4444

*Most programmes transmitted by Channel Four are provided by independent production companies.

Channel Television Ltd
Television Centre
St Helier, Jersey
Channel Islands JE2 3ZD
tel. 01534-816816

GMTV Ltd
The London Television Centre
Upper Ground
London SE1 9LT
tel. 020 7827 7000

Grampian Television Ltd
Queen's Cross
Aberdeen AB15 2XJ
tel. 01224-846846

Granada Television Ltd
Quay Street
Manchester M60 9EA
tel. 0161-832 7211

HTV Group Ltd
HTV (Cymru) Wales
The Television Centre
Culverhouse Cross
Cardiff CF5 6XJ
tel. 029 2059 0590

HTV West
The Television Centre
Bath Road
Bristol BS4 3HG
tel. 0117-972 2722

London Weekend Television Ltd
The London Television Centre
Upper Ground
London SE1 9LT
tel. 020 7620 1620

Meridian Broadcasting Ltd
Television Centre
Southampton SO14 0PZ
tel. 023 8022 2555

Scottish Television plc
Cowcaddens
Glasgow G2 3PR
tel. 0141-300 3000

Tyne Tees Television Ltd
The Television Centre
City Road
Newcastle-upon-Tyne
NE1 2AL
tel. 0191-261 0181

Ulster Television plc
Havelock House
Ormeau Road
Belfast BT7 1EB
tel. 028 9032 8122

Westcountry Television Ltd
Langage Science Park
Plymouth PL7 5BG
tel. 01752-333333

Yorkshire Television Ltd
The Television Centre
Leeds LS3 1JS
tel. 0113-243 8283

Ireland

Radio Telefis Eireann
Donnybrook
Dublin 4
tel. 00-353-1-2083111

ITV Network Centre

200 Gray's Inn Road
London WC1X 8HF
tel. 020 7843 8000

Some programmes transmitted by the commercial companies on Channel 3 are provided by the Network Centre which commissions and purchases programmes for the licencees collectively. The centre, however, is not a production unit. Programmes and scripts for programmes likely to be acceptable for networking are submitted by companies who have facilities to make them.

Independent production companies

The collective organisation of Independent Production Companies, formerly the Film Producers' Association (FPA) was in 1992 subsumed into the Producers' Alliance for Cinema & Television (PACT), with currently 11,400 members. Although many make films for TV as well as documentaries, travel, educational, instructional, musical and children's programmes, others are involved only in commercial promotion and advertising work (see Corporate television below). The output of all but the largest of these independent companies is, however, small and many use only scripts written in-house while others are not actively in production most of the time. But the scene is constantly changing. Producers who make only public relations films this year might well be making dramas for television next year or may have ceased trading altogether.

For this reason it would not be helpful to list here the names of the many companies. You will find a full and comprehensive list published and regularly updated in *The Directory of Independent Production Companies* published annually by PACT and in other year and reference books in libraries or bookshops. Many of the companies listed indicate they are willing to look at unsolicited manuscripts but writers are well advised to check by phone or letter to ascertain if they are likely to be interested in the theme of their script and, if they are, to what sort of time schedule they might be working. The last thing a writer wants is his work caught up for a couple of years in a log-jam.

PACT (Producers' Alliance for Cinema & Television), 45 Mortimer Street, London W1N 7TD tel. 020 7331 6000

Corporate television

The use of audio visual media for public relations, sales promotions, staff training, customer instruction, and for communicating political and social messages continues to expand. Many film and TV production companies, once concerned primarily with documentaries and commercials, now concentrate their efforts and talents on this lucrative market.

Some writers could profitably do the same.

Programmes for film and video tape have to be scripted and while many are 'in-house' productions, made by directors and staff, freelance screenwriters are often commissioned for this work.

But this is not an area for the dilettante. A writer seeking commissions of this kind needs to be well organised; a businessman able to present both himself and his work in a totally professional way, no less than one who has fully mastered the techniques of scripting TV and other audio visual presentations. He must also be able to take a brief; often to assimilate highly technical information in order to present the first draft script.

Some agents now represent writers working in this field. Markets are production companies and in-house units but also companies without in-house units who commission programmes outside: i.e. public relations firms, design groups, marketing consultancies, conference organisers, training organisations and so on. Outside the London area a lot of corporate work is commissioned via the advertising agency which handles the client's account.

The *Audio Visual Directory* lists 2,400 companies producing corporate television.

Trade Association:

International Visual Communication Association. Bolsover House, 5–6 Clipstone Street, London W1P 7EB tel. 020 7580 0962

Yearbooks and reference books

Audio Visual Directory
EMAP McLaren Organisation
McLaren House
19 Scarbrook Road
Croydon
Surrey CR9 1QA
tel. 020 8565 4200

**Audio Visual Presentation
Handbook**
EMAP McLaren Organisation
McLaren House
19 Scarbrook Road
Croydon
Surrey CR9 1QA
tel. 020 8565 4200

**British Film and Television
Yearbook**
published by
British Film Institute
21 Stephen Street
London W1P 21N
tel. 020 7255 1444

**Freelance Scripting in the
Corporate Television Market**
published by
Writers' Guild of Great Britain
430 Edgware Road
London W2 1EH
tel. 020 7723 8074

ITC Factfile
published by the
Independent Television
Commission
33 Foley Street
London W1P 7LB
tel. 020 7255 3000

**Kemp's Film, TV & Video
Yearbook**
published by
Variety Media Publications
6 Bell Yard
London WC2A 2JR
tel. 020 7637 3663

**The PACT Directory of
Independent Production
Companies**
45 Mortimer Street
London W1N 7TD
tel. 020 7331 6000

Writers' & Artists' Yearbook
published by
A & C Black
35 Bedford Row
London WC1R 4JH
tel. 020 7242 0946

The Writer's Handbook
published by
Macmillan
25 Eccleston Place
London SW1W 9NF
tel. 020 7881 8000

Agents

Every new writer asks the question – Does one need an agent?

That depends on the personality of the writer; whether he finds trying to sell himself and talk money an embarrassment or a challenge. There are writers who do it very successfully and they give a lot more time and effort to marketing their work than any agent would ever give except, perhaps, to a really big-time writer who was making big-time money for them.

The problem for a television writer without an agent is keeping up with what is going on in the industry. When the day's work demands such concentration and so many hours shut away writing there is little time to make new contacts and chase around trying to discover just what different producers and production companies have in prospect. And, in the series market in particular, by the time they announce details of their production plans it is usually too late. The scripts have all been written.

The principal service an agent can perform for a television writer is to keep him briefed about who is looking for what so that he has a chance to submit scripts, storylines and ideas to editors and producers who are at that point actually looking for material. If you should happen to find yourself with an agent who is not regularly doing that you should pause and take stock of what exactly he is doing for you in return for the money you pay him. A good agent should also be introducing the writer's name and work to producers who have not previously used him.

Before you ask any agent to represent you, find out who else he is representing. A long list of successful writers may impress you but it won't do you much good if all his time and effort goes in promoting them. Again some agents have too many clients in competition with each other and are content to sit back leaving the writer to get his own work while they do nothing more than act as a postbox forwarding the cheques after duly deducting ten per cent. They don't even negotiate the fee except for 'name' writers in big demand. The 'going rate' for film and television scripts is laid down in national agreements negotiated between the employers and the Writers' Guild. The agent is not often able to increase the fee paid to a new writer sufficiently to cover the commission. If, however, the agent really is working to promote you the money it costs you could be a good investment.

Selling scripts overseas – as opposed to productions – is something very few writers are able to do without an agent who has expert knowledge and close contacts with overseas producers, particularly in Europe. Productions – the tape or film of the programme is not yours to sell. That includes the contributions of the actors and everyone else concerned in the making of the programme. Only the production company can sell the entire work and if and when they do the writer is paid a royalty under the terms of the agreements negotiated between the producers' organisations and the Writers' Guild – and it would be paid to you, too, even though you are not, at that time, a member of the Guild.

Selling rights

The Writers' Guild of Great Britain is to be found at 430 Edgware Road, London W2 1EH, tel: 020 7723 8074. It is a TUC-affiliated trade union, founded in the late sixties to protect the interests of television writers by established screenwriters, like the late Ted Willis, Denis Norden, Brian Forbes and other well-known writers. At that time there was no standard fee for a TV script. I well remember Brian Forbes telling a Guild meeting that he was paid £50 for one of his first television scripts. And for that handsome sum the producers took all rights.

Which brings me to a very important point of which you should be aware. I have talked throughout about 'selling scripts' but that needs clarification. Film companies traditionally bought scripts and took the total copyright. The commercial TV companies fell in with the practice of the BBC who bought a licence to exploit the work for a limited period of years (seldom less than three or more than seven). However, with the introduction of satellite and cable TV and the involvement in the European market of international media giants, the BBC and ITV companies – both with a financial interest in the UK Gold channel on the Sky satellite – have been seeking to persuade writers to sign away their entire copyright in return for a percentage royalty based on the income they receive for the satellite transmission.

When the writer signs a contract 'selling' his copyright he loses control of his work and for this reason the Guild and many leading members are opposed to the development.

Nevertheless it is necessary to recognise we are living in a changing world and face the proliferation of both satellites and the number of channels each can carry. It is now almost impossible to individually monitor and collect payments for programmes transmitted from satellites and picked up in remote parts of the world. A royalty deal may be the only sure way for the writer to collect payments for the use of his work.

Under EU law writers' copyright has been extended to 70 years and in negotiations it has been agreed the licence period granted to the BBC shall be 25 years.

It is impossible for the individual writer to monitor programmes that are picked up off air, or from satellites, and piped through European cable networks – much less collect payment for them. Fortunately we now have in this country a collecting agency, Authors' Licensing and Collecting Society (ALCS), which monitors and collects payments for writers in the way that the Performing Rights Society collects for musicians.

When you sell your programme to the BBC or an Independent you should join ALCS who keep computerised records of writers' credits. Many TV writers regularly receive from ALCS totally unexpected chques for transmissions of programmes they'd almost forgotten in places they scarcely knew existed as well as larger payments from major markets.

The BBC usually require the right to transmit a programme via any or all UK transmitters. The Network Centre want rights for the ITV national network. A regional television company may want the right to transmit in their own area only. This is covered by a special opt-out clause in the Writers' Guild agreements.

Copyright, where it is retained by the writer, is divisable. Beyond the regional and network rights there are repeat rights and overseas rights (in some agreements specifying the different areas of the world individually). The producer may make a specified payment for each of these rights.

Further rights, for the use of which the writer is due payment, include Pay TV, Satellites, Cable, Videogram use and cinematograph exhibition. There are other rights too. Book rights if a publisher gets involved. Spin-off rights, if you are the originator of a (usually) series and the producers decide to do another and different series based on the same, or some, of your characters. There are also merchandising rights. These are particularly important when a writer devises children's programmes where the sales of toys and tee-shirts could become very lucrative.

It would be wrong, however, if you gained the impression that every script you write will earn you money from the sale of all these different rights. It won't so don't go trying to persuade your bank manager to give you an overdraft on the strength of the cinematograph exhibition rights in your first success or the merchandising rights for cute new puppets you have created. When your script has been accepted and the programme is in production you can only safely rely on the money from that first sale. After that there is a fairly good chance that you may get a UK repeat fee. Then some money for UK Gold but seldom a US Network and relatively few writers have been lucky enough to get payment for merchandising, although some have been unlucky enough – or unwise enough to sign contracts granting these rights to the producers only to find, when it is too late, they are being profitably exploited.

One of the battles writers have had over the years has been to hold on to these many different rights.

With ever changing technology; cable TV and satellites, new companies, new stations and, sadly, not least new Government legislation the writer's copyright and thereby his income is under constant threat of erosion. It is in this area the services of an agent and advice and guidance from the Guild is invaluable.

The Writers' Guild, which was founded as The Screenwriters' Guild, is an organisation of professionals who, in the mid seventies, extended the membership to embrace authors and stage playwrights. Members receive updated information about all new script fees, a monthly newsletter, notice of craft meetings they may attend and of 'surgeries' which are conducted from time to time by established writers to advise and assist new writers.

Members may also call on the Guild office for information and guidance about contractual problems which is particularly valuable to newcomers trying to find their way around in the jungle of show business. But the Guild is not an agency. It does not sell scripts or recommend writers to producers. It would be invidious for a trade union to be pushing the work of one member against another.

Comedy writers and aspiring comedy writers may also find membership of the Comedy Writers Association UK, helpful. Their address is 61 Parry Road, Ashmore Park, Wolverhampton, West Midlands WV11 2PS, tel. 01902-722729. The Association organise seminars with talks by script editors and leading comedy writers.

Below are examples of some of the network fees paid to beginners in accordance with the terms of agreements between the Writers' Guild and Producers. It should be noted, however, that some of these agreements are negotiated annually and new agreements when signed should show a modest increase in the fees paid.

BBC Television fees for new writers

Original plays (60 mins)	£4,703
Per minute rate	£78
Series/Serials (50 mins)	£3,880
Per minute rate	£78
Dramatisations (50 mins)	£2,707
Per minute rate	£54
Adaptations (50 mins)	£1,632
Per minute rate	£33
Educational drama	£50.62 per minute
Light Entertainment sketch material	£34.18 per minute
Attendance payment for read-through and rehearsals	£67 per day

ITV Television fees for new writers

Original plays:

not less than 90 mins	£9,437
75	£7,562
60	£6,296
30	£3,775

Series episodes:

46 to 60 mins	£5,038
31 to 45	£3,779
21 to 30	£2,517
up to 20	£1,921

Serials: storyline provided

21 to 30 mins	£1,674
up to 20 mins	£1,250

Serials: script and storyline:

45 to 60 mins	£4,031
31 to 45 mins	£3,025
21 to 30 mins	£2,012
up to 20 mins	£1,511

Finite series or serial: writer provides script and storyline:

episode length 90 mins	£9,437
75	£7,562
60	£6,296
30	£3,775

Dramatisations

not less than 60 mins	£4,000

Adaptations	£2,517

Established writers: Guild members new to television

Original plays:

not less than 90 mins	£9,855
75	£7,891
60	£6,568
30	£3,940

Series episodes:

46 to 60 mins	£5,254
31 to 45	£4,515
21 to 30	£2,627
up to 20	£2,010

Serials: storyline provided		Finite series or serial: writer provides script and storyline:	
21 to 30 mins	£1,750	episode length 90 mins	£9,855
up to 20 mins	£1,300	75	£7,891
		60	£6,568
Serials: script and storyline:		30	£3,940
45 to 60 mins	£4,204		
31 to 45 mins	£3,152	Dramatisations	
21 to 30 mins	£2,101	not less than 60 mins	£4,173
up to 20 mins	£1,574		
		Adaptations	£2,627

Original teleplays: fictional drama specially written for children's educational or religious programmes

per minute transmission time   £85.70
Attendance payment rehearsals   £74.40

Both the BBC and ITV companies make further payments for repeat screenings and overseas sales. Fees specified above represent payment for a network transmission. If a programme is transmitted in only one ITV region the payment due is 50% of the fee. Other regions attract additional payments up to the maximum 100% of the agreed network fee. Payments are staggered. The writer receives 50% of his total fee from both BBC and ITV when the work is commissioned. ITV then pay a further 25% on delivery and the balance upon acceptance. The BBC pay the balance upon acceptance when any rewrites required are completed.

Producers' Alliance for Cinema & Television (PACT)

The agreement with PACT is quite different. The fee paid to the writer relates to the budget of the film. The agreement is currently under negotiation and should be finalied during the next few months. The current total fee for a film budgeted at or below £750,000 is £14,000. From £75,000 to £2 million it is £19,000.

Higher budget fees relate to feature films made for cinematograph exhibition but we are concerned here only with the lower budget films made for television.

Payment for series or serial episodes is, however, based on screen time. Here the minimum payment for a sixty minute episode is £5,500 and pro-rate for shorter lengths.

The contract stipulates 'stage' payments:

Treatment:	£1,375
Commissioned first draft:	£1,375
Delivery first draft:	£1,375
Acceptance second draft:	£1,375

The total minimum payment buys one UK Network Television transmission. There is a schedule of payments for other uses. The company have the right to cancel the agreement if they are not satisfied with the script.

The right to terminate an agreement is also embodied in the BBC and ITV agreements which lay down guidelines as to how much rewriting may be expected from the writer and the extent to which a producing organisation may alter a writer's work (e.g. they may not make structural alterations). These agreements contain clauses that deal with the problem of a producer not being satisfied with the work of the writer they have commissioned. If, with series episodes, despite the writer's attempts to make his script acceptable the editor and producer are still dissatisfied but believe it can be improved by another writer, the original writer may lose his final stage payment and this money be used to bring in someone else to rewrite the script. This, however, does not apply to totally original plays where the whole concept and copyright belongs to the writer. In this situation a play the producers were unhappy about would be abandoned with the writer retaining the money he had at that point been paid.

When writers and producers or script editors fall out over this kind of thing they generally turn to the Guild who, by agreement with the Producers' Alliance, appoint an arbitration committee to sort out the problem and see justice is done.

Pensions

One of the drawbacks for any 'would be' full time writer, if he is safely established in some other profession or business, is the prospect of losing his retirement pension. It is impossible to know twenty-five or thirty years before you reach retirement age whether you will actually earn enough by your writing to make regular payments into a private pension fund.

The freelance writer is self-employed. There is no regular monthly contribution from an employer into his pension fund, so thirty years ago the Guild decided that television producers, who reaped the benefit of the freelance system prevailing in the industry should, in all justice, make a pension contribution in respect of each script commissioned from Guild members.

It took a few years to get them all to agree but today any Guild member working for the BBC, ITC or PACT has a pension contribution paid over and above the script fee negotiated. As with TV company staff pensions the beneficiary is also required to make a personal contribution – currently the PACT contribution is 6% against the writers' 4%, the BBC contribution is 7½% against the writer's 5% while the ITC companies pay 8% against the writer's 5%. The writer's contribution is deducted from his fee and sent by the company with their contribution to the Writers' Guild Pension Fund and invested by leading pension brokers in the name of the writer concerned.

If as a writer you are very successful and are offered the opportunity to work in Hollywood, membership of the Writers' Guild here will smooth the path for you since they have an affiliation agreement with the Writers' Guild of America. The Canadian Writers' Guild and Writers' Guilds in Australia and New Zealand are also affiliated. All give professional advice and assistance to members of the other affiliated organisations.

A word of caution

The freelance writer working on his own, endeavouring to sell his work to companies and producers, about whom he knows very little is particularly open to exploitation; so let me add a final word of caution. A character to be avoided is the independent film producer who is neither independent nor is he really a producer.

After one of your plays has been on television, you may be called by someone (in my experience usually American) who tells you how impressed he was and wants to know if you would be available to accept a commission to write a film.

This *could* be genuine so tread carefully.

If it is less than genuine you will be invited along for morning coffee or afternoon tea (it's never lunch or dinner) in the main lounge of a big London hotel. This is both to impress you and save the 'producer' the expense of an office. He will tell you about this film he is going to make and what he proposes is that you should write the script and will be paid a large sum of money on the first day of shooting. He won't be offering you a commissioning fee but he'll make it sound so important with the names of the stars he's got lined up that you'll want to do it anyway.

What he is after is work. For himself as a producer – and he hopes to obtain this via a script he can hawk around the distributors and financiers in an attempt to raise the money to make the film.

It's an old trick. A great many writers have been excited at the prospect only to find they have spent weeks working for nothing on a script that gets nowhere.

Experience among writers has shown that this kind of speculative work is usually abortive and it is strictly against the agreements the Writers' Guild have with the producers' organisations. If you are a member of the Guild or if you have an agent you should ask advice before you get involved with these characters. In any event you should try to check on the track record of your 'producer' and judge how genuine he is by his willingness to pay you for the work he asks you to do – and that is pay you at least half the fee before you write a word.

Another group who sometimes approach writers to do speculative writing are out of work actors. Even star names are sometimes unemployed. You may some day be flattered to hear on the phone a well known voice calling you, and inviting you to meet him. He has an idea for a script or more possibly a series on which you and he could work together.

It sometimes comes good. More often the writer finds himself doing a great deal of writing that finishes up in the wastepaper basket or collecting dust on a shelf.

So be careful.

15. What not to write

No book on writing for television would be complete without some guidance to a new writer on the matter of censorship. The problem is that the boundaries of taste and language are constantly moving. What is acceptable one year may provoke protest a few years on and what may have created an outburst of indignation ten years ago may, today, pass without general offence.

Twenty years ago, bad language was the cause of the majority of complaints to the Independent Television Authority. Recent BBC research has shown that of programmes where more than five per cent of those surveyed expressed disapproval, complaints about sex outnumbered complaints about bad language by almost three to two. In the next month, however, a survey of all programmes showed strong disapproval of bad language exceeding 'strong' disapproval about sex by close on three to one.

It has been well said, there are liars, damned liars and statistics. Possibly all these surveys are strongly influenced by programmes those surveyed have most recently watched. Clearly a single scene or a single word in a single play can influence the results of a particular survey to the extent that it cannot be taken as a totally reliable guide and it is very difficult for television producers and writers to know with certainty where the boundaries of good taste and tolerance lie at any given time. Neither language nor public morals remain static for long. There are no absolutes.

Very obviously many of the once taboo words of the English language have been devalued by everyday usage to the extent that they are now widely accepted in 'polite' society without the hostess having an attack of the vapours. But a television audience is not a gathering of selected, sophisticated guests that the writer might invite to his dinner table safe in the knowledge that no words he uses, no topic of conversation he or other guests introduce will discomfort them.

The ten million audience who may be watching your work comprise a cross section of the public with all the inhibitions, prejudices, temptations and fears to which men and women are subject. The writer must never overlook this and should endeavour to avoid giving gratuitous offence.

Strangely, in a society that currently expresses itself very concerned about real life violence, the BBC survey on the 'boundaries of taste' showed only seven per cent were concerned about violence, against twenty per cent who were concerned about sex.

The values of the Victorians who made sex a dirty word but practised and tolerated such violence to children; to felons; to down and outs and other unfortunates, die hard indeed.

It is likely that any specific advice one gives to writers on what is, and what is not, permissible on television will be outmoded by the time you read this book. It is perhaps best, therefore to deal in general principles and point you in the direction of the BBC at Broadcasting House, London W1 1AA and the Independent Television Commission, 33 Foley Street, London W1P 7LB, from both of whom you can obtain copies of their codes if you find yourself in need of up to the minute guidance.

Children's programmes

Both the BBC and the ITV companies operate a 'watershed' policy, making 9 o'clock the pivotal point of the evening's viewing, before which time, in normal circumstances, all programmes should be suitable for child viewers. A writer scripting programmes intended for early evening screening is making problems for himself if he ignores this.

We have already touched on the writer's special responsibility with regard to children but it is important to recognise the essential differences between the things that distress children and those that distress adults. Such matters as family insecurity and marital infidelity which may be commonplace to adults can be deeply disturbing to children. The main danger points the writer needs to watch are:

Situations which threaten a child's emotional security, arising out of adoptions, desertions, cruelty in the home, unwanted children and friction between parents. All these things apply more in contemporary settings, because the child is better able to identify with the present-day world.

Portrayal of injury, illness or disablements, especially when used to sharpen a dramatic crisis (e.g. nightmares); and of embarrassing personal disabilities (e.g. stuttering).

Examples of weapons and other devices which the child could easily imitate. The BBC programme *Grange Hill*, for example, has always rejected storylines about child suicide. Few British children have access to guns or exotic poisons but knives are all too readily available and it is very easy to stretch a piece of wire across a path which may result in the victim breaking a leg or worse.

Bad habits in good characters. In programmes written for children don't have your hero smoking, drinking alcohol excessively or hitting people below the belt.

Scenes in which pleasure is taken in the infliction of pain or humiliation on others. Suffering by children, women or animals.

Situations in which children get the impression they are entering a world in which they can count on nothing as settled, reliable and kind, in which they must make their way at the expense of others, resorting to physical or mental violence whenever it will pay them.

Scenes which children might copy with resultant injury to themselves. It was reported that, some years ago, a number of small children imitated Batman and jumped out of windows.

Adult programmes

Violence for its own sake is not permissible. Neither the BBC nor ITC will permit stories that dwell upon the calculated infliction of pain. A hand fight or a shoot out are acceptable providing the physical confrontation is a natural development of the story. With fights, beware of depicting one person held by another while a third hits him. People must not be under restraint while being hit.

In a paper for the BBC 'Violence on Television', Robin Midgely, Head of Television Drama, Pebble Mill suggested there should be a distinction drawn between 'serious' and 'entertainment' drama and that if limits were set to the proportion of drama containing violence, it is to the 'entertainment' drama we should in the main look in our efforts at such containment.

This is a view which a great many people find acceptable. It is impossible for a serious dramatist to depict the everyday life and circumstances of men and women living at present with any degree of accuracy if all violence is censored out of contemporary writing. Truth in serious drama is no less important than truth in news reporting and the play often has currency long beyond yesterday's news.

A vital rule is the need to show the consequences of violence. The human body is frail and vulnerable. A man thrown through the windscreen of a car does not escape relatively unharmed. People can not be subjected to brutal beatings without real injuries. Truth in serious drama would not disguise this. All too often in 'entertainment' drama the consequences of such violence are ignored or trivialised.

Programmes like *Miami Vice* present the simple solution to a problem: to shoot. The Wyatt Committee, an internal committee set up to review BBC guidelines on violence, sensed that the easy ambience of violence portrayed in *Miami Vice* had a glamorising effect.

It is, however, all too easy to lay blame for the violence in society today at the door of television but research has shown that since the 60s, as crimes of violence have multiplied, violent acts per hour depicted on the television screen have been substantially reduced, a fact that points to other influences and causes, and perhaps not least the desperate anxiety of parents, teachers and politicians to off-load on to television the responsibility for the results of their own shortcomings and failures.

Be that as it may. The writer has to work in the climate as it exists and he can be sure his work will be rejected if he ignores it. Most television producers and directors keep to both the spirit and the letter of the codes.

Despite the protests, the climate concerning sex is changing, albeit slowly. The pendulum swings. After the permissive years of the late sixties and early seventies there was a positive reaction, but shocked as some viewers may have been at unwelcome words and scenes being projected into their living rooms there is little doubt that television has played a part in making the subject of sex less embarrassing for many people – particularly the young.

But it would be a mistake to imagine that Mrs Mary Whitehouse and the supporters of her association are a tiny minority of cranks and bigots. The truth, that every TV writer needs to recognise, is that Mrs Whitehouse does represent the views and feelings of many millions of people in this country. Television for them means family viewing. They are not necessarily puritans or of any particular religious persuasion. They do not have to be old, old-fashioned or stupid, for bad language, nudity and gratuitous sexual references to embarrass them. As with violence, however, it is trivialising that is most offensive. A serious, well written play that needs outspoken language to make an important and relevant point will provoke fewer objections than a dirty joke.

A writer should never overlook that fact that attitudes to sex and sexual morality are deeply ingrained from childhood. If you were brought up in a totally uninhibited atmosphere you may have little understanding of the embarrassment to others for whom the subject has always been taboo. You need to tread carefully if you wish to hold your audience.

I touched briefly on the problem of libel when talking about finding material for your stories but in this chapter on 'What Not To Write' it is worth adding an additional caution.

I once knew a writer who thought it a great joke to give the names of his friends to characters in his scripts. His friends thought it funny too – at first. Soon they got fed up with people they worked with and acquaintances making further jokes at their expense or assuming the antics and behaviour of the character in the script was actually a biographical episode. Happily the writer's friends were not litigious and he realised the risk he'd been running before it was too late.

But names you dream up can also be dangerous. Way back in 1909 there was a famous libel case that illustrates the point. A Sunday newspaper published an amusing article about the behaviour of an Englishman who crossed the Channel to attend a motor festival at Dieppe. The writer gave his character the unlikely name Artemus Jones. In a light hearted way the article claimed that a woman had recognised Artemus Jones 'with a woman who is not his wife and must be, you know, the other thing!'. 'Who would suppose by his goings on he was a churchwarden in Peckham?'. The piece went on to continue the story in the same light hearted vein.

Now it happened that there was a gentleman named Artemus Jones. He wasn't a churchwarden and he didn't live in Peckham; he wasn't married and he had taken no part in the Dieppe Festival; but witnesses stated they had referred the story to him. The jury awarded him damages and the High Court upheld the judgement.

The moral is don't use unusual names. Common every day names shared by hundreds of people are far safest. And don't be more specific about any detail than is absolutely essential to your story.

Defamation need not only be in dialogue. It can be visual. If your housewife character complains that her sewing machine is constantly breaking down, and if we see a sewing machine, the shape of which identifies it as a particular make, the manufacturer could get very upset – although that is the problem of the producer rather than the writer since writers are not responsible for props unless the script stipulates them by name.

Only use dead telephone numbers. If you use your own number you may get people ringing to see if the character in your story answers the phone. If you use any number you think up it could be worse as some Smart Alec starts phoning there to the annoyance of the innocent telephone subscriber.

British Telecom issue special numbers to cover this situation and you can contact them by phone on 020 7604 3940 for a number you can safely use.

If the registration number of a motor car is important to your story you should write to the Licensing Department, DVLC, Swansea SA99 1AR and ask for a number you can use. It is not safe to just think up a number. Someone may have it and find themselves identified with the driver of the car in your story and the same thing applies if you try to play safe and use your own car number. One cautionary tale has it that a writer once used his own car number in a story about a child molester and, as a result, found himself attacked in the street by angry mothers.

Race relations and writing of minority groups are matters where the writer needs to be socially conscious to avoid not only the penalties of law but more importantly, giving unintentional offence. For many years now the black members of Equity have urged television companies and writers to give them greater work opportunities portraying them in present day society, not simply as busmen, station porters and other labouring workers but also reflecting their involvement in business, commerce and professional life. Most television writers today see this as a desirable and important contribution that they can make towards racial harmony but a writer who has not close experience of the life, attitudes and customs of the different immigrant communities should not attempt to write about them without proper research.

Most American television series these days include different ethnic characters because the American sponsors do not want to lose the sale of a single bar of soap. Except for a few 'enrichment stations' all American television is commercial, and many complete programmes are sponsored. This means a whole one hour drama or entertainment slot is brought to you by courtesy of a manufacturer, and he is determined not to offend anyone, while at the same time pandering to everybody in every way possible. It is even said that one writer was required to remove the line 'Step on the Gas' from a script sponsored by an Electricity Company.

Happily in this country although we now have TV programmes

sponsored by manufacturers we do not yet suffer such commercial interference. It can have a disastrous effect on creativity.

Finally, the most important of the 'What not to writes'. Don't write a letter to your employer giving him notice to terminate your job on the strength of your hope to become a television writer – nor in a flush of excitement the day after your first script is screened. Selling one script – even two or three – will not keep you for the rest of your life and there are a lot of bills to pay between the day you get the money for that first script and the time you are sufficiently well established to be able to afford even basic necessities on your income from scripting.

Lord Goodman once said, 'One of the least impressive liberties is the liberty to starve. This particular liberty is freely accorded to authors.'

It was not a liberty of which I cared to avail myself. I worked evenings, weekends and holidays for over two years before I got my first script accepted, then I worked evenings, weekends and holidays for another eighteen months and did not give up my regular job until I had secured a contract from a television company that promised, for the next year, more than twice what I was earning at my day job. Only then did I throw away my security.

A lot of writers have earned a good living in television and a lot of writers have earned a lot of money for a short time only to find, for whatever reason, they are unable to get new commissions or sell work sufficiently often to provide adequate income to support themselves and their families. Some have been forced to sell their houses and cars and take whatever job they could get.

Many of the most successful and prudent television writers I know do not put all their eggs in one basket. They diversify – writing books, short stories, stage plays, radio plays and magazine articles. If they are also actors they remain available to accept acting parts. Some who are teachers do some part-time teaching, while lecturers often continue to do a couple of days a week at college. The wise take the precaution of ensuring they have some additional string to their bow.

Writers always have to make sacrifices of one sort or another to achieve success but I am sure it is very hard to think creatively about the script one is trying to write with the bailiff banging at the door.

16. So start the clock

It is not only in the scenes of a writer's television play that marriages get broken up. It can happen all too easily in the writing of the script. If you are living with someone it is important that they should be an understanding partner – or at least you should have an understanding with your partner. Writing is a lonely, selfish occupation. It shuts out everyone else and the loneliness has to be endured mostly by those closest to you. You will be fully occupied playing God, creating your own world and deciding the destinies of the folk who inhabit it; loving or hating them; sharing the intensity of their suffering or pleasures and finally deciding for each whether their lives shall be heaven or hell and whether they should live or die. There is no room in that world for intruders. Others may enter and share it only when the work of creation is done.

Writing for television as a full time freelance writer is not so much a job, it is more a way of life. Achievement calls for sacrifice. To succeed you have to be willing to give up most of your other interests and pursuits. Very few writers I know can run it as a nine to five business, shutting shop on Friday night and not giving it a thought again until Monday. The big illusion of those who think enviously of the way of life of a self employed writer is to imagine that you work only when you are in the mood and take time off whenever you wish – like a small boy who once lived next door to me and told his mother that he intended to be a writer when he grew up because he thought it a lovely life taking the dog for walks when everyone else was at work.

For a scriptwriter it isn't like that. As Burton Rascoe said, 'What no wife of a writer can ever understand is that a writer is working when he is staring out of the window.' – or taking the dog for a walk. And what only another writer understands is that conversation – be it ever so short or trivial – can fracture a train of thought and leave the writer struggling to retrieve an idea like a man clutching to recapture a balloon floating away in a fog.

When you have a commission to write a script you have a deadline to meet. The production team are waiting on you and if the words

173

and ideas don't come to mind as fast as necessary you have no choice but to work on, sleeping only long enough to disperse the weariness to make it possible to go on again until the script is finished. I knew one writer who, when he was writing, kept a camp-bed in his office. He shut himself in and chopped his week into segments of eight hours. He wrote for eight hours, then slept for eight hours, then wrote again for eight hours and went on regardless of day or night until the script was completed. Such a schedule wouldn't suit everyone. Some writers I know get up around four in the morning. Others go regularly through the night. This is the kind of pattern of life for most of us when under pressure.

And if you imagine the heat is off when you have no work commissioned and no delivery date to meet you couldn't be more wrong. The pressure then is to find a new ideas and write a new script and sell it.

'A freelance writer has to be a self-starter. There is no discipline beyond his own training and need for money', wrote Paddy Chayefsky in the foreword of his book of television plays.

Need for money? If you have a full time job the immediate need for money is possibly not the driving force. As I said earlier, we all start as amateurs and write because we enjoy it and sometimes because we hope to escape from some uncongenial or unsuitable occupation to spend our working lives doing something we find more satisfying. Or maybe you are looking for fame and fortune. If you really have the talent and determination you could make it. Whatever the reason, getting started requires a single minded dedication; more particularly if you are tied up working all day for your living.

Did someone say, they don't have time? If there is one thing that really makes writers furious it is the person who says, 'I'd love to write if only I had the time'.

None of us have the time unless we give up other interests, neglect our family and friends; refuse most social invitations and regard weekends and holidays as ordinary work days. The only question is whether the desire to write is stronger than the desire to play games, take weekend breaks, go for drinks with friends, visit relatives – even play with your kids.

If I am making script writing sound tough, it is – at times. It is also, for the writer, very enjoyable – at times. You get great pleasure seeing the people you have created materialising on the screen, displaying the emotions you have demanded and saying words you have put into their mouths. And when you see a truly talented actor or actress playing a role that you have written, it can really be very thrilling.

And if, as frequently happens, the critics give the actor or actress all the credit for 'your' success, you can be sure they won't overlook your disasters. Screenwriter William Goldman whose credits include among other such outstanding films as *Butch Cassidy and The Sundance Kid* and *All The President's Men* had this to say in his book *Adventures in the Screen Trade* published by Macdonald. 'You get a rave and the writer is not mentioned but you get top billing in a pan. You're the one who screwed it up.'

But if you really want to write scripts none of this will deter you. Nor should it. If you are successful it will possibly take you a few years to get established so you should start right away. Don't wait for ideal conditions. A window that looks out on a brick wall is better for a writer than a panoramic view. I think it was Somerset Maugham who advised a young writer seeking advice to find himself a room with a window overlooking the Mediterranean and then turn the desk so that he faced the wall. It was good advice. Some years ago I found what seemed to me the perfect setting to write – a house with a quiet wooded garden. Then I sat at my desk with a bird identification book and binoculars at hand and was shortly compelled to take Maugham's advice and turn the desk to face the wall.

A writer needs to shut out all distractions – although it is not absolutely essential for you to go quite so far as to follow the advice of Pundit Nehru who said, 'All my major works have been written in prison. I would recommend prison to aspiring writers.'

As a beginner write, write, write and enjoy it, because when you are a professional and your services are in demand you will sometimes find yourself writing scripts that you don't much care about and angrily rewriting scenes and scripts that you really do. But you will have a fascinating life meeting interesting actors, actresses and directors. You may make a lot of money but have little time to spend it on holidays or other interests.

All too often you are likely to find yourself stuck at your desk writing all day and working on through the night into the early hours of the next morning.

But as you struggle to keep awake; shiver at the dawn and wonder why the hell you are doing it you'll be able to console yourself, as I do, with the thought that it's a whole lot better than work.

Situation comedy

Father Ted

Graham Linehan and Arthur Mathews

In comedy writing, the bounds of acceptability have been stretched far beyond anything thought possible a few years ago. Even the sacred cow of religion is less sacrosanct than it was – and perhaps I could have put that better.

Recalling former series, *Oh Brother* (set in a monastery), *All Gas and Gaiters* (the Church of England) and *The Vicar of Dibley* updating to the emergence of female clergy, it is clear that Faith now finds itself in the comedy firing line. Of all such shows, however, *Father Ted* has received the greatest audience appreciation and critical acclaim. The apparent mockery usually implies a degree of affection and the strengths of religions can surely be measured by the degree of laughter they can absorb – reference *The Canterbury Tales*.

The *Father Ted* series, a Hat Trick Production for Channel Four, was sadly curtailed by the untimely death of its eponymous star Dermot Morgan and we are grateful to the writers, Graham Linehan and Arthur Mathews; Mary Bell, Executive Producer, Hat Trick Productions Ltd; and Channel Four Television, for permission to reproduce this excerpt.

---

*Some slight adjustment to the original layout has been made to all the scripts in the Appendix, in order to save space.

ENTERTAINING FATHER STONE

<u>SCENE 14 INT. EVENING 1</u>

<u>SET BEDROOM</u>

<u>STUDIO</u>

(TED AND DOUGAL ARE IN THEIR BEDS, STARING AT THE CEILING.)

DOUGAL:

I can't take much more of this, Ted.

TED:

I know, I know . . .

DOUGAL:

Six years. You'd think that by now he'd have got the message. Do you remember that time, Ted, when we knew he was coming and we pretended to be in Rome.

TED:

God, yeah. That was amazing. Anyone else would go, 'fair enough', and just not turn up. God . . . five days in the attic. No food, no water . . . rats everywhere. If only we'd thought of it this year.

DOUGAL:

How'd you meet him in the first place?

TED:

He was introduced to me by Father Jim Dougan. We were at a conference – Dougan came up and said, this is Father Stone, and ran out of the building. Just ran straight out of the building. So we started talking . . . well, I started talking. You know the way he is. And just to break the silence I invited him to stay . . . just for something to say, you know? The next day, the next <u>day</u>, he arrived on the island. Oh God, if he'd only say something! But he just sits there! I mean what does he get out of it!

DOUGAL:

Well, I hope he's gone before your birthday party, anyway.

TED:

Oh, he'll be gone long before then. What is it, three weeks away?

<u>SCENE 15 INT. NIGHT 2</u>

<u>SET PAROCHIAL HOUSE</u>

<u>STUDIO (3 WEEKS LATER)</u>

WE SEE FATHER STONE SITTING IN WHAT IS BY NOW HIS USUAL CHAIR, WEARING A PARTY HAT . . .

GRANT UNTO HIM ETERNAL REST

<u>SCENE 6 INT. NIGHT 1</u>
(INCORPS. 7)

<u>SET CRYPT</u>

<u>STUDIO</u>

TED ENTERS THE ROOM WITH A RUCKSACK AND A PILE OF CANDLES.
HE HAS A BANDAGE OVER HIS EYE.

DOUGAL:
Oh, how's your head, Ted?

TED:
Not too bad. It's true what they say though, about these career
women, they're very aggressive.

DOUGAL:
Yes, she was very agressive wasn't she Ted?

TED:
Oh, the language out of her! You wouldn't hear that from a docker.

DOUGAL:
Ah, you would Ted. They use very bad language.

TED:
Effing this, and effing that.

DOUGAL:
It was worse than that, Ted. She was saying fu . .

TED:
Dougal! But anyway, who would have thought Father Jack had half
a million pounds?

DOUGAL:
And he never said a word about it.

TED:
. . . there it was, lying in a bank account all these years . . .

DOUGAL:
How did he get it all in the first place?

TED:
Well as I understand it, he was just an astute saver. He tried to
avoid giving money to charity, he wouldn't wear trousers during the
summer – that obviously saved a couple of bob on wear and tear –
all sorts of little savings here and there all over the place. It all adds
up you know.

TED:

(ABSENTLY) I suppose, we only really knew him in his twilight years. But I think we saw the best of him. A really lovely man, a true Knight of the Church . . . gentle, lovely sense of humour, patient, good natured . . .

DOUGAL:

Sorry, Ted, who's this now?

TED:

(PAUSE) Who do you think I'd be talking about at this particular moment Dougal?

DOUGAL:

I'm not sure. I didn't catch the start.

TED:

Jack, of course!

DOUGAL:

Oh, right. Yes.

TED:

A great priest.

SCENE 7B INT. NIGHT 1

SET CRYPT

STUDIO

DOUGAL:

First priest to denounce the Beatles.

TED:

That's right.

DOUGAL:

He could see what they were up to.

TED:

And he loved children, of course.

DOUGAL:

Oh he did, yes.

TED:

(PAUSE) They were terrified of him, though.

Comedy sketches

Gerald Kelsey

Tramps have long been favourite characters for comedy writers switching, as many tramps do, from craven humility to aggressive arrogance as they plead, cheat or bully a cup of tea and a wad out of gullible or soft-hearted strangers. This sketch I wrote as a comedy scene for part of a drama script.

EXT: BUSY STREET   DAY

A tramp loiters outside a large store trying for a handout from shoppers. A BMW pulls into the kerb and parks tight against the car in front. An expensively dressed woman gets out and starts towards the shop. The tramp intercepts her.

TRAMP:
(Holding out a begging hand)

Can you spare a quid or two lady for . . .

The woman ignores him and goes on her way.
The tramp looks after her mouthing oaths.
He is joined by a second tramp.

2nd TRAMP:

No luck?

1st TRAMP:

Miserable cow. I hope she wins the lottery.

2nd TRAMP:

Eh?

1st TRAMP:

And finds she's lost her ticket.

They wander off together.

ANOTHER ANGLE

The woman loaded with parcels is returning. She puts them in the boot and gets into the car.

ANOTHER ANGLE

The 1st tramp approaches from rear of car. As he reaches it the reversing light comes up as the woman backs clear of the car in front . . . The tramp leaps in the road, gives the rear of the car a resounding kick, lets out a loud yell and falls into the road. The woman stops, leaps out and runs to rear.

1st TRAMP:

Oh me leg . . . Oh, oh oh!

WOMAN:

I'm sorry. Are you hurt badly. I didn't see you.

2nd TRAMP (ARRIVING):

I saw that. Reckless driving, that's what that was. Someone call an ambulance.

1st TRAMP:

No need for an ambulance. Don't worry, lady, I'll be all right.

2nd TRAMP:

You can't be sure. If he dies you could be done for manslaughter.

WOMAN:

Oh dear. You'd better get a check up with your doctor.

2nd TRAMP:

His doctor? He won't get an appointment for a week. He'll have to go private. Get him in your car. We'll take him to that clinic round the corner where the Arabs go.

1st TRAMP:

No, I don't want to bother the lady. I'll just limp home. I'd take a taxi if I had the money.

WOMAN (OPENING HER BAG):

How far is it? Would ten pounds cover it?

1st TRAMP:

Ten? Oh tah yes.

TAKES MONEY

2nd TRAMP:

What about me?

WOMAN:

You? You weren't involved.

2nd TRAMP:

I saw it all. I'm suffering from shock. Trauma, they calls it. Very nasty. I need compensation.

FX: Siren of approaching ambulance.

WOMAN:

Oh thank heavens. Here comes the ambulance.

1st TRAMP (RECOVERING):

Oh, shame to have called them out. I feel better now.

2nd TRAMP:

He looks better too. Come on, mate. I'll see you home. Good day, Lady. THEY HURRY OFF.

Comedy sketches

Hale and Pace

Comedy is a broad church. The previous example is of a 'naturalistic-it-can-happen' nature. The following is positively surrealistic. It is from a Hale and Pace show. It owes its humour to the absurd, the impossible, the ridiculous but the funny. We are indebted to Gareth Hale and Norman Pace for permission to reproduce this example.

TYRE OUT

SC. 1 EXT. TYRE AND EXHAUST CENTRE

A man in a Kwik Fit type uniform walks outside the garage with an old tyre in his hand.

MAN 1:
Retread.

MAN 2:
No it's knackered, sling it on the scrap heap.

MAN 1 THROWS THE TYRE OUT AND WALKS INSIDE. WE SEE THE TYRE ROLLING ALONG OUTSIDE, IT WOBBLES AND THEN IT STOPS AND LOOKS AROUND. MAN 1 COMES OUT THE BACK, THE TYRE FALLS OVER AND PLAYS DEAD. WHEN THE MAN WALKS BACK IN, THE TYRE JUMPS UP, BOUNCES ON THE SPOT AND ROLLS OFF INTO THE BIG WIDE WORLD.

SC. 2 EXT. STREET

THE TYRE ROLLS ALONG DOWN THE STREET. WE SEE A BLIND MAN STANDING AT A PELICAN CROSSING. THE TYRE STOPS AND ROLLS OUT OF SHOT. WE CUT TO THE BLIND MAN BEING LED ACROSS THE ROAD BY THE TYRE.

SC. 3 EXT. STREET

AN OLD LADY IS BEING MUGGED. THE TYRE NOTICES THIS AS HE ROLLS ALONG THE STREET. HE ACCELERATES OUT OF THE SHOT, BOUNCES ON THE KERB, WE HAVE A SHOT OF THE TYRE ROTATING END OVER END THROUGH THE AIR. THE TYRE LASSO'S THE MUGGER SO HIS ARMS CANNOT MOVE. THE OLD LADY RUNS AWAY. THE MUGGER THROWS THE TYRE OFF. OFF IT GOES AGAIN ON ITS JOURNEY.

SC. 4 EXT. STREET

WE SEE A LITTLE BOY SITTING ON THE KERB CRYING. THE TYRE SEES HIM AND ROLLS UP TO HIM. HE NUDGES THE LITTLE BOY. THE LITTLE BOY BECOMES INTERESTED IN THE TYRE. HE STARTS TO ROLL THE TYRE BACK AND FORTH, THEN HE STARTS TO ROLL THE TYRE DOWN THE STREET, FASTER AND FASTER. OH DEAR, THERE IS A HILL.

THE MUSIC BECOMES VERY DRAMATIC, THE TYRE ROLLS OUT OF THE BOY'S CONTROL AND DOWN THE HILL. IT GETS FASTER AND FASTER. A POSTMAN DIVES OUT OF THE WAY, HIS LETTERS FLY EVERYWHERE. A MOTHER SNATCHES THE TODDLER FROM THE PATH OF THE TYRE.

THE TYRE RACES PAST A POLICEMAN. THE POLICEMAN SEES IT'S OUT OF CONTROL. HE SPEAKS INTO HIS WALKIE TALKIE AND GETS IN HIS POLICE CAR.

WE SEE A SHOT OF THE POLICE CAR CHASING THE TYRE DOWN A BUSY STREET. WE SEE THIS FROM THE P.O.V. OF THE POLICE CAR. THE TYRE APPROACHES A STATIONARY CAR AT THE TRAFFIC LIGHTS. THE TYRE ROLLS OVER THE TOP OF THE CAR LEAVING TYRE MARKS ON THE TOP OF THE CAR. THE COP CAR HAS TO SWERVE TO AVOID RUNNING INTO THE CAR IN FRONT.

THE TYRE GOES ACROSS THE BUSY CROSSROAD, MISSING A CAR COMING THE OTHER WAY BY INCHES IN THE CLASSIC MANNER OF CAR CHASES IN MOVIES. THE COP CAR TRIES TO RUN THE TYRE OFF THE ROAD, PULLING ALONGSIDE TRYING TO BUMP IT. THE TYRE TURNS RIGHT, THE COP CAR SCREECHES TO A HALT AND HAS TO REVERSE. AS THE COP CAR TURNS RIGHT WHERE THE TYRE HAS GONE WE SEE A SIGN SAYING 'BREAKER'S YARD'.

SC. 5 EXT. BREAKER'S YARD

THE COP CAR SCREECHES TO A HALT IN THE BREAKER'S YARD. THE POLICEMAN AND HIS MATE RUN OUT OF THE CAR. THEIR FACES SAY 'OH NO'. FROM THEIR P.O.V. WE SEE THOUSANDS OF TYRES STACKED UP. OUR LITTLE FRIEND THE TYRE POKES HIS HEAD OUT FROM BEHIND A STACK OF OTHER TYRES.

THE POLICEMEN EXIT.

OUR TYRE ROLLS OUT WITH A WHITE-RIMMED TYRE AND TWO SMALLER TYRES.

'GREAT ESCAPE' MUSIC PLAYS OVER THE TOP.

A dissection.

Note that this is almost entirely visual with no more than brief establishing dialogue.

In scene one the tyre acquires a life of its own. Ridiculous.

In scene two, the tyre displays a social conscience. What? A tyre?

In three, it displays civic responsibility. Now this is truly daft. What will happen next? We are beginning to like and laugh at this tyre. And so on.

The police give chase and finish up looking for a pebble on a beach. But when they have gone, our tyre shows himself to be a jack-the-lad with a little blonde lady tyre and two kid tyres. All visual and deriving from a long tradition of nonsense humour.

ROCKY PANTALOON

SC. 1 FOOTAGE

1930s NEW YORK, TIN PAN ALLEY, BACK STREETS ETC.

CUT TO: OPENING TITLES

'SOMEBODY UP THERE WEARS BIG TROUSERS' STARRING: JAMES CAGNEY AS ROCKY PANTALOON AND EAMONN O'IRISHMAN AS EVERYBODY ELSE.

SC. 2 INT. JAIL

AN IRISH COPPER (GARETH) UNLOCKS A CELL AND POKES A SLUMBERING DRUNK WITH HIS TRUNCHEON.

COPPER:
Come on, wake up you no good drunken bum.

HE PICKS THE DRUNK UP BY THE COLLAR. IT'S ROCKY PANTALOON. 15 EMPTY WHISKEY BOTTLES FALL OUT OF ROCKY'S COAT. CLOSE UP OF ROCKY BEING SHAKEN. WE HEAR MORE BOTTLES FALLING OUT OF HIS ATTIRE.

COPPER:
You two bit no good tramp.

CUT WIDE TO SEE A LARGE PILE OF BOTTLES SURROUNDING ROCKY AND THE COP.

COPPER:
Why if I had half a mind I would ram this night stick with great force clean up your . . . . . as I live and breathe, didn't you used to be Rocky Pantaloon, boxing champeen of the whole wide world?

SC. 3 INT. BOXING RING

CLOSE-UP OF ROCKY'S FACE. MIX THROUGH TO A SHOT OF A BELL AT THE START OF A ROUND.

OLD FOOTAGE OF BOXERS PUNCHING EACH OTHER.

SHOT OF A WIDE BOARD SAYING 'ROUND TWO'.

WE HEAR V.O. OF CROWD.

VOICE:
Get him with the old 'one two' Rocky.

WE SEE NORMAN AS ROCKY. HE SITS IN HIS CORNER, A SECOND WIPES HIS FACE WITH A WET FLANNEL.

4. INT. JAIL

CUT BACK TO ROCKY IN JAIL. A BUCKET OF WATER IS THROWN OVER HIS FACE. WE CUT TO SHOW THE POLICEMAN HAS THROWN IT. ROCKY JUMPS TO HIS FEET AND STARTS BEATING THE SHIT OUT OF A PILLOW. FEATHERS FLY EVERYWHERE.

ROCKY:
Come on you sap or I'll punch your lights out.

THE COP CALMS HIM DOWN.

COPPER:
Rocky, calm down.

ROCKY:
(CONFUSED) Where am I? Who are you? Who am I? Why do fools fall in love? What's it all about, Alfie?

COPPER:
(HITTING ROCKY WITH HIS TRUNCHEON)
It's all right Rocky, it's just the booze rotting your brain.

ROCKY:
Oh yeah, the booze that's it. I remember, it's all coming back to me now. I was boxing champeen of the world. I had it all, money, flash cars, dames and the biggest pair of pantaloons west of the Ganges.

COPPER:
So tell me for the sake of the plot – where did it all go wrong?

ROCKY:
Well it was 1928 in New York City when things started to go all wavy . . . .

THE PICTURE GOES ALL WAVY (FLASH BACK)

FLASH-BACK

SC 5. EXT. SPEAKEASY

ROCKY APPEARS WITH TWO CHORUS GIRLS ON HIS ARMS. A PRESS PHOTOGRAPHER WITH A PRESS CARD IN THE BRIM OF HIS HAT STOPS THEM.

PRESS PHOTOGRAPHER:
Just one picture, Mr Pantaloon.

PHOTOGRAPHER'S BULB FLASHES AS ROCKY POSES. ALL THREE FACES TURN BLACK WITH THE FLASH.

HE DECKS THE PHOTOGRAPHER.

Here we have another example which depends upon a degree of recollective sophistication of the part of the audience who can remember all of the soon-to-be cliché-ridden films of the 1940s and earlier. It harks back to *On The Waterfront* ('Charlie I coulda bin a contender') and to many James Cagney pictures and to the countless journeys into the situation of comedian, boxer, journalist who hits the skids via the bottle. But its absurdity comes from the 'pantaloons'. Simply, it is a send-up of a genre. That jarring off-note of the pantaloons makes it funny and not tragic.

Comedy sketches

Ken Rock

We have to thank comedy writer Ken Rock for the following examples of very short sketches for which there is a steady demand from professional comedians who use up their material at a rate of knots. These all have been sold to and used by top artists.

RUSS ABBOT SHOW

A BURGLAR IS REMOVING A RADIO FROM A CAR.

V.O. This man can remove your car radio in less than sixty seconds.

CUT TO CAR MECHANIC LOOKING PUZZLED AS HE TRIES TO RE-FIT THE RADIO.

V.O. So why does it take this man – more than seven hours to put it back again!?

RUSS ABBOT SHOW

SET: A LOUNGE   INT

1ST PERSON: I've given up my job. I'm writing full time now.

2ND PERSON: Have you sold anything?

1ST PERSON: Yes, my TV, video, stereo, table, chairs, furniture . . .

PULL BACK TO SHOW THEY ARE SITTING ON TWO
WOODEN BOXES AND THE ROOM IS COMPLETELY EMPTY.

DAVE ALLEN AT LARGE

SET: A CONFESSION BOX   INT

CLOSE-UP OF A MAN SITTING IN A CONFESSION BOX.

MAN: Bless me Father for I have sinned.

PULL BACK TO THE OTHER SIDE OF THE CONFESSION
BOX WHICH IS EMPTY EXCEPT FOR A TELEPHONE
ANSWERING MACHINE.

VOICE: I'm sorry I am unable to take your call at the moment but
if you would like to leave your name and number . . .

NAKED VIDEO

SET: A CAR INTERIOR

A COUPLE ARE EMBRACING EACH OTHER IN THE FRONT
OF THE CAR.

MAN: (SIGHS) Fiona . . .

WOMAN: Yes, my love?

MAN: Fancy getting in the back?

WOMAN: What for?

MAN: You know what for.

WOMAN: (SIGHS) Why do I have to do this every night?

MAN: You know why . . . because there's more room in the back.

WOMAN: Tsk! Alright then. (SHE CLIMBS OVER INTO THE
BACK SEAT AND LIES DOWN.) Will you promise me something,
Simon?

THE MAN MOVES POSITION AS IF TO JOIN HER BUT
INSTEAD STRETCHES OUT LIKE HER ON THE FRONT SEAT.

187

MAN: What's that my darling?

WOMAN: (ANGRILY) Go and put our names on the
housing list tomorrow. It's been six months now since our wedding!

THE MAN MUMBLES.

CUT TO OUTSIDE OF CAR WHICH HAS WHITE WEDDING
RIBBONS TIED ROUND THE BONNET.

DIETER & CARY SHOW
(German TV)

SET: A LOUNGE   INT

A WORKMAN IS MAKING SOME REPAIRS. HE IS ABOUT TO
HAMMER A NAIL INTO A WALL.

WORKMAN: (LOOKS IN HIS TOOLBAG) Oh no!

OWNER: What's wrong?

WORKMAN: I've left my hammer behind at the depot.

OWNER: Can't you go and fetch it?

WORKMAN: No, it's too far away. Can I use your telephone?

OWNER: Certainly. Help yourself.

WORKMAN PICKS UP THE TELEPHONE RECEIVER AND
HAMMERS THE NAIL INTO THE WALL WITH IT.

Series drama

Heartbeat

Excerpt from 'Baby Love' by Anthony Read

This drama series produced by Yorkshire Television is one of the most successful series on television – which is not, perhaps, surprising since it incorporates in the one programme two of the most popular TV themes, Docs and Cops. For good measure it also includes light comedy scenes, always relevant to the plot, with the local 'Artful Dodger' Claude Greengrass, played by Bill Maynard.

The excerpt we include is written by Anthony Read, a writer with considerable experience of popular drama series.

Note particularly how he has indicated which day, and what times of day, the events in the scene take place. Where the time element is crucial to the story, as it often is in police and mystery stories, it is important that the writer makes this clear.

Our thanks are due to Yorkshire Television for permission to reproduce this excerpt.

---

14. INT. MOORSIDE LODGE, LOUNGE   TIME: 10.10 DAY 2

PAULA IS SLUMPED IN AN ARMCHAIR, READING A MAGAZINE AND LISTENING TO POP MUSIC ON THE RADIO.

EDIE HOLLERNSHAW, A PLAIN LITTLE WOMAN IN HER FORTIES, IS CLEANING THE ROOM, SINGING ALONG HAPPILY. SHE STOPS AS BRADLEY COMES IN.

BRADLEY: Morning.

PAULA: Morning, constable.

BRADLEY: Hello, Edie. I didn't know you worked here.

EDIE: Oh, aye. I started six month since. After me dad died. Just mornings, you know.

BRADLEY: Like it?

EDIE: Oh, I do. It's better nor sittin' in that empty house. Have you come about our pervert, Mr Bradley?

BRADLEY: We don't know if he is one yet, Edie.

EDIE: Course he is. Stands to reason. There's nowt worth robbing here.

BRADLEY: Well, maybe. I don't suppose you've seen anybody hanging about these last few days?

EDIE: No.

BRADLEY: How about you, Paula?

PAULA SHAKES HER HEAD.

PAULA: Think he'll come back?

BRADLEY: You never know.

PAULA: You could come and give us some protection . . .

BRADLEY: Yeh, we'll have to see what we can do.

BRADLEY LAUGHS. EDIE RAISES HER EYES, A BIT SHOCKED AT PAULA'S FORWARDNESS. DEBBIE COMES IN, CARRYING HER BABY.

PAULA: Oh, hi, Debs.

EDIE: Hallo, love. And how's young Robert this morning?

DEBBIE: He's fine, thanks, Edie.

EDIE: Let's have a look at him, then. Aaah, in't he sweet?

SHE GAZES FONDLY AT THE BABY.

Oh, he's lovely . . . lovely . . . Ee, I don't know how you can bear to part wi' him . . . It'd break my heart.

DEBBIE HOLDS THE BABY TIGHTLY TO HER. HER FACE CRUMPLES, AND SHE DASHES FROM THE ROOM.

EDIE: Oh, dear – I've put my foot in it, haven't I?

30. INT. POST OFFICE   TIME: 12.25 DAY 3

AT THE COUNTER, MARY IS TALKING TO BLAKETON AND GLADYS.

GLADYS: You're not safe anywhere, these days. I mean, a mother and baby home, of all places . . .

MARY: I never even knew there was a home up there.

BLAKETON: That's the whole point of those places. They're supposed to be discreet.

MARY: So the girls can hide their shame, d'you mean? Shut them away and sweep everything under the carpet?

HAZEL COMES IN, AND STOPS TO LOOK AT THE CARDS OR WHATEVER, ON DISPLAY INSIDE THE DOOR.

GLADYS: It's their parents I feel sorry for.

MARY: Don't you think they should be taking care of their own daughters? What would you do, Oscar, if you had a daughter who got into trouble?

BLAKETON: Thankfully, I've only got a son. But I imagine it could be a very difficult decision.

GLADYS: Of course, the chaps who got them into trouble should be made to marry them.

MARY: If they can.

GLADYS: Yes. Mind you, marriage isn't always a bed of roses . . .

SHE SIGNALS WITH HER EYES TOWARDS HAZEL, WHO IS MOVING TOWARDS THE POST OFFICE COUNTER. MARY NODS KNOWINGLY.

BLAKETON: Will you see to Mrs Mansfield, Gladys?

GLADYS SMILES AND MOVES TO THE POST OFFICE COUNTER.

GLADYS: Hello, Hazel, love. Come to pick up your family allowance, have you?

HAZEL: Yes, please, Gladys.

SHE HANDS OVER HER ALLOWANCE BOOK.

GLADYS: And how's little Peter?

HAZEL: He's a bit better today, thanks. I've actually got him off to sleep in his pram.

31. EXT. AIDENSFIELD STREET   TIME: 12.30   DAY 3

GREENGRASS'S LORRY IS PARKED A LITTLE WAY DOWN THE STREET. MAGGIE'S LAND ROVER PULLS UP OUTSIDE THE POST OFFICE. MAGGIE GETS OUT.

32. INT. POST OFFICE   TIME: 12.31   DAY 3

HAZEL IS PUTTING HER CASH AND ALLOWANCE BOOK IN HER HANDBAG. MARY IS STILL WITH BLAKETON.

MARY: I'm always telling our Gina it's time she got married and settled down. She'd make somebody a lovely wife.

BLAKETON: Oh, yes? Have you got anybody particular in mind?

MARY: I might have. But you wouldn't expect me to tell you, would you?

MAGGIE ENTERS, BREEZILY.

MAGGIE: Morning, everybody.

BLAKETON: Morning, Maggie.

MAGGIE LOOKS AT HAZEL IN SURPRISE.

MAGGIE: Hello, Hazel. Where's Peter?

HAZEL: He's in his pram, asleep, thank goodness.

MAGGIE: No. No he isn't. I just looked.

THERE IS A MOMENT'S STUNNED SILENCE. THEN HAZEL DASHES FOR THE DOOR, WITH MAGGIE CLOSE BEHIND HER.

33. EXT. POST OFFICE   TIME: 12.32   DAY 3

AS BEFORE. BUT GREENGRASS'S LORRY IS NO LONGER THERE.

HAZEL COMES OUT OF THE DOOR. SHE LOOKS FRANTICALLY INTO THE PRAM. IT IS EMPTY.

HAZEL: My baby! Somebody's stolen my baby!!!

END OF PART 1

37. INT. MANSFIELDS' HOUSE   TIME: 13.15   DAY 3

MAGGIE IS WITH HAZEL, WHO SITS HUNCHED ON THE SETTEE, CLUTCHING A CHILD'S CUDDLY TOY AND STARING AT THE EMPTY PLAYPEN.

HAZEL: It's my fault, Maggie. All my fault. It's a judgement on me.

MAGGIE: Hazel, you mustn't say that.

HAZEL: I've been horrible to him just lately. I've found myself wishing we'd never had him . . .

MAGGIE: Do you think you're the only mother who's ever thought that?

HAZEL: It's like wishing him dead.

MAGGIE: No. No, it isn't.

HAZEL: And now I'm going to be punished . . . I'm never going to see him again, am I? Never . . .

AND SHE BREAKS DOWN AGAIN.

39. INT. POLICE HOUSE   TIME: 13.25   DAY 3

BRADLEY JUMPS TO HIS FEET AS CRADDOCK STEAMS IN, WITH BELLAMY TRAILING BEHIND.

BELLAMY: Hey up, Mike. Cavalry's here!

CRADDOCK: That'll be quite enough of that, thank you, Bellamy.

BELLAMY: Sorry, sarge . . .

CRADDOCK: Now then, Bradley. Any new developments?

BRADLEY: No, sarge. I've looked round the whole village and I can't see hide nor hair of any baby.

CRADDOCK: Hmmm. How old did you say this child was?

BRADLEY: About thirteen months.

CRADDOCK: Couldn't have wandered off on his own, then. You'd better fill me in on the exact details, before I go and talk to the mother.

BELLAMY: What d'you want us to do, sarge?

CRADDOCK: You can make a start on house-to-house inquiries. Knock on every door, see if anybody knows anything, if anybody saw anything. Can I trust you to do that without getting distracted?

40. INT. MANSFIELDS' HOUSE   TIME: 13.45 DAY 3

HAZEL SWALLOWS A PILL, GIVEN TO HER BY NEIL. MAGGIE WATCHES.

NEIL: There you are, Hazel. That should help a little. Now, I've got to go, but Nurse Bolton will stay with you for a while.

HE BEGINS MOVING TOWARDS THE DOOR.

You've had a very nasty shock, but you must try to keep calm.

THERE IS A KNOCK AT THE FRONT DOOR.

NEIL: You stay there. I'll see who it is.

HAZEL: I don't want to see anybody.

NEIL OPENS THE DOOR TO CRADDOCK.

NEIL: Hello, Sergeant.

CRADDOCK: Doctor.

MAGGIE: It's Sergeant Craddock.

HAZEL: Oh, no . . . What's happened?

CRADDOCK: Nothing's happened, Mrs Mansfield. We're still looking for Peter. I've got reinforcements coming to help with the search.

HAZEL: You've got to find him. He's not well . . .

CRADDOCK: Doctor?

NEIL: He'll be fine, Hazel. I promise you.

CRADDOCK LOOKS AT HIM, INQUIRINGLY. NEIL DROPS HIS VOICE AND SPEAKS QUIETLY TO HIM, AT THE DOOR.

He has a bit of childhood asthma. Nothing to worry about under normal circumstances.

CRADDOCK: But these aren't normal circumstances, are they?

NEIL: No, but . . .

CRADDOCK: What are the risks?

NEIL: Well, if he's not looked after properly, he could get chest infections, maybe pneumonia.

CRADDOCK: And that would be dangerous?

NEIL: Yes, of course.

CRADDOCK: Thank you, docotor.

NEIL NODS, AND GOES. CRADDOCK CLOSES THE DOOR BEHIND HIM THEN TURNS BACK INTO THE LIVING ROOM.

CRADDOCK: Now then, Mrs Mansfield.

HAZEL: He's going to die . . . I know he's going to die . . .

CRADDOCK: It's my experience, Mrs Mansfield, that people who steal babies generally take very good care of them. Isn't that right, Nurse Bolton?

MAGGIE: Er, yes. Yes . . .

CRADDOCK: If you think about it, the only reason anybody would steal a baby is because they're desperate for a child. For something to love, you see?

HAZEL: They can't love him as much as I do. Nobody could. Not his real mother. Not anybody . . .

MAGGIE: Sssh, ssh . . . of course they couldn't. You've done a wonderful job, you and Alan . . .

CRADDOCK: Er, excuse me – what do you mean, his real mother?

HAZEL: Peter's not ours. He's adopted . . . It's her isn't it?

CRADDOCK: Who?

HAZEL: His natural mother . . . I always knew she'd come back for him.

CRADDOCK: Who is she?

HAZEL: I don't know . . . I don't know . . .

AND SHE BREAKS DOWN IN TEARS AGAIN.

---

92. INT. EDIE'S HOUSE   TIME: 10.59 DAY 4

EDIE SITS NURSING BABY PETER.

THE DOOR OPENS QUIETLY, AND BRADLEY ENTERS.

BRADLEY: Hello, Edie.

SHE LOOKS UP AND SMILES AT HIM.

EDIE: Hello, Mr Bradley.

BRADLEY: What are you doing with the baby, Edie?

EDIE: He's lovely, in't he?

BRADLEY: Yeh, but he's not yours, is he?

EDIE: Oh, yes. Yes, he is now.

BRADLEY: No, Edie. He's got to go home.

EDIE: He's got a good home here. You can't take him away. I won't let you . . .

---

93. EXT. EDIE'S HOUSE   TIME: 11.01 DAY 4

CRADDOCK AND BELLAMY ARE WAITING. NEIL AND MAGGIE ARRIVE IN NEIL'S CAR. CRADDOCK CROSSES TO THEM, GESTURING THEM TO BE QUIET.

94. INT. EDIE'S HOUSE   TIME: 11.01 DAY 4

RESUME BRADLEY, EDIE AND PETER

EDIE: She's not his real mother, you know. I've got as much right to him as she has.

BRADLEY: No Edie. You haven't.

EDIE: He's better off wi' me. Them two, they're always rowing and shouting. I've heard 'em. And she doesn't look after him proper. You should hear him coughing and wheezing. I had to hold him most of the night, 'cause he kept crying. I never got a wink of sleep.

BRADLEY: Neither did Hazel Mansfield, Edie. She's been worried sick about him.

EDIE: Has she?

BRADLEY: Yes. I've never seen anybody so upset. She loves him so much . . . She really does.

EDIE: Oh . . .

SHE PONDERS ON THIS, BUT STILL CLINGS TO THE BABY.

95. EXT. EDIE'S HOUSE   TIME: 11.03 DAY 4

CRADDOCK, BELLAMY, NEIL AND MAGGIE ALL WAIT, NERVOUSLY.

96. INT. EDIE'S HOUSE   TIME: 11.03 DAY 4

RESUME BRADLEY, EDIE AND PETER

BRADLEY: Why did you take him, Edie?

EDIE: I . . . I was on my way to the shop and I saw him in his pram . . .

BRADLEY: Yes?

EDIE: I picked him up . . . just for a little cuddle, like I do sometimes with the babies up at the home . . . and I couldn't put him down again . . . I'm sorry.

BRADLEY: OK, Edie. It's all right. If you just give him to me now, we'll sort everything out.

EDIE: This house has been so empty since my dad died . . . You don't know what it's like, when you've had somebody to look after all them years, then all of a sudden there's nobody . . . nobody . . .

BRADLEY: Is that why you took a job at the home? To be with babies?

EDIE: Not really. I never thought owt about it till I'd started. Then there they were – all them lasses wi' babies they didn't want. And I could never have one. I'd left it too late, wi' looking' after me dad, and all . . . It don't seem fair, does it?

BRADLEY: No, Edie. It doesn't.

EDIE: I've looked after him real careful . . .

BRADLEY: Yes, I'm sure you have. But he does need to have his medicine, now.

EDIE: OK.

BRADLEY: It's time for him to go home.

EDIE NODS, AND LOOKS AT THE BABY IN HER ARMS. SHE HANDS HIM GENTLY TO BRADLEY.

Series drama

The Bill

Devised by Geoff McQueen
Excerpt from 'No Comment' by Christopher Russell

We are indebted to Producer Michael Chapman, writer Christopher Russell and Thames Television for permission to reproduce this excerpt.

Of the series Michael Chapman has said, 'It is an attempt to show policemen being policemen rather than investigators in someone else's story.'

Realism is the keynote. There are no convenient happy endings. Right does not always triumph. Dedicated hard work frequently ends in failure and frustration for the men of Sun Hill.

In this episode an old man has been killed in his flat. Meadows interviews the two suspects but makes no headway because they know they have a right to silence. Everyone is left wondering about the rights of the victim and his family.

25. INT. SUN HILL. INTERVIEW ROOM NUMBER TWO. 12.50. DAY 1.

MICHAEL OSMAN, WEARING A CUSTODY SUIT, IS SEATED AT TABLE. TENSE, APPREHENSIVE, HE LOOKS UNCOMFORTABLE IN THE INTERVIEW SITUATION. MORGAN, HAVING CLOSED THE DOOR, IS PUTTING TWO FRESH TAPES IN THE MACHINE. MEADOWS SITS DOWN OPPOSITE OSMAN, LOOKING CALM AND RELAXED. GLANCES UP AT CATTLIN WHO IS STANDING TAKING NOTEBOOK, PENS AND LEGAL AID FORMS FROM HIS BRIEFCASE.

MEADOWS: (NODDING AT A CHAIR SOME DISTANCE AWAY FROM OSMAN AND OUT OF HIS EYELINE) If you'd like to sit over there, Mr Cattlin.

CATTLIN: (MILDLY, NOT CONFRONTATIONAL) I'd rather sit next to my client, if you don't mind.

HE FETCHES THE CHAIR AND SITS NEXT TO OSMAN. MEADOWS GIVES HIM A LOOK BUT MAKES NO COMMENT.

MORGAN: (HAVING STARTED TAPE, SPEAKS FOR ITS BENEFIT) Tape interview with Michael Osman. Those present DCI Meadows, DC Morgan and Mr Osman's legal representative Brian Cattlin. Time now is 12.50.

MEADOWS WAITS FOR CATTLIN TO SIT DOWN BESIDE HIM BEFORE

196

SPEAKING PLEASANTLY BUT QUITE QUICKLY TO OSMAN.

MEADOWS: Michael, I must remind you that you're still under caution – that is, you don't have to say anything unless you wish to do so but what you do say may be given in evidence . . . understand?

OSMAN LOOKS TO CATTLIN.

CATTLIN: Could you confirm to Mr Osman that if he chooses not to speak, no adverse comment may legally be made about his silence by the prosecution at any trial that might take place. In other words, his silence cannot be used against him.

MEADOWS: (NODS BUT NOT OVER-KEEN TO SPELL IT OUT) That is the legal position, yes.

CATTLIN: Thank you.

MEADOWS: But it should also be explained to Mr Osman that if he doesn't speak, only one side of the story is going to be heard.

MEADOWS REGARDS CATTLIN A BEAT, EXPECTING HIM TO REPLY BUT HE DOESN'T.

MEADOWS: (CONT'D) You do understand that, Michael?

AGAIN OSMAN LOOKS TO CATTLIN.

CATTLIN: My client understands.

MEADOWS: (TO OSMAN. CALM, ALMOST FRIENDLY) Right then, Michael . . . I think you know why we need to speak to you. Could you tell me where you were at eleven o'clock this morning?

OSMAN LOOKS AT CATTLIN, WHO GIVES THE SLIGHTEST ENCOURAGING NOD OF THE HEAD.

OSMAN CLEARS HIS THROAT AND SPEAKS HALTINGLY AS IF RECITING SOMETHING LEARNT BY ROTE.

OSMAN: Having taken legal advice . . . No comment.

END ON MEADOWS.

END OF PART ONE

27. INT. SUN HILL. INTERVIEW ROOM. NUMBER TWO. 13.05. DAY.

MEADOWS, MORGAN, OSMAN AND CATTLIN AS BEFORE. THE TAPE MACHINE IS RUNNING. CATTLIN IS MAKING NOTES.

MEADOWS: (INITIALLY RELAXED, ALMOST CASUAL, OUTWARDLY AT LEAST) Tell me about the dusters, Michael. You and Ian go round selling them, do you? Knocking on people's doors. Is that what you were doing in Silbury Court. Trying to sell dusters?

OSMAN LOOKS AT THE TABLE. DOESN'T ANSWER.

MEADOWS: (CONT'D. BUILDING SLIGHTLY) Did you knock at the door of number two. And did an old man open the door? (BEAT PAUSE) What happened then? Did you go in? Did you go into the flat, Michael?

OSMAN GLANCES NERVOUSLY AT CATTLIN WHO AGAIN GIVES THE
SLIGHTEST OF NODS.

OSMAN: (A BIT HUSKY BUT MORE FLUENT THAN BEFORE) No reply.
Having taken legal advice.

MEADOWS: (UP A NOTCH MORE BUT MAINTAINING CONTROL) The
old man did open the door, didn't he, Michael. And then what? Did you persuade
him to buy something? Did Ian persuade him? Did the old man go back into the flat
to get some money? Is that when you went into the flat? Or perhaps it was just Ian
who went in – and you stayed outside. Is that what happened? Ian followed the old
man into the flat.

OSMAN BLOWS A SIGH. SHIFTS UNCOMFORTABLY IN HIS SEAT.

MEADOWS: (PRESSES ON SENSING A SNIFF OF A CHANCE DESPITE
CATTLIN'S PRESENCE) He did, didn't he, Michael?

OSMAN RUBS HIS FACE WITH HIS HAND.

MEADOWS: (CONT'D) For the benefit of the tape, Mr Osman is rubbing his
face with his hand and looking very uncomfortable with this question.

CATTLIN: (CALMLY BUT CLEARLY) For the benefit of the tape, the air
conditioning in this interview room is faulty and the atmosphere is oppressive. We
are all uncomfortable.

MEADOWS: (VERY SHORT) Then I suggest we take a break. (AS HE
STANDS UP ABRUPTLY) Interview suspended at 13.07. (SWITCHES OFF TAPE
MACHINE) Get Michael a cup of tea and a sandwich please, Jo. (INDICATING
DOOR) Can we speak, Mr Cattlin?

CUT TO:

28. INT. SUN HILL. INTERVIEW ROOM. NUMBER ONE. (OR OTHER
CONVENIENT EMPTY ROOM) 13.08. DAY.

MEADOWS STALKS IN, TURNS AS CATTLIN COMES IN BEHIND HIM,
CATTLIN CLOSES DOOR.

MEADOWS: (WITHOUT PREAMBLE) Look. The only thing I'm interested in
is the truth. Aren't you?

CATTLIN LOOKS AT HIM.

CATTLIN: Oh come on, Mr Meadows, don't pretend to be naive. A solicitor's
only duty is to his client, I'm sure you're aware of that.

MEADOWS: (ATTEMPTING TO BROW BEAT HIM) Your legal duty yes, but
what about your moral duty?

MEADOWS IS OVERSTEPPING THE MARK WITH THIS AND CATTLIN
REACTS SLIGHTLY.

CATTLIN: I don't think my moral duty is for you to dictate –

MEADOWS: Osman or Prior killed that old man.

CATTLIN: The point is: you don't <u>know</u> that.

MEADOWS: I do know it and so do you. And I'll bet my pension Osman's admitted as much to you.

CATTLIN: What he's told me in private is none of your business. I can't permit him to tell lies to you but that doesn't affect his right to say nothing. <u>Both</u> men are innocent of this crime till proven guilty and neither of them is required to help you prove that guilt. That's my 'moral duty', defending that principle.

MEADOWS: (IMPATIENTLY DISMISSIVE, HEADING FOR THE DOOR) Yeh, fine, forget it, thanks for the lecture . . .

CATTLIN: (NOT PREPARED TO LEAVE IT) And all solicitors are either lefty or bent, yes?

MEADOWS: (ROUNDING ON HIM BUT RESTRAINED) I sometimes wonder why else anyone devotes a career to helping pond life. Frankly.

CATTLIN: (UNFLINCHING) Who decides who <u>is</u> pond life, then, you?

MEADOWS: (MILDLY) Broadly speaking, Mr Cattlin, we deal with scum in here. You know that. Joe Public wants protecting from scum. That's my job. You can't expect a pat on the back for stopping me from doing it.

CATTLIN: And if <u>you</u> were Michael Osman? Vulnerable, inarticulate, scared stiff. With the full weight of the police and CPS bearing down on <u>you</u>?

MEADOWS: (LEVELLY) An innocent man has nothing to fear.

CATTLIN: (RETURNING THE LOOK) I beg to differ.

CUT TO:

29. INT. SUN HILL. CUSTODY AREA. 16.50. DAY.

IN THE OFFICE. BOYDEN SEATED AT DESK, WRITING, AS CONWAY COMES IN.

CONWAY: What's the score?

BOYDEN: (GLANCING UP. AIRILY) About ten nil to the legal fraternity and the criminals, sir. The DCI's hanging in there in the forlorn hope of an own goal.

CUT TO:

30. INT. SUN HILL. FRONT INTERVIEW ROOM. 16.50. DAY.

CARVER AND HARDING SEATED AT TABLE, CARVER WITH HIS NOTEBOOK OPEN IN FRONT OF HIM. CROFT IS ALSO PRESENT. HARDING IS MORE COMPOSED NOW.

HARDING: (FROWNS) Wearing gloves? I honestly dunno.

CARVER: But you got a good look at them, yeh? They went out of the building past you.

HARDING: Yeh but I wasn't looking at their hands. I mean, black hands, black gloves . . . (HOW WOULD I HAVE NOTICED)

CARVER: (CONTROLLING HIS FRUSTRATION MOVES SWIFTLY ON) Yeh, never mind, thanks . . . (REFERRING TO NOTEBOOK) What about your dad's front door? You told PC Jarvis you didn't see the two men actually coming out of the flat. Can I ask you to think again about that please?

HARDING: How d'you mean, 'think again'? I do know what I saw.

CARVER: Yeh, but these things happen so quickly. We often find when witnesses have had time to think about it they remember more clearly. You're quite sure you didn't see them coming out of the flat?

HARDING: I saw them outside the flat. Both of them. The door was shut.

CARVER: But if it was open –

HARDING: (REACTING, BECOMING AGITATED) You keep asking and I keep telling you. You've nicked the scumbags who were there, why aren't you asking them?

CROFT: We are, Mr Harding, but under the law they're not obliged to say anything.

HARDING: Obliged? Not obliged? My old man had his head smashed in!

CROFT: Yes –

HARDING: But they're 'not obliged' so I've gotta tell lies so you can screw the bastards, is that how the system works?

Continuous serial

Brookside

Brookside is a continuous serial, devised by writer Phil Redmond, who also created *Grange Hill*, the popular children's serial screened by BBC2.

The programme is made on video tape and shown by Channel Four. Screened Tuesday, Wednesday and Friday, with an omnibus repeat on Saturday, *Brookside* covers the everyday lives of its people and does not hesitate to tackle the kind of disturbing emotional problems that are usually reserved for the 'serious' play.

We are indebted to Mersey Television, Phil Redmond and writer, Jane Pritchard, for permission to include this example. The background to the excerpt is that Jimmy Corkhill, desperately anxious to better himself, has forged his degree qualification to obtain a teaching position. So far he has got away with it but when his wife discovers what he has done the truth threatens to wreck their marriage.

Sc. 2199.14 (INT) CORKHILLS' LIVING ROOM DAY 10.18am

AS <u>JIMMY</u> COMES IN FROM HALL – LEANING BACKWARDS TO SHOUT UPSTAIRS . . .

1   <u>JIMMY</u>: (O.O.V.) I just want to see if nana's OK – and then I'll batter bunny again.

HE HEADS FOR THE KITCHEN – BUT HESITATES AT THE EXTENSION DOOR – WONDERING IF HE SHOULD JUST LOOK IN – BUT DECIDES NOT TO . . . LOOKS AT THE DEBRIS OF *THE GUARDIAN* STILL ON THE FLOOR – BUT DECIDES TO PUT THE KETTLE ON FIRST – THEN TACKLE THE CLEAN UP WHILE IT IS BOILING . . .

HE GOES AND TESTS THE KETTLE FIRST – IT ALREADY HAS WATER – AND HE IS SWITCHING ON THE KETTLE WHEN <u>LINDSEY</u> COMES OUT – BUT SEEING HIM, LOOKS BACK – AND DECIDES THEY ARE NOT READY TO MEET YET – SO CLOSES THE DOOR – WHILE . . .

2   <u>LINDSEY</u>: I was gonna do that.

1   <u>JIMMY</u>: Is she on the road to recovery then?

2   <u>LINDSEY</u>: Yeah.

BUT HER HESITATION ALERTS <u>JIMMY</u>.

4   <u>JIMMY</u>: What's going on, Linds?

4   LINDSEY: (BUT SHE DECIDES TO DUCK THE ISSUE) She just needs a bit of time, that's all.

5   JIMMY: (NODS – STARTS GETTING THE THINGS TOGETHER)
Funny, isn't it. I was always dreading getting into trouble at school over me dodgy degree – never expected to get so much grief off your mother.

LINDSEY HAS AUTOMATICALLY STOPPED TO GATHER UP SHREDDED *GUARDIAN* – AND USES THIS AS AN OPPORTUNITY TO DIVERT THE QUESTION.

6   LINDSEY: Dad, I can understand you using a false name and address to get your degree – but – Well, I thought the schools they did more thorough checks than that.

1   JIMMY: (GRINS – THEN) They do – but – you never get anywhere in life without a bit of luck. Do you? (TURNS TO HER) Drugs.

2   LINDSEY: How?

3   JIMMY: You remember when the parade blew up?

4   LINDSEY: Am I likely to forget it.

5   JIMMY: And I was missing? (LINDSEY NODS) I was boxing off this fella who's responsible for doing all the police checks in the Council.

6   LINDSEY: Oh, you weren't dealing

7   JIMMY: No-o. He was a punter, wasn't he. A friend Brian Kennedy – that fella who got me into the game in the first place. All the police checks go through him – all I did was point out that he had as much to hide as me . . . Well, Martin James Corkhill got a nice big tick next to his name. Bit like the "old smack head network" really. I just didn't want your mother knowing all those gory details.

8   LINDSEY: Which is exactly the point, dad. You didn't trust her.

1   JIMMY: No, I didn't trust her to trust herself. She's too good a woman for me.

2   LINDSEY: Oh dad, don't say that.

3   JIMMY: Well – she deserves better than me. She should have gone off with someone like that scaffolder used to live down her way.

LINDSEY NEARLY DROPS HER CUP – BUT DOESN'T SAY ANYTHING.

4   JIMMY: (CONT/G) He's done alright for himself I've heard. He was always sniffing around your mother. (GRINS) Made me dead chuffed when she copped for me . . .

5   LINDSEY: Don't you mean copped for me?

6   JIMMY: No . . . we were . . . "committed" before that . . .

7   LINDSEY: Oh, so forging your degree wasn't your first introduction to "illegitimacy" then?

8   JIMMY: (MATTER OF FACT) That was expediency.

9   LINDSEY: What!?

1   JIMMY: Well, it was either that or do another three or four years as a student. I wouldn't have even been half way there now, and seeing as we're all going through an honesty rush at the moment, well, I don't think I could have stuck it. Back to the scally in me. Wanted the rewards – but not the graft.

AS HE HAS BEEN SPEAKING SHE HAS BEEN LISTENING INTENTLY – ADJUSTING THE METAPHOR TO HER OWN POSITION – SOMETHING HE READS ON HER FACE . . .

2   JIMMY: (CONT/G) Which is exactly why you want to jump into bed with the Finnegans? The easy route in.

3   JIMMY: I mean – where we were brought up, you were taught to get what you could when you could – live for today. Grab a slice as quick as you can.

4   LINDSEY: You're not soft, are you?

5   JIMMY: You had no idea that you could graft for a few years to get a bigger slice of the cake, did you? Not like Karen and her lot.

THE KETTLE NOW BOILS AND JIMMY STARTS MAKING TEA . . .

1   LINDSEY: Deferred gratification?

JIMMY NODS – NICE ONE . . .

2   LINDSEY: See, not totally illiterate.

3   JIMMY: None of us are, love. I mean, sometimes we get forgetful. We sometimes forget where we come from.

4   JIMMY: I mean, our problem, well, perhaps my problem, is that I saw Karen, and her mates – and I wanted to be part of that "club" I keep on about. Only we belong to the "club" of dockers and bus drivers. I mean, I don't mind that – I'm proud of it really, at least I know what life is *really* about. Survival.

5   LINDSEY: You see, I know which club I'm supposed to belong to – and I know the club I want to join. And I don't want to wait either.

6   JIMMY: Yeah . . . but . . . Linds. Like I said it before, I'm just breaking a few rules here and there. You know what the likes of the Finnegans can break!

7   JIMMY: Callum was a Finnegan.

1   LINDSEY: Dad, I know what I'm doing. And I know what I want.

2   JIMMY: (NODS – ACCEPTS THIS – BUT) And what about Jacqui Dicko and Susannah?

3   LINDSEY: (HARD) Well Susannah, I mean – she's harmless – but Jacqui – oh, she'll end up in exactly the same position. She soon dumped her own father when Barry took over Bar Brookie. Right?

SHE LOOKS HIM IN THE EYE – A HARD, COLD DETERMINED LOOK HE'S SEEN BEFORE AND KNOWS HE WON'T DEFEAT . . . SO HE NODS HIS ACCEPTANCE . . .

SHE NODS BACK – BOTH ACKNOWLEDGING THE REALITY OF THEIR CHANGING WORLDS – THEN SHE GOES TO PICK UP THE TEAS . . .

BUT HE TAKES THEM . . .

4   JIMMY: You're alright . . . leave them, I'll do it – you go and check on the bunny bashers. I think there's a few things I need to say to your mother.

AS SHE NODS AND WATCHES HIM GO . . . THIS TIME IT IS SHE WHO IS WONDERING WHAT WILL HAPPEN NEXT . . .

CUT TO:

Sc. 2199.15 (INT) CORKHILLS' EXTENSION DAY 10.20am

JACKIE IS STANDING AT THE WINDOW AS JIMMY COMES IN – ALMOST A REPEAT OF THEIR POSITIONS WHEN SHE CHALLENGED HIM ABOUT GOING AFTER RUFUS.

SHE TURNS AS THE DOOR OPENS – AND HER FACE STIFFENS WHEN SHE SEES IT IS JIMMY . . . WITH THE TEA . . .

1   JACKIE: Where's Lindsey?

2   JIMMY: Seeing the kids . . . (OFFERS TEA) Seems like I've spent most of the morning doing this.

3   JACKIE: Good for something then?

JIMMY TAKES THE JIBE . . . THEN . . .

4   JIMMY: Right, come on then . . . how bad is it – are you leaving me or what?

5   JACKIE: Are you serious?

6   JIMMY: Are you?

THEY BOTH HESITATE – WONDERING IF THEY SHOULD GET INTO THIS . . . UNTIL . . .

1   JACKIE: Would you blame me if I did go?

2   JIMMY: (HESITATES – THINKS – THEN GOES AND SITS ON SETTEE) Well . . . actually . . . no.

JACKIE LOOKS AT HIM – SEARCHES HIS FACE FOR SIGNS OF SINCERITY – AND HE APPEARS GENUINE . . . SO SHE MOVES TO FACE HIM DIRECTLY . . .

3   JACKIE: Easy to say.

4   JIMMY: Is it?

5   JACKIE: And where would I be expected to go? Jimmy? Not having any options? Not even that one.

6   JIMMY: Well, I could go.

THIS CATCHES HER – SHE WASN'T EXPECTING THIS . . . WHICH HE SEES . . .

7   JIMMY: (CONT/G) What's up? Do you think I'm "too far above you" to know what you're thinking anymore?

8   JACKIE: It's not that. I just didn't think you'd be brave enough – or honest enough to face it.

1   JIMMY: Well, that's what's good about life, isn't it? Full of surprises.

2   JACKIE: It has been with you.

THEY LAPSE INTO AN AWKWARD SILENCE AGAIN AS THEY BOTH
KNOW THEY ARE REACHING THE EDGE – AND FACING THE
PRECIPICE . . . UNTIL . . .

3   JIMMY: Look Jackie . . . I have said I'm sorry. I know I've said it (TO HER) a
million times, yes – but – I am. I am. And if you don't believe me . . . well, that's
me own stupid fault.

JACKIE STILL DOESN'T KNOW HOW DEEP THIS CONTRITION IS . . .

4   JIMMY: I don't want to lose you, Jack . . . I . . . well . . . I love you, don't I?

5   JACKIE: Do you?

6   JIMMY: (SLIGHTLY OFFENDED) Trust me Jack, everything will be fine. You
do trust me don't you?

7   JACKIE: I trust you more than you trust me – otherwise you wouldn't keep all
these secrets from me, would you?

1   JIMMY: (SARCASTIC) Alright . . . so what would you have said, Jackie?
If I'd come to you and said "Ey Jack, what do you reckon to me forging
qualifications and becoming a teacher?"

JACKIE HOLDS HIS STARE FOR A MOMENT – BEFORE NODDING
SLIGHTLY . . .

2   JACKIE: I just wish you wouldn't go developing these crazy schemes without
talking to me first about what the real problem is.

3   JIMMY: Which is what?

4   JACKIE: Our different dreams.

5   JIMMY: About what?

6   JACKIE: I don't want "it all" Jim? I'm not like Lindsey – I'm not like you. I
just want what most people want. You know, I just want to feel comfortable.
And I just want to feel safe. And I just want a bit of . . . of . . . normality.

7   JIMMY: Right yeah . . . Like, we're poor but proud and happy, yeah?

1   JACKIE: (GIVING UP – SHE STANDS) Oh well, almost – but if I'd wanted to
be happy – I wouldn't have stuck with you, would I?

WITH THAT SHE WALKS OUT AND LEAVES HIM TO THINK ABOUT
IT . . . WHICH HE DOES . . . THE MORE HE DOES . . . THE MORE HE
REALISES WHAT A MESS HE HAS MADE OF THINGS . . . BUT HE CAN'T
QUITE FIGURE IT ALL OUT YET – IT SHOULD ALL BE GREAT – BUT IT
ISN'T . . . AND THE MORE HE THINKS THE NEARER THE SURFACE
THE TEARS ARE . . .

END OF EPISODE TWO THOUSAND ONE HUNDRED AND NINETY NINE

A pilot script

The Further Adventures of Tom Jones

Return of the Prodigal
(In which our hero learns that
Good Intentions are not enough)

by Terence Feely

This is the pilot script of a rumbustious period comedy. It is clearly a very expensive production calling for special costumes but it is the work of one of our most experienced television film writers and, with a great many successes behind him, producers are prepared to find the necessary budget.

Written for production entirely on film it is of particular interest for the way it exploits screen techniques, using a narrator to interject exposition without breaking the action and the particularly amusing use of the technical device of the WIPE (the picture is wiped from the screen).

It is an English/French/American co-production and we are indebted to Terence Feely and Serprocor Estab. for permission to reprint the following scenes.

THE FURTHER ADVENTURES OF TOM JONES

Return of the Prodigal

(In Which Our Hero Learns That Good Intentions Are Not Enough)

Pilot Script by Terence Feely

Copyright: Serprocor Estab.

4. EXT. COUNTRYSIDE. DAY.

Tom Jones and his servant, Ned, gallop briskly on fine horses across the lovely landscape.

Tom is fresh, handsome, rugged, with a kind of invincible joyous innocence.
He's 21 years old.
Ned is a bull, sitting his horse like a fall of rock, a mad twinkle in his bright brown eye belying his stolidity.
He's about 30.

206

NARRATOR

Our story, gentle viewer, is of Tom Jones, a good
and simple young man more sinned against than
sinning. Not one of the towering intellects of the
age, but instinctively wise in the commonsense
matters that lie at the heart of life.
Passionate by nature and much beset by women all
his life, he rides now to fair Somerset to wed his
beloved sweetheart, Sophia Western, forswearing all
women else. Not an easy decision, for he can no
more help attracting those divine creatures than the
candle-flame the moth.

* * * * * *

A lovely girl in a gracious riding habit rides past in the opposite direction.
She gives Tom a dazzling come-on.
Tom averts his eyes.

TOM
(grimly joyful)
I'm a rock. I am ice. I am snow on the mountain top.

An even lovelier girl rides past, gives Tom a sizzling smile. Tom again looks away.
Behind her comes her chaperone, a toothlesss old crone. She gives Tom a frankly
lecherous leer.
Tom gives a weak smile back then scowls at Ned, defying him to laugh.
Ned, containing himself, looks dead ahead, his eyes dancing. Tom eyes him
narrowly then snatches off his hat and starts to beat him with it.
Ned's laughter explodes and he kicks up his horse and takes off, Tom chasing him,
brandishing his hat.

TOM
You damned American Irishman! I can always
throw you back to the Navy, you know! They don't
like Colonials who jump ship in London.

NED
(REINING IN)
I never did thank you for your help in the fight
with the Press Gang.

TOM
I needed a cheap servant.

They grin at each other, not as master and servant but as man to man.

CUT TO

5. ANOTHER LOCATION. COUNTRYSIDE. DAY.

Tom and Ned, sober again, ride side by side.

NARRATOR
On the long journey from London where – thanks
to his perfidious cousin Mr Blifil –

207

INSERT – TOP RIGHT CORNER OF FRAME – BLIFIL, SNEERING. HOLD.

> – he has been in exile, he has conducted himself like
> a cold and holy friar. Now with his faithful servant,
> Ned, Tom returns to the home of his uncle, the
> good Squire Allworthy, the kindest, best-hearted
> man in all the kingdom –

INSERT – TOP LEFT CORNER OF FRAME – SQUIRE ALLWORTHY, SMILING BENIGNLY. HOLD.

> It was Squire Allworthy who found Tom as an
> abandoned baby on his doorstep –

REPLACE TOP LEFT INSERT WITH TINY, UNDETAILED CAMEO OF ALLWORTHY PICKING UP A BUNDLY BABY FROM HIS DOORSTEP

> – and discovered him to be his true heir and
> nephew, thus earning for Tom the undying enmity
> of Allworthy's more distant nephew, Blifil, who was
> thus disinherited.

BLIFIL'S IMAGE – TOP RIGHT CORNER – PULSES WITH RAGE.

SQUIRE ALLWORTHY RETURNS, SMILING, TO THE TOP LEFT.

> On Squire Allworthy's estate Tom now means to
> marry his beloved Sophia, niece of Allworthy's
> good neighbour, Squire Western, whom you have
> already met.

CUT TO

6. WHOLE TOP HALF OF FRAME INSERT, LOSING ALLWORTHY AND BLIFIL.

A heart-shaped bubble over Tom's head.
Inside the bubble a CLOSE SHOT of the delicious SOPHIA, dressed as a bride.
She's 18 years old and a knock-out.
In character she's the Grace Kelly of 'High Noon', but quietly even feistier and more hardy.

NARRATOR

> Lovely Sophia, chaste product of a lofty moral
> upbringing in New England, a province of the
> quaint little colony of America.

The bubble enlarges to show that SOPHIA is walking in a lovely garden.

> There her father – Squire Western's brother – went to
> find his fortune and lost his scalp. Cool to the untutored
> eye yet there are banked-down fires within Sophia.

An enigmatic smile starts to curve Sophia's bee-stung lips.

The bubble now enlarges to encompass nearly the whole frame and Tom bounds into shot, dressed as a bridegroom.
The scene is mute. They meet lovingly.
Tom starts to kiss Sophia, first on the cheek, then on the lips. His hands start to slide her dress slowly off her shoulders.

NARRATOR

The keynote of our humble narrative will be
refinement and due decorum –

Tom is now kissing Sophia's ear, kiss-kissing his way to her neck.
The dress is now nearly off her shoulders.

Though Tom, in his youthful exuberance (SPEEDING
UP) may sometimes overstep the bounds of that
moderation which is the mark of true gentility,

The dress is now fully off her shoulders and travelling South.

we, gentle viewers – rest assured – will not.

The bubble abruptly narrows – like a camera aperture closing down – and is
extinguished.

CUT TO

7. RESUME COUNTRYSIDE. DAY.

Tom blinks at the sudden extinction of his fantasy. Ned points ahead.

NED

Look there.

Barely in frame in the distance is Squire Western's coach, leaning crazily by the
lakeside at the edge of the trees.
Tom and Ned gallop towards it.
As they do so, Squire Western, a gross and corpulent scarecrow, stripped of all his
clothes except his combinations, detaches himself from the coach and starts
windmilling his arms and roaring.

WESTERN

Robbery! Murder! Damnation, rape and plunder!

TOM

That's Squire Western or I'm a Dutchman!

WESTERN

Holloa! To me! To me, brave lads!

Tom and Ned thunder up and dismount.
Western clutches Tom breathlessly.

WESTERN

Highwaymen! Took all my money, the squint-eyed
bugs. All Sophie's jewels and finery for your
wedding. We'll have to postpone it.

TOM

Never!

There's a stir in the trees behind them.
Tom and Ned wheel.

CUT TO

8. ANOTHER ANGLE.

Seth and Rory have ridden quietly out of the forest.
They are still masked, their pistols cocked and ready.

> SETH
> Well now – look what we've got here.

> RORY
> The stricken partridge always brings its fellows.

> WESTERN
> Those are the scoundrels!

> RORY
> (pointing his pistol at Tom)
> Your money or your life!

> SETH
> (leering)
> And then your clothes.

Tom and Ned look at each other, their minds in sync.
There's a kind of joy in their eye.

> TOM
> My life is a poor thing, gentlemen. As for my purse,
> poorer still.

He gets out his money bag.
Ned does the same.

> If you can squeeze a sovereign from it, you're welcome.

They hand their purses up to the highwaymen.
As Seth and Rory reach down for them, Tom and Ned move in unison, grasping the extended hands and ripping their owners tumbling from the saddle.
Ned grabs Rory by the front of his shirt, shakes him like a rag doll and hurls him to the ground.
Tom ducks a roundhouse right from Seth, doubles him up with a blow to the solar plexus, straightens him by pulling him up by two fingers delicately hooked into the nostrils and gives him his quietus with a right cross.
Ned picks up Rory and rattles him again.

> NED
> The Squire's belongings. Where are they?

> RORY
> (gasping)
> At the inn. 'The Fox's Lair'.

Tom makes to move off.

> TOM
> Come, Ned.

> WESTERN
> That's that trollop Beth Archer's place. She knows you.
> (Meaningfully) And with good reason. They'd see you coming.

> TOM
> No, they won't.

He rips the masks from the bandits' faces, gives one to Ned. They do not yet put them on.

WESTERN
Besides, you were to return to Somerset discreetly,
with no alarms.

Tom vaults into the saddle.

TOM
I'll be as anonymous as a monk.

He and Ned thunder out of shot.
Western shouts after them.

WESTERN
And see you keep your mind on your task! I know you!

He turns bad-temperedly and, as a kind of afterthought, kicks Seth and Rory, who
have dragged themselves to their feet and stand swaying, into the lake.

CUT TO

8A. EXT. COUNTRYSIDE. DAY.

Tom and Ned gallop across the lush green acres.
In the distance we see the inn, 'The Fox's Lair'.

TOM
I see my cousin Blifil's hand in this. He not only wants
Squire Allworthy's fortune, he wants Sophie, too.

NED
And you, Master Tom, what do you want?

TOM
(SIGHS)
I want my Sophie, then I just want to till the good
earth and bring up our children close to it.

9. EXT. INN. 'THE FOX'S LAIR'. DAY.

Tom and Ned gallop up, don their masks and dismount.
Ned kicks open the door with a mighty boot.

CUT TO

10. INT. INN. DAY.

A villainous crew of unshaven cut-throats and grimily alluring molls raise a cheer of
greeting as Tom and Ned enter, masked. We pan across them, briefly favouring a
recruiting sergeant, busily getting a prospective candidate drunk as he lines up
another tankard in front of the unfortunate, to add to the three that are already
brimming before him.

CHORUS
What, Rory! How now, Seth!

They raise their tankards.

FIRST VILLAIN
Had more sport, have you?

Tom and Ned level their pistols and swords.
The villains are taken completely by surprise.
There's a rhubarb of astonishment.

TOM

Pistols in the barrel. Blades on the bar.

The villains throw their guns into a barrel of wine, lay their swords on the counter.
Tom slaps a table with his sword.

TOM

Squire Western's things. Put them here.

Beth Archer, a pretty gangsters' moll in an incongruously expensive, low-cut dress, detaches herself from the rest and moves provocatively forward.
She has magnificent breasts.
Tom's eyes gleam behind the mask. He tries to avert them.
Beth picks up a laden sack and brings it to the table.
Tom taps the table again with his sword.
Beth delves into the sack and pulls out clothes, money bags, jewellery, one by one.
The way she leans into the sack does nothing to hide her magnificent frontal development.
She keeps her eyes provocatively on Tom as she does it.
She fancies him strongly: she knows he fancies her, even behind the mask.
She finishes.
Tom briefly mops his brow to relieve the heat she has wrought in him.
Ned is watching him, knowingly.

TOM
(sternly)

And the Squire's niece – where are her things?

BETH
(slow smile)

They're upstairs, mysterious sir.

Tom gestures towards the stairs with his pistol.
Beths sets off towards the stairs, her bottom twitching saucily.
Tom follows, eyes gleaming.
Ned, keeping the others covered, clears his throat with heavy significance.
Tom turns and snaps at him.

TOM
(testily)

I know, I know!

He follows Beth up the stairs

CUT TO

11. INT. INN BEDROOM. DAY.

The stairs lead straight into it.
A pile of dresses and jewellery is heaped on a bed between Beth and Tom.
She is adding to it from a sack.

TOM

Is that all?

BETH

Just this, strange sir. And this. And this. And this.

Again she leans forward to mind-blowing effect as she empties the sack.

212

> My name's Beth Archer. Mayn't I know yours,
> pretty stranger?

Tom is being rock-like.

TOM

> Anything else?

Beth indicates the dress she is wearing.

BETH

> Only this, secret sir.

TOM
(hesitates)

> Take it off.

Beth smiles wickedly.
Her eyes locked on Tom's, she starts to shed the dress.
Tom licks his lips nervously, looks over his shoulder toward downstairs then –
unable to resist any longer – he starts to shed his own clothes, his hat and cloak
first, then elaborate coat, elaborate waistcoat.
Instantly, the narrator is on the air.

NARRATOR

> It will be our custom, gentle viewer, on your behalf,
> to draw a veil over scenes such as these.

A wipe starts to blot out the picture.
It gets halfway across frame, stops, struggles, then is forced to retreat.
Beth is smiling lasciviously, as she matches her strip – she has a blizzard of garments
– to time with Tom's.

NARRATOR

> I said we will draw a veil!

Again the wipe starts and appears to be winning, but again it fails to make it and is
forced back.
Tom is down to his shirt.
We see a costly gold locket around his neck underneath the shirt.
Beth reaches out and fondles it.

BETH

> Pretty!

The Narrator breaks in again. He sounds as if he is physically struggling to draw
the wipe across.

NARRATOR
(clenched teeth)

> I . . . . . said . . . . draw . . . a . . veil!

Again the wipe advances but again it's defeated, this time with a kind of finality.

NARRATOR
(grim)

> Very well! Different times, different manners. But
> you won't like it!

The undressing has got faster and faster – and so has the music.
Tom starts to unbuckle his breeches.

As he does so we move in so that we can only see Tom and Beth above the waist.
Tom drops his trousers and launches himself eagerly towards Beth.
As he does so, her eyes go down.

> BETH
> Why, 'tis Tom Jones!

CUT TO

12. FREEZE FRAME.

Tom is arrested in mid-flight, his head turned and his masked face, open-mouthed, gazing directly and guiltily at the viewer.

WIPE TO

13. EXT. FIELD. DAY.

Two village maidens run excitedly towards each other.
They speak simultaneously.

> BOTH
> Tom Jones is back!

WIPE TO

14. INT. BARN. DAY. (MUTE)

Close on girl expertly milking a cow.
Another milkmaid runs in to her.
The scene is mute, but we read her lips.

> MILKMAID
> Tom Jones is back!

The first girl looks dreamy, her hands on the cow's udders.

WIPE TO

15. INT. SALON. DAY. (MUTE)

Two elegant ladies are taking tea.
One leans confidentially towards the other.
Again we read her lips.

> LADY
> Tom Jones is back!

Her friend smiles secretly and pours more tea from an aggressively spouted tea pot.

WIPE TO

16. EXT. COUNTRYSIDE. DAY.

Tom gallops furiously with the sacks of loot, conscious of Ned's eyes on him.
He bursts out.

> TOM
> I'm not a statue!

> NED
> I thought you said you were.

Tom bad-temperedly spurs his horse on and outdistances Ned.

WIPE

Glossary

The words included are peculiar to British television. Some are borrowed from the theatre and other arts, and of these some are given a slightly different meaning in television. In some instances only the slang word is listed because that is the one everyone uses. The number in brackets following a definition refers to a page in this book where the word is used or is explained in more detail.

ALCS Authors' Licensing & Collecting Society.
AV Audio visual. Film or video productions incoporating both sound and vision.
actuality Reportage of an event taking place at the time of showing, or recorded for showing at a suitable time with minimal editing.
adaptation Converting into a television script a dramatic work originally written for stage or radio.
angle The scene from the camera position.
anthology A series of plays thematically linked.

BAFTA British Academy of Film & Television Arts.
BARB British Audience Research Bureau
BBC British Broadcasting Corporation.
BCU Big close-up (e.g. a section of a face).
BECTU Broadcasting Entertainment Cinematograph & Theatre Union.
BFI British Film Institute
BP Back projection (34).
backing A piece of scenery stood behind doors, windows, etc., to stop the camera 'shooting off', i.e. seeing the studio through some aperture in the set.
book The script.
boom Sound boom (8).
brief The policy stated by a management regarding a production or series of productions, e.g. a programme may be intended to obtain high ratings cheaply or expensively; or a programme may be intended to gain prestige for the organisation making it.

215

business Any activity for a character, e.g. pouring tea, polishing nails, dusting shelves, etc.

CAN 'In the can' Recorded.

CGI Computer Generated Imagery.

CSO Colour separation overlay (36).

CU (and C/U) Close-up, i.e. only the face, or a hand, or a hotel label on a suitcase.

camera script In electronic television, the version of the script after the director has 'blocked out' his camera shots and moves. It is normally only distributed to the cameramen and other technicians (13).

camera set-up The position the camera is situated. See also set-up.

cheat A falsification in production giving an impression of truth, e.g. an actor looking off the screen to give the viewer the feeling that he is looking at an object, although he is in fact not doing so.

Chroma-key The ITV term for CSO (36).

cliff-hanger Exciting ending to a scene or episode designed to attract the audience back after the commercial break or the next episode in the case of a serial.

clip A short piece of film from a longer film.

closed circuit When both camera and receiver are linked by cable, and the electrical impulses are not transmitted through the air.

copywriter A writer who writes commercials.

cornerpiece A very small set with a limited or non-existent acting area.

'Corporate Television' Programmes made for marketing, promotional, image-building, educational, social, political and other purposes.

crane-shot Scene shot by an elevated camera for high or overhead angles.

credits Title and names of writer, director, actors and others involved in the production.

cue A signal to an actor or technician to take the action rehearsed. It can be the end of a line of dialogue (which is the other actor's cue to speak his lines), a wave, a nod, or a nudge.

cut (1) If your script is too long you may be asked to cut it, or to make a cut, or a number of cuts. (2) In electronic television, to change from the view of one camera to that of another. In TV/film, to change from the view of one set up to that of another set up.

cut away A quick shot of something away from the main action.

digital Method by which a programme is transmitted (7).

director The person accountable to a producer for putting the show 'on the floor' (4).

dissolve An overlapping change from one scene to another. Also known as a MIX.

documentary A non-fiction programme other than a newscast or an actuality OB.

double A look-alike actor or extra engaged to take the place of a principal player in long shots or night scenes while the principal is engaged in major scenes elsewhere.

dramatisation Rendering a work not written as drama (e.g. a novel or short story) into dramatic form.

dress (1) A set is dressed by its details, e.g. picture on the wall, flowers in vase. (2) Prior to the production there is a full dress rehearsal simply called 'the dress'.

drop (Also back drop). A canvas curtain depicting the background to a set, e.g. houses opposite, garden, open country. It serves the same purpose as a backing (see above). However, a backing is a free-standing flat, whereas a drop is 'flown' (hung from the grid).

dry When an actor completely forgets his lines and stops altogether it is a dry, or you can say that he dried.

dubbing mixer Only in filmed inserts, for which he gets a screen credit. After the film has been edited, he mixes in the appropriate sound tracks that were recorded at the time of the filming. There is a similar process for edited video tape; this is done by the sound supervisor, who gets no credit.

ETV Educational television.

EXT Exterior

editing (Film) The selection of disconnected shots and the assembly of those, or the parts of those, chosen for the final film.

editing (VTR) An electronic process whereby material considered redundant can be cut out; the assembly by electronic means of separate scenes previously recorded, in or out of the final sequence.

editor (Features (see below)). The manager accountable for the material used in, say, a magazine programme.

editor (Film) The technician who edits film.

editor (VTR) The technician who edits vision tape.

effects Sound effects.

entrance The moment an actor appears on a set he has made an entrance.

Equity Actors' Equity, the actors' and variety artistes' trade union. Also represents stage managers (SMs) and assistant stage managers (ASMs).

exit The moments leading up to, and the actual moment of, an actor leaving a set.

extra Small part actor (67).

FAP Front Axial Projection.

F/U Fade up. Starting from a blank screen or silent sound, bringing up the picture and/or sound to the required level.

FX Sound effects.

faction A dramatised documentary mixing fact and fiction.

fade-in The materialisation of the picture from a blank screen. Also used in respect of sound. See F/U.

fade-out The reverse of above. From picture to blank screen or aural effects to silence.

feature player Actor supporting the principals.

feature programme BBC term for a documentary.

fishing rod Boom from the end of which hangs a microphone.

flat A single backing; a painted board or canvas.

floor Studio floor.

fluff An actor who forgets a word or phrase, but covers it by continuing correctly, is said to have fluffed.

format Document explaining an idea (78).

fourth wall The non-existent fourth wall of a tape television or theatrical set.

frame The field of vision limited by the bounds of the picture.

fudge round To cheat (using that word in its television and theatrical sense) something in the plot or writing. If a writer hasn't the time or inclination to check a fact (e.g. date of the Battle of Waterloo), he can fudge round by not being specific. Given the choice, it's better to fudge round than to be inaccurate.

gaffer Chief electrician.

gag A comedy line or situation.

get out The time allocated for the removal of all the sets from a studio.

grams Generic term for sound sources playing back into the production (music, effects, etc.).

grips Men who move the heavy objects on and off set.

group shot (Group-s) Usually four or more people.

The Guild The Writers' Guild of Great Britain.

HTV Harlech Television Limited.

hand props Properties carried by artists (wallet, handbag, gun) as different from properties which dress the set (telephone, flower vase).

heavy A big and mostly villainous character in the script.

hook See teaser.

IBA Independent Broadcasting Authority.

INT Interior.

INT/EXT An exterior set located in a studio. An alternative is: EXT/STUDIO.

ITA Independent Television Association.

ITC Independent Television Commission.

ITN Independent Television News.

ITV Independent Television, which is an unofficial umbrella term for commercial television organisations.

IVCA International Visual Communications Association.

idiot card Slang for 'prompt card'. This term tends not to be used by actors who need them.

in frame For a person to be in the camera's view.

inlay An optical effect whereby something is added to the visual on the screen (36).

insert (1) A short piece of film. (2) Script writer's term to denote a cut away.

in shot Same as 'in frame'.

in the can To have been recorded or filmed.

LIP SYNC Matching lip movements to a sound track.

LS Long shot, showing the whole scene.

lazy arm A sound boom with a limited field of operation.

live There are three forms of television production in Britain: live, tape and film. Nowadays, only the news, weather forecasts, and some outside broadcasts (sport, coronations, etc) are live (i.e. transmitted as they happen). All drama is taped or filmed. But drama used to be transmitted live (16).

location Any place other than the studio or studio lot.

MCCC Motion Control Computerised Camera.

MIX Transition from one scene to another, in sound and/or vision, by fading the end of one scene while fading in the beginning of another. In film they use DISSOLVE.

MLS Medium long shot (e.g. the whole figure).

MS Mid or medium shot, e.g. cutting above the head and above the waist.

MU Musicians' Union.

magazine A type of regular, generally non-fictional, programme directed at a specific audience.

matte A mask that obscures part of the field of view.

mike Microphone.

mileage The amount of story material; twists and turns in the plot.

mobile scanner A small control room on wheels.

monitor Television screens within the studio and control rooms, allowing those staff who need to see the action (director, lighting, sound mixer, floor manager) to do so.

move An actor's change of position within a set.

N/S Non-speaking character.

Noddy A non-speaking character, because at one time low paid non-speakers were allowed to nod, but not to utter any sound, if spoken to. (See current Equity definitions on page 67.)

OB Outside broadcast (17).

OOV Out of vision, not in shot.

O/S Out of shot, not in vision.

one off An original play, also called 'single shot'.

outline A storyline.

over If your script is too long for the slot, you may be told it is 'over' or, say, 'two minutes over'.

PA A director's assistant (9).

PACT Producers' Alliance for Cinema & Television.

POV Point of view. Sometimes the term 'eyeline' is used.

PRS Performing Rights Society.

paint-box Electronic system of masking part of the shot.

pan Short for panoramic. Originally, and still in film, the act of turning a camera horizontally but now in television also applied to up and down movements of the camera.

period A production placed in the historical past.

pick ups Shots made in filming to assist in editing, e.g. the interviewer listening.

piece, the The script.

play-time The time scale within a play.

practical A property or part of a set required to function as real life, e.g. a door that opens and isn't simply painted on, a gas oven that really works, etc.

post synchronisation Adding dialogue, music, or sound effects, after the mute or partially sound picture (tape or film) has been shot. Slang: 'post sync'. Slang past tense: 'post synked' or 'post sunk'.

producer's run A complete rehearsal in the rehearsal room for the benefit of the producer. By this time actors should be word perfect, i.e. don't need their scripts to remember.

prompt card A card or note bearing the actor's lines, placed where the camera can't see it but the actor can.

prompt copy The producer's master copy of the script, in which all dialogue and other changes agreed during rehearsals have been noted.

properties Items used for dressing a set.

props (1) Same as properties. (2) Name given to the technician in charge of properties.

ratings The estimated number of viewers of a particular programme. The figures are arrived at by checking the past week's viewing pattern of panels of viewers who are believed to be a cross-section of the population as a whole.

reader A person employed to read unsolicited material.

read through The first time the cast of a play meet and read aloud the whole play. Normally the producer, director, wardrobe and make-up people will be present, as well as the writer.

rehearsal script The printed version of the script that is distributed to the writer, cast, and various non-technical departments. Pages 10 to 12 is the rehearsal script. The term is used to differentiate it from the camera script (13–15).

rehearse record TV studio production scenes rehearsed individually and then shot in the way films are made.

residuals Additional money the writer may receive from the producing company if they sell the tape or film abroad.

ripple An optical effect whereby the picture on the screen is seen as though through rippling water. It may be used for a subjective view by someone who is semi-conscious, or to go into a dream sequence or a flashback.

run, the The production, or VTR, from beginning to end.

running time Length of a production.

rushes The first prints of filmed scenes.

STV Scottish Television Limited.

scenario A film described scene by scene in full detail. Also called the shooting script.

second unit Another camera crew complete with director, lighting and sound technicians.

serial A succession of drama presentations which unfold one complete story.

series A number of drama presentations using the same theme and leading characters. Each episode has a self-contained story.

series/serial A number of drama presentations using the same theme and leading characters, each episode being an entity, but the series as a whole containing a serial element or overall story thread.

set and light That period of time allocated by the producer in consultation with specialists for the erection of the sets and the basic lighting rig.

set up The scene in the frame of a camera placed in a particular position.

sets Representations, stylised or realistic, of interiors or exteriors, in a studio.

scene hands Operatives who set and strike the sets.

shooting script See 'scenario'.

single shot See 'one off'.

slot Period of time allocated for a programme, e.g. one hour, thirty minutes, etc. However, the actual running time may be much shorter to allow for commercial breaks. This also applies to the BBC when they hope to sell the tape to commercial networks overseas where commercials will be introduced.

special talents An actor's ability to sing, ride a horse, etc.

split screen A divided screen used, for example, for telephone conversations to show both parties and their reactions at the same time.

spread If your script is 'under' (see below) you may be asked to write a spread, i.e. an extra thirty or sixty seconds, or whatever is required.

stabilise Correct running speed for a VTR machine.

stage Studio floor. The set.

stage directions The writer's description of sets, artists' moves and business, and in some cases thought processes.

stock Film clips, obtainable from film libraries which may be inserted, e.g. busy street, storm at sea (28).

stooging Characters in shot but without business or lines are stooging, i.e. doing nothing but stand around.

storyline An extended synopsis, but not as detailed as a treatment.

strike When the show is in the can (recorded) they strike (dismantle) the sets. In some cases, props may be struck during a production, if the story so requires.

studio lot Land and other property that is part of the studio complex – the exteriors of the office buildings; exteriors of storage sheds, roadways, gardens, main entrance gate etc.

study The act of learning lines; an actor who can learn quickly is a 'good study'.

synopsis A brief outline of a story (73).

T/C Telecine (4).

TIC Tongue in cheek.

T/K Telecine (4).

take out The rounding off of a scene.

teaser (or hook) as it is sometimes called. A short pre-credit sequence designed to grab audience attention and ensure they continue to watch after the first commercial interruption – which in the USA comes within the first two or three minutes of the start.

telephone backing A scene-heading term meaning a neutral backdrop for a close up of someone on the phone in a two-way telephone conversation,

    e.g. 3. INT. TELEPHONE BACKING. DAY.

three shot A frame in which only three people are seen. The term 'four shot' is used, but more than that number is generally termed a 'group shot'.

thrown An actor who is mis-cued, or has his concentration broken in some way, and is unable to react quickly enough to cover up the error, is said to have been thrown.

tight An actor who can't 'give' plays tight.

tilt In film, the act of moving the camera vertically during shot.

titles Your name, plus others, on the screen.

Tom Technical operations manager; the technician accountable for the technical operation of the studio and the studio staff.

took An actor who gets a fit of the giggles is said to have been took, or to have corpsed.

track To move the camera forwards or backwards.

treatment A detailed story synopsis, often describing the story scene by scene with scene headings. Some writers include a few lines of dialogue in their treatments if that helps to convey their story idea even more vividly.

two hander A scene, or a play, in which there are only two characters.

two shot (2-shot) Two characters in the frame.

under The opposite of over (see above), meaning too short.

VTR Video tape recording.

video tape The tape on which is recorded both sound and vision electrical impulses.

vision mixer The person who physically presses the buttons that cut from one camera to another to link selected camera output to the video tape recorder or (if 'live') to transmission.

vision tape Same as video tape.

WGGB Writers' Guild of Great Britain.

walk-on Small role actor (67).

whip pan Instead of indicating a cut or mix from one scene to another, you can suggest a whip pan. This is a very fast pan blurring the scene, then cutting to another camera finishing a whip pan on to the new scene.

wild track A clip of sound tape used for background effects, e.g. open air sounds, birdsong, airport concourse hubbub.

wing Making up dialogue or business to cover a fluff, dry, or corpse.

wipe The picture is wiped from the screen.

working title A temporary make-do title to help identify a script for discussion or commissioning reasons.

Bibliography

Archer, Wm, *Play-Making – A Manual of Craftsmanship* (Dover Publications Inc.)

Bartlett, Sir Basil, *Writing for Television* (Allen & Unwin)

Brandenburger, Barbara, *Working in Television* (Bodley Head)

Charlton, James (ed.), *The Writer's Quotation Book* (Robert Hale)

Chayefsky, Paddy, *Television Plays* (Simon & Schuster)

Contacts (The Spotlight)

Cotton, Bill. '*Violence on Television*', *Guidelines for Producers* (BBC)

Farre, Rowena, *Seal Morning* (Arrow Books)

Field, Syd, *Screenplay* (Delta Books)

Goldman, William, *Adventures in the Screen Trade* (Macdonald & Co.)

Halliwell, Leslie with Phillip Purser, *Halliwell's Television Companion* (Paladin)

Herman, Lewis, *A Practical Manual of Screen Playwriting* (Forum Books, World Publishing Co.)

Kerr, Walter, *How Not to Write a Play* (Max Reinhardt)

Lewisohn, Mark, *Guide to TV Comedy* (Radio Times)

Maugham, Somerset, *A Writer's Notebook* (William Heinemann)

Mercer, David, *The Generations, a trilogy of plays* (John Calder)

Miller, Merle & Rhodes, Evan, *Only You Dick Daring* (Wm Sloane Associates)

Morris, Colin, *Drawing the Line. Taste & Standards in BBC Programmes* (BBC Books)

Owen, Alun, *Three TV Plays* (Jonathan Cape)

PACT Directory of Independent Production Companies

Paice, Eric, *The Way to Write for Television* (Elm Tree Books)

Quirk, Professor Randolph, *The Use of English* (Longman)

Serling, Rod, *Patterns* (Bantam Books)

Turner, Barry (ed.), *The Writer's Handbook* (Macmillan & Co.)

Writers' & Artists' Yearbook (A & C Black)

Index